UNWANTED

UNWANTED

SUZ EVASDAUGHTER

MIRROR BOOKS

First published by Mirror Books in 2020

Mirror Books is part of Reach plc
10 Lower Thames Street
London EC3R 6EN

www.mirrorbooks.co.uk

ISBN 978-1-912624-96-6

Typeset by Danny Lyle

Printed and bound in Great Britain by
CPI Group (UK) Ltd, Croydon, CR0 4YY

A CIP catalogue record for this book is available from the British Library.

Every effort has been made to fulfil requirements with regard to
reproducing copyright material. The author and publisher will be
glad to rectify any omissions at the earliest opportunity.

3 5 7 9 10 8 6 4 2

Cover images: Mirrorpix, iStockphoto

For all children who have
lost a parent too soon

Contents

Prologue – Flowers, 1957

When I was five I killed my mother. She took a year to die.

Did I know she was ill? I think so; young as I was, I think I knew and was determined to thwart, reverse, deny and spurn whatever powers I believed control our world, but I failed. I challenged them to do their worst, and they did.

*   *   *

On a narrow path between high banks of white stars on tall stalks I stop and stoop.

'What ya doin'?' asks my friend, who sometimes shares this part of the way home from infant school.

'Pickin' these flowers for our mam.'

'You can't pick them, they're called Mother Die. If you take them in your 'owse yer mam'll die.'

'That's daft,' I say, 'course she won't die. You can't kill your mam with flowers.'

'Don't say I didn't warn you,' she says, skipping off.

Mam gives me a big smile when I get in and a hug. 'What have you got there, love?' she asks. I give her the bunch of white lace. 'Oh, thank you sweetheart, what a lovely present for Mam. I'll put them in a vase.'

*   *   *

If only I could have retained the confidence I felt back then, when I had a mother, how different my life might have been. I was carefree. I didn't stop to think that my mother would have known that same superstition. Then, with the confidence her constant presence gave me, I believed that I would never lose her.

PART ONE

BETTY, 1941

Mam's first job when she left school was the same as mine: she was a waitress. She worked at the Sunlight Cafe, close to the Denaby main pit in Conisbrough, a small mining village with the remnants of a magnificent castle near Doncaster in South Yorkshire. Like me, she also left home when she was young.

The war provided the means to escape the suffocating smallness of her northern pit village. She joined the NAFFI, opting for RAF Hunmanby Moor near Filey, a Butlins holiday camp that was leased to the RAF for the duration of the war. Had she stayed in Conisbrough she might have had to take a job in the Powder Works, where her two nieces were to be employed some years later. The girls had to be 18 before they were allowed to work in 'Dets', the section of the factory which made detonators for the pits, because the work was so dangerous. Betty must have been delighted to trade the suffocating smog of home for the freedom offered by the ozone rich rolling hills of North Yorkshire by the sea.

I imagine her life at 16, in a gaggle of young women, having a laugh, exchanging make-up tips, talking about the latest fashion and films and their dreams of finding Mr Right. She might have saved some of her meagre wages to buy a handbag, or fabric from the market to make a new summer frock. In my imagination, when they got a day off, she and her friends would have a picnic on the beach and, tucking their skirts and underslips into their knickers, they'd run through the sea squealing from the cold splashes. In the evening they would go to the cinema or a dance hall in the town. With her shapely figure, small waist and dark curls, Betty would draw admiring glances. I really hope that Mam had some carefree fun in her life.

Betty was charmed by a smart uniform and a Highland accent. Her mother's only teachings on birth control that 'men are only after one thing' and 'it's up to a man to ask and a girl to refuse', proved ineffective. The young man returned home to Scotland and Betty never heard from him again. She checked and rechecked her dates but, in the end, there was no other possibility. She confided in her friend, Elsie, a wireless operator.

'Is there no way you can get in touch with the lad, get his address?' said Elsie.

'No, I don't think so, I daren't ask, they might ask me why I want to know.'

Elsie could see the sense in this so she changed tack.

'You'll have to tell your mam.'

A shadow crossed Betty's face but she knew Elsie was right. On her next free weekend, she would have to go home.

* * *

The long bus journey gave her ample time to torture herself with thoughts of how her mother would react. She felt so ashamed for letting down the family. She had heard her mam complaining about having to go through the same thing with her sister Alice and she dreaded every moment of the meeting she was about to endure. Her tortured mind went over and over it in slow motion.

Catherine Swift was the size and shape of Queen Victoria in her golden years. She was not only the head of her family but also, through her ownership of the fish and chip shop and her no-nonsense reputation, the matriarch of the whole of this small mining community. Her domain encompassed five rows of smut-darkened terraced houses. In other words, all of her customers. No one dared cross her or stand up to her.

Two of her six sons still lived at home: Cyril, a miner, and Arnold, an extremely large, bald diabetic, who worked for ICI and rode a Lambretta scooter. Two younger members of the Swift family, also lived in the house in Athelston Road. They were actually Catherine's grandchildren, born out of wedlock, that Catherine had passed off as her own. They were the children of Betty's only sister, Alice.

Once Betty arrived home, she had to dam up her anguish until she got through all the welcomes. She mashed some tea and then sat around the range with her mam and dad. She fixed her eyes on the glowing fire and forced herself to blurt it all out before her brothers came in from work. Then she held everything tight inside, ready for what she knew would follow, what she knew she deserved.

'Betty Swift, I would never have believed it of you, bringing shame on this family. What did I tell you before you went away? You've been a very selfish and silly girl,' her mother said. 'How could you do such a wicked thing to us, Betty?'

Tears filled Betty's eyes.

'It's no good rourin' now. There's nothing else for it, you'll have to get rid of it.'

'Oh no Mam, please!' she stammered, her thoughts turning to the woman who lived at the bottom of their street, the woman that all the local lasses lived in terror of ever having to visit, the woman with the coat hanger.

She looked pleadingly at her dad but he kept his own counsel. She forced herself to look at her mother. 'Please Mam, can't I keep it? I'll come back home and I'll look after it. You did it for Alice...' Betty hadn't wanted to bring her sister into this, she knew it would only make her mam angrier and it felt disloyal to Alice.

'No, I've had enough of bringing up bairns. I've already got 10 and folk would soon be callin' about another one at my age. You can't bring it home. Think what the neighbours would say about this family, lasses laddin' it and 'aving bairns, and no lad would ever look at you with a bairn in tow. You'll have to get rid of it and that's final. Not around here though. Do it where you are.'

Betty's older sister Alice had given birth to three children before she married their father. Catherine made her have her first son adopted but when she went on to have a girl and then another boy, Grandma passed them off as her own. When Alice married the children's father, her mother would not give their children back, as that would have confirmed the rumours of their illegitimacy. The pair of acquired children were devoted to their grandmother, who they called Mam.

Without a welfare system, who was there to keep children if there was no man earning a wage? The danger and heartbreak as well as the burden of blame and shame, was shouldered by women.

'But Mam—' Betty was terrified, but she was no match for her mother, who continued unabated.

'You'll have to go to the authorities where you're staying and let them find a family for it. Or get one of them lasses you work with who's married and wants a babby to tek it, and if no one wants it it'll have to go to the orphanage. Now that's it, I want to hear no more about it, and as soon as you start showing you can stay away from here.'

Her mam's word was final. Betty kept all her feelings inside while she helped make the tea for the lads. That night she sobbed herself to sleep and the next day, on the long journey back to camp, tears of self-pity and injustice, exacerbated by her hormones, began flowing again. Though Betty was downhearted at the thought of parting from her baby she felt lighter because she'd faced her worst fear, her mam. At least

Mam hadn't thrown her out like one of the other lasses at the camp, who had to go to a mother and baby home. Or maybe she had. She had told her not to come back until after it was adopted, but where would she go until then? While she was at work, Betty tried to put the baby to the back of her mind. Every night she prayed for a solution.

Elsie, her wireless operator friend, was waiting for Betty one Sunday when her shift finished. Elsie had just returned from a visit home and was unable to contain herself. 'I've asked our Lily, my sister, about your babby,' Elsie said, 'and she and her husband Joe want to take it. I'd already written to her about it and she'd said she would talk to Joe but I didn't want to get your hopes up. They can't seem to have kids of their own so they want to adopt one.'

'If they did take it, do you think they would let me see the babby sometimes?' asked Betty.

'I don't see why not,' said Elsie, 'you are its mother after all.' This seemed a very good reason to the girls.

When Betty began to show, the friends went to Woolworths in Filey and bought a cheap wedding ring for Betty to wear. No longer able to visit her own home, Betty went with Elsie to see Lily and Joe when they had a day off together. Betty asked them about the only part of the arrangement that was important to her. 'Do you think I would be able to visit the babby? It wouldn't be too often, just a few times a year. Birthdays and before Christmas perhaps?'

'Are you sure you'll want to, Betty?' Lily said. 'Don't you think you will want to put this whole sorry affair behind you and get on with your life, meet a nice young man and get married and have children of your own?'

'It feels like knowing I can still see it is the only way I can let the babby go.'

'Well, from what I hear, you don't really have a choice, but I'm sure we can sort something out,' said Lily. 'I thought you could go to the Jessop in Sheffield when your time comes and then you'll come back here with the babby so you can feed him for a few days and get well enough to go back home to your mam.'

Betty tried to feel satisfied with the arrangements, though her hormones disagreed. She had a solution to her predicament and she told herself she must be grateful.

Everything went as planned and, on 26 November 1942, with the war still raging around the steel producing city of Sheffield, at the age of 17, Betty gave birth to a little boy.

As planned, Betty and the baby went to Lily and Joe's, and it was there that someone from Child Welfare came to sort out the paperwork. The council official issued Betty with a form that confirmed she would not be applying for a 'bastardy order' – a claim against the biological father for maintenance payments – because the child would be adequately supported by Lily and Joe. The adoption certificate noted that Joe and his father, who lived with them, brought in a good wage each, and that Lily kept the three-up, two-down, in a 'very clean and tidy condition'. Betty fed the baby for the next two weeks and the two mothers agreed on visits and promised to write to each other.

Some weeks later, Betty returned with her mother for the baptism. Following the service, over potted meat sandwiches and butterfly buns, Catherine tried to tell Lily how the child should be raised. But Catherine had met her match. Lily's mother was from the same generation of matriarchs who had learnt to use hard graft and their tongue to ensure the survival of their offspring in the harsh male world of the pit village. Every bit as feisty as her opposite number, Lily's mother abandoned the facade of politeness due to guests at a christening and told Catherine, amongst other things to, 'Buggar off back to Conisbrough.'

THE LAST GOODBYE, 1945

Betty is 20 and thrilled to be seeing her little boy on his third birthday. She has saved each week from her small wage packet to buy a toy train and a little bag of coloured wooden building blocks to make a toy town. She arrives in the mining village of Cudworth, four miles outside Barnsley, and very similar to the one where she grew up. She knocks on the door of the terraced cottage. As soon as he hears her voice, Norman runs to his 'Auntie' Betty, arms lifted. She picks him up for a loving cuddle. Then, after greetings are exchanged with Lily and Joe, the two of them, mother and son, kneel down on the mat in front of the fire. They set up the blocks, drive the engine through them and make train noises, accompanied by much giggling and fun. After a short while, Lily asks Betty, 'Would you like to come into the front room?' She's holding a tea tray in her hand.

Betty is a little apprehensive at this request as they usually all have tea together, but she gets up to follow Lily, telling Norman, 'I'll be back soon, sweetheart.'

'I want to play with my auntie Betty,' Norman wails when he sees his favourite auntie disappearing.

Joe begins making train noises and gets down onto the floor to take Betty's place and Norman settles. He doesn't usually get to play with his dad.

Lily pours the tea into the two bone china cups, then places the knitted cosy over the pot. As she offers Betty the plate of homemade strawberry jam tarts she says, 'Betty, I'm sorry, but Joe and me have been talking and we're going to have to ask you to stop coming.'

Everything inside Betty clenches up as the scene in the little parlour freezes in her mind forever – the tart in her hand, the usually comforting smell from the cups of freshly poured tea and, most of all, Lily's face mouthing words she can no longer hear. She's stunned; her mouth and throat dry up and, although her head is swimming with questions, she finds herself mute. What will she do if she can't keep seeing her little boy? She loves him more than anything in the world.

Lily's voice continues from somewhere that seems far away. 'Our Norman is becoming quite attached to his Auntie Betty, and Joe and me don't want him to be confused. We're sure you would like to be free to get on with your own life. You're only 20 and you're bound to meet someone and have bairns of your own.'

Tears fill Betty's eyes. She manages a nod – it's not in her nature to argue, even for something as important as this, and what can she do about it anyway? She signed the adoption certificate; officially Norman is theirs.

'Have a drink of your tea, it will make you feel better,' says the older woman, and Betty takes an obedient gulp but feels no different. She's still being told she'll never see her little boy again, never see him go to school, never see him in long trousers, or come to another of his birthdays, or hear his sweet voice call her 'Auntie Betty' again. What will he think has happened – that she has abandoned him, that she doesn't love him any more? It's more than Betty can bear. All she can think of is that she must get back to him now and squeeze in a few more precious moments before she is sent away.

'Is it all right for me to go back and play with him now?' Betty manages to say.

'All right, but we think you should get the next bus. It goes at quarter past.'

Gripped in what feels like claws of panic, Betty moves in a haze back to the living room where her little boy is holding up his new engine and smiling at her, glad that she's back to play with him.

'Auntie Betty,' he says, 'can we go to your house on the train?'

She has to take a moment to find her voice and get around the massive lump in her throat. 'Yes, we can do that sweetheart, can this be my house here?' she says, pointing to a wooden block with a red roof top and trying desperately to hide the break in her voice.

'I have to leave soon darling,' she says to the infant. 'I have to go home, on the bus, so can you give me a cuddle before I go?' Norman puts his small soft arms around her warm neck. She holds him tight for a long moment and then they play pat-a-cake and eye-nose-cheeky-cheeky-chin and peek-a-boo until her little treasure is rolling around with laughter.

'You had better get your coat on now, Betty,' Lily says.

'I have to go now, darling,' says Betty, trying to disguise her faltering voice once again. Then she holds the child close for one last time and whispers in his ear, 'Remember your Auntie Betty, won't you my darling? I love you so much and I always will.' As she stands up the child cries and, with the leaden feet of a prisoner ascending the gallows, Betty gets her coat, then turns to wave for the last time.

'Wave ta ta to Auntie Betty,' says Lily.

But the child will not wave, instead he wails inconsolably, for himself and for his mother.

Always Summer, 1946-1956

For months, Betty can think of nothing else but her lost little boy. RAF Hunmanby Moor is now closed, and the camp where it was based has reverted to a Butlins holiday camp where Betty continues to work as a waitress for the summer season. Elsie is a frequent visitor to the camp. There are cafes and bars and dancing but Betty is still distracted and has little appetite for fun on the beach or in the dance hall.

'You've been moping about for weeks,' says Elsie one evening. 'You have to get on with your life. Your baby is well cared for and loved and you'll have other bairns. Why don't we go dancing for once, take your mind off things?'

'Well, I…'

'No, I won't hear any more excuses. We're getting dressed up and you're coming out and that's final.'

They begin going out again, but Betty is very careful not to get too close to anyone. Then one night the girls are sitting with a lemonade each, when they both notice a tall, dark, rugged man looking over at them. He has broad shoulders and a Clark Gable dimple in his chin. He seems shy. From his tanned face Betty thinks he might be a farmer. There are mostly farmers around now.

'He's looking over, I wonder which one of us he'll ask to dance,' says Elsie, nudging her friend.

The farmer is Arthur Cooke, he is 19, just a year younger than Betty. He lives with his parents on his uncle's farm in Gristhorpe, a quaint little village made up of a few clusters of cottages and the farm, nine miles to the north of the Butlins camp and close to the sea. Arthur asks Betty if he can buy her a drink. He is not keen on dancing. The two of them begin courting. Betty is invited back for tea. The crab fresh from the sea is a luxury she had never tasted. Betty loves his parents, so different from her own. His mother, Mary, is gentle, softly spoken and delicate; she's slightly built with a long, full plait of hair tidied into a bun. His father, James, is always pleasant and kind.

The couple become serious and decide to marry. Betty moves into the family farmhouse, Manor Farm in Gristhorpe, and shares a bed with Arthur's sister Dorothy. The holiday season is over, and so she helps Arthur's mother on the farm and helps out by waiting at table at the Manor House in the village when they have extra visitors.

Two days after Christmas 1948, aged 20 and 21, the couple are married, and that night Betty at last feels it is safe to tell her new husband that she already has a son. Perhaps Arthur, her big strong farmer, will find a way for her to be able to see him again, and anyway, there shouldn't be any secrets between a husband and wife. It's been eating away at her since they got engaged. She's sure it will all be all right, that Arthur will understand.

But Betty is wrong: Arthur is angry, he never wants the matter spoken of again. Betty, distressed that he is so upset and that it's her fault, forces herself to let go of hopes of seeing Norman again and concentrates instead on their new life together and the new baby that is already growing inside her.

* * *

Now that he has a wife, Arthur needs more than the bed and board and spending money that he's received from his father since he left school. Grandad, the farm manager, asks his brother-in-law, the farm owner, for a wage for Arthur, who is now 21, and is told, 'If tha wants a wage for t' lad tha mun gi' it 'im outa thi own pay.'

Oh, if only folk hadn't stopped using horses for everything from deliveries to pulling ploughs, then Grandad would still have had the income from his two blacksmiths forges and been able to set Arthur up with a business of his own.

Arthur looks for a farm of his own to work on and finds one in Lebberston, just two miles away from his parents in Gristhorpe. While Arthur works on the fields and poaches a few rabbits, Betty does bed and board for the farm labourers, and continues to 'wait on' when needed at the 'big house' as well as taking care of the chickens and turkeys. It is here, at

8 Council Houses, that my elder brother – whom they also name Arthur – and myself, are born.

My life in these early years is idyllic. It is always summer and I am always happy. When it's not summer outside I have the snugness of the fire and my mother and the beaming rays of my father, the doting balm of my grandparents and the radiating warmth of the love of my two maiden aunts, Grandma's sister Auntie Renee and her friend who she lives with, Auntie Anna. I have all the animals to watch, play with and talk to. My two lovely aunties take me to the beach where the sand is soft and golden and there are lots of shallow pools to splash and paddle in. Dad would lift me and my big brother onto the hay rick pulled by the big horse. I have dollies' tea parties in the barn with my friend and I help Mam to feed the hens and collect the eggs. As a baby, I copied the turkeys and tried to eat a worm. Mam would say, 'Sweep a chimney' and I would waggle a chubby arm through the sleeve of a soft top that had been warmed on the fireguard. When we are older, Dad takes us out onto the rolling hillside, then leaves us while he goes over the dry-stone wall into the next field to catch rabbits.

'If tha sees anybody, tell 'em thi father's in t'next field,' Dad would say and I knew that we would be safe and they wouldn't touch us, because they would be scared of him because he is big and strong. When Dad comes back with some rabbits and I ask him how he caught them he tells me you have to put salt on their tails. I always know that my daddy is nearby and he comes home for his breakfast or dinner and tea with us. Sometimes he looks after me when Mam has to help out at the big house.

I can see the sea from our house. Dad has made us a swing from an old tyre and hung it up in the barn so we can play on it whenever we want. I can run and play and I have the whole farm, the hens to talk to and play with, the sweet-smelling straw bales in the barn to climb on and get lost in and hide in with my friends.

Arthur takes me scrumping for apples. We climb over the wall and pick up all the windfalls that aren't bruised. Mam plays skipping with me. She gets me to stand in front of her, both facing the same way and we jump together in the same rope as she turns it and it makes a thrushing sound along the stone slab floor. Sometimes we go to Grandma and Grandpa's for tea or Sunday dinner and its really lovely to be a big family all together, especially because they have got Rhonda the dog. Dad says he's a Welsh spaniel and that's why he has that name.

After we have been in this farm for a few years we move to another one in Haywold, 28 miles away, then another in Reighton, six miles down the coast from Lebberston. This is where Nicky is born. Arthur and I are told that the doctor brought the baby in his black bag. It is while she is breastfeeding the baby that Mam finds a lump in her breast and goes to the doctor.

'Oh, that's nothing to worry about,' he tells her, 'it's just a touch of mastitis. Just forget about it and it will go away.'

So she does.

* * *

'Where's Mam?' I ask Arthur, when it seems like we have been waiting a long time. We're on a visit to Grandma Swift's and Mam has taken us to the market in Doncaster. Mam was buying something at one of the stalls and people were pushing past Arthur and me. My big brother grabs my hand. A lady takes us to a little blue house and another lady with lots of shiny silver buttons sits us by a lovely warm fire and gives us milk and biscuits. I've got Arthur and I know Mam won't be away from us for long, so I take a big bite of a Jammy Dodger. I've drunk half my milk when the lady says, 'Is that your mam?'

I look across to where the lady is pointing and there is Mam's lovely face smiling at us through the wooden square above the counter that the policemen lift up when they come inside. She's done it. I knew she would come like they said; she's done something magic, found us in a different place. Arthur puts a chocolate digestive in his blazer pocket and snatches up a pink cream wafer. Bits fly in my face as he rams it in his mouth. I drop my biscuit, leave my milk and run over to Mam.

LEEDS ROAD,
HUDDERSFIELD, 1956

Farming doesn't pay enough now there are three of us kids. Dad's sister Dorothy, who's 10 years older than him, has moved to Huddersfield, about 90 miles away, and thinks Dad could earn more money there. Grandma Swift says she will pay for a deposit on a house once Dad is settled into a job that pays enough for the mortgage. Dorothy finds a house for us to live in until then. The rent is cheap because it's a condemned slum, set between a busy main road and a canal. We leave the farm and our tied cottage, the seaside, all the happy days and the loving attention of our grandparents and great aunties, in search of a better life.

It's really exciting sitting in the cab of the big lorry that's moving all our stuff to our new house. But when I climb down the big step and Dad lifts me on to the pavement, I see that everything looks wet and dark and dirty. The 'new' house is really old, a little two-up, two-down, black stone cottage on Leeds Road. It's just next to the main road and the sound of the big lorries and cars is frightening. There's no sea, no trees and no animals just this dark old cottage with stone steps that are worn down in the middle that go up to the bedrooms. There's just one tap in the whole house but we've got our own lav in the back yard, just like at the farm. The house feels cold and dark. There's no sunshine here.

While Mam and Dad do the unpacking, I put my hand behind my back and snap off a bit of the whitewash on the walls. Mam says that if we play out, we're not allowed to go near the canal at the back or the main road at the front. I'm glad because I don't even want to go out. There's nowhere nice to play and no village and no aunties and no grandma or Rhonda. Mam must be able to see I look sad because she says we are just living here for a bit, until Dad gets a good new job so we can have a lovely house in a place with trees and fields.

They know where the house will be but it's not even built yet. We are going to have a brand-new house built just for us, Mam says. I want us all to go back to the farm and can't understand why we had to leave, but I want to live in the new house that is going to be built just for us. There's no barn here, and no friends, just a little yard with some grass and a shed at the end of it. Dad hangs a dart board on the shed for us to play darts on.

Where we live here is all hard edges and black stone and lots of other houses and walls everywhere. It smells dirty and its smoky like at Grandma Swift's. Where we lived on the farm was all soft edges and green and you could see forever – right down to the sea.

*　*　*

After we've been here a bit and I've started school, Mam stops picking me up for a cuddle when I run to her and we don't do fun things like 'ring a roses, we all fall down' any more. She just about manages to lift the baby, now two years old. Then, one Saturday, Mam says, 'Come on love, let's go to town, just you and me.'

I never go anywhere with just Mam, she always takes all of us, but today Dad's at home and Arthur is throwing darts at the board hanging on the shed in the back yard and Nicky is watching, always wanting to do everything Arthur does. Mam helps me into my best blue coat. She gets her shopping bag and her purse then she holds my hand when we go for the bus and I smile up at her. This is lovely.

I like my feet not being able to reach the rubber mat. This long seat is my favourite, there's lots of room for me to swing my legs. I can look out of the open door and when we go around corners, I can see flashes and crackles above us. The trolley bus has giants' arms and it's like they are holding sparklers. Mam's got her arm around me. I feel all warm inside and I can feel her warm body even though we both have our coats on. Her lovely face is smiling down at me and I want to melt into her, like butter into toast.

When we get off the bus, she holds my hand again and we go into a shop. It's a flower shop, and the different colours smell soft and sweet and we look at the patterns they make. Mam asks which I like best and she buys some for us. It feels so special being out with my Mam on my own, without the others, just her and me. We've never done this before, just us two.

NOT JUST MASTITIS

'Hello Betty, the cafe's closed today so I thought I'd come over to see how you're getting on. You didn't look very well when you all came over for tea on Sunday,' says Aunt Dorothy as she lets herself in. Dorothy, Dad's sister, has a transport cafe on the main road into town. She's an independent woman, self-educated, and knows what she wants. She has taken up with a married man who has left his wife to live with her. She is slender, smartly dressed, has designer gowns for going dancing and has thick, prematurely grey hair which she wears in a stylish, blunt cut. She and her partner Jimmy don't have children; they go on holidays to Italy and Spain. Dorothy is the antithesis of her salt of the earth younger brother.

It's Monday, washing day, and Betty is on her hands and knees struggling to turn the handle on the mangle. 'Oh, get up off that stone floor for heaven's sake, what is the matter?'

'I'm sorry Dorothy, I just can't seem to manage any more, it's just too hard. I don't seem to have any strength.'

'Well, you have three young kids to look after so that's not surprising.'

Betty struggles into a nearby armchair and immediately the baby, just two years old, clambers on her lap. 'I think it might be this,' she says, as she moves her apron aside and opens her blouse to show Dorothy her breast. It is swollen and puckered like orange peel. Dorothy's face doesn't give away the wave of fear that has just passed through her. 'But it can't be anything serious,' Betty continues, 'because it started at the farm, when I was breastfeeding the baby. I went to the doctor and he said it was just mastitis. He said at 31 I was too young for it to be anything more serious.'

'Well it must be the mastitis that's got worse then,' says Dorothy, unable to put conviction into her tone. 'But you're having the doctor anyway. You can't go on like this. It's free now, you know, with the National Health Service. I'll send young Arthur round to the surgery with a note when he gets in from school.'

Dorothy waits for us to come home from school and makes tea for all of us. When the doctor comes round he examines Mam and gently pinches the skin on the back of her hand. 'This is neglect, just sheer neglect,' he says.

Mam is sent to a specialist and put on a pointless barbaric treadmill of radium and radical surgery. After she gets back from the hospital she stays in bed all the time. Uncle John, Mam's oldest brother, comes from Conisbrough with our older cousin, Pat, his daughter, to visit us. When he finds that Mam is too poorly to look after even herself, he takes her back with him to Grandma Swift's house to be looked after by her.

* * *

Grandma Swift often told me the story of the doctor's visit, emphasising the neglect comment. I never asked her who she thought was neglectful – Dad or the first doctor? Under all that blame she probably just wanted it to have been different, for Mam not to have died so young.

As an adult, I believe that ignorance rather than neglect caused my mother's untimely death. The same ignorance that caused the scandal of Thalidomide. If my mother had not given birth in a hospital where drugs were freely dispensed, then I believe she would have lived to see her children grow up. In 1942, it was common (and remained so up until 1977) to prescribe the synthetic oestrogen diethylstilbestrol for anything from (unsuccessfully) preventing miscarriage, to ensuring a bouncing baby and preventing breast engorgement when the mother had no baby to take her milk. It was not until daughters born to women given this drug during pregnancy developed rare forms of vaginal cancer that its use was stopped in humans. This drug is now known to be a carcinogen, linked to breast cancer. It is still given to cattle.

I have no evidence to prove that my mother was given this drug but it seems likely. Breast cancer in a woman so young was extremely rare in the 1950s.

They didn't tell patients that they had cancer back then. She must have guessed what was wrong though, but I expect she tried to believe the family when they said, 'Just let them doctors sort thee out lass and tha'll be as reet as rain.'

FLOATERS AND SWINGS

'Dad, can we save one for Mam?' I ask.

'Nay lass, we'll mec a fresh un for 'er when she comes 'ome.'

Dad's making us something special for a treat. Arthur just got back with two wafer blocks from the ice cream van. There's a *screwk* noise as Dad unscrews the cream soda bottle. The sweet bubbles tickle my nose as he pours some into each of our four glasses. I'm allowed to unwrap the wafer blocks but not to hold the knife. Arthur is eight and I'm five, Nicky is just two. I keep the blocks in the paper on the wooden table and Dad cuts them both in half, then he picks up the paper and plops a half in each of the glasses, making the pop fizz even more. Dad says they're floaters. We've never had one before. He hasn't said anything but it must be a special day. Maybe it's to cheer us up because Mam's gone.

I want to ask if we can have another one when Mam has hers and when will it be but Dad tells me to sit on the sofa with Arthur and the baby. We slurp and lick. Nicky gets it everywhere and fizzy ice cream gets mixed with slaver and snot and drips down onto the nice blue pullover that Mam

28

keeps for best. Dad says I have to look after Nicky now, while Mam's not here, so I try to help but get pushed away and there are even more slops.

Dad gets the little black and white telly going and we watch *William Tell*. Tell beats Lamburger Gessler just like he does every week then they play the song – 'Come away, come away with William Tell…' – and it's the end and our ice-cream floaters have finished as well. I want to watch *Robin Hood* but Dad says it's not on now. He tells us to wash our hands and faces. I find a flannel in the kitchen. 'Give me your pandy,' I say to the baby, 'and the other one, that's it.'

This is what Mam does, but I don't seem to manage very well. Nicky pulls away and is still messy. I run back to the tap and rinse the flannel and wipe my own face and hands. Arthur has done his already, he knows he'll get a clout if Dad has to tell him twice.

'Now let's put thi coits on, we're off for a ride,' says Dad.

I manage to put on my blue coat by myself and Dad helps our little one. Dad told us to get dressed in our best clothes and sandals when we got up so we must be going somewhere nice. Dad lifts me and the baby up into his work's van with the sliding side door and big letters on it: DAVID BROWNS TRACTORS. Arthur gets in after us. It's nearly as good as when we came in the removals van from the farm. After working on the buses for a bit and hating it because, 'After thas done all t'fares, up and down stairs, that lot get off an' another

29

lot ger on, all day,' Dad got a job with David Brown's and now travels all over the country and up to Scotland fixing new tractors made in his works. Dad got the job because he knows everything about tractors.

'Dad, when's Mam coming home?' I ask.

'Soon, lass, soon, I've telled thee already, she's poorly and she'll be back as soon as she's better.'

The van joggles over the bumpy cobbles. I do a big smile at Nicky and bounce up and down in the seat to make the bumps even bigger. Nicky giggles. Then we're on the smooth main road that we are not allowed to go near when we play out.

After a bit Dad stops the van outside a big old building. This place is bigger than school and it has massive big windows. There are some giant stone steps to a huge door. Maybe it's a witch's castle or a hospital like the one Dad says Mam went to to make her better. Dad slides open the door and we wriggle across the seat and he lifts me and the baby out. Arthur gets out by himself. I take Nicky's hand to help with the steps while Dad rings the bell.

In a minute a lady opens the great big door. She looks more like a mum than a witch. She's a bit bustly, as if she's got lots to do and wants to get on with it. She's dressed in a blue overall with poppers all down the front and is wearing stockings and shiny shoes. Mam never wears her best stockings and shoes if she's at home. The lady says she's called Mrs Downing and we all follow her inside.

Dad comes in last. When we go through the big door, we're in a place with lots of other doors. It's bigger than a passage but too small to be a room. The lady takes Nicky's hand out of mine and wants Dad to go with her through one of the doors. She says to Arthur and me, 'Now, why don't you two go and play out on the swings in the back yard?' and she points to what looks like a back door down a passage.

I look up at Dad to see what he says but he's already disappearing through the door with the lady, so I follow my big brother. The door that Mrs Downing had pointed to is just a normal door, not like the massive one at the front. Outside there's three swings and nothing else except for the metal stairs that zig-zag up the outside of the building and a few trees. There's a smell of school dinners from an open window. I want to play on the metal steps because I know they'll make a loud clang when you jump on them but Arthur has gone on the swings, so I follow him.

I manage to get up onto one of the swing seats by myself. Mam usually pushes me on the swing but she's not here and Dad's not here.

'Give us a push,' I ask Arthur.

'Do it yerself,' he says.

'I don't know how to, I'm too young.' I feel sad because it feels like something big has changed. There's nobody to help me now. He should because he's older than me and I help Nicky who is younger than me. It's not fair! I try to waggle backwards and forwards. The swing's chains creak and rattle. The wooden seat's hard and damp against my bare cold-blotched legs.

'No, you're not doing it right, do it like this, look.' Arthur gets the swing he's on to go higher and higher. He's showing off. I'm fed up. I start to snivel. I don't know what happens at this place but it doesn't feel right and he won't look after me.

'Like this, look,' he says again and shows me how to bend my legs and push back with my feet at the right time.

I don't want to do it myself, I want him to push me, but I also want to do what he can so I copy him. I push my body forwards but nothing happens, I just woggle about. I look at Arthur again and move my legs the way he does and after a few goes I'm as high as half the zig-zag staircase and my tummy feels really nice when I swing, just like when Mam pushes me. But it's not the same. It makes me feel sad.

We've been out here ages. I'm fed up and cold and now my tummy's hurting. Did Dad see where we went? Is this a hospital? Is Dad with Mam and are we going to see her next? The sky's getting closer and the birds are singing and then, at last, we hear the lady's voice: 'Come in now, you two, it's time for supper.'

Supper, here? Why? I follow Arthur inside.

Where are you Dad? I can't see you anywhere. Please come out of that door. Please come and take us to see where Mam is or take us home now. I don't want to have supper here. He's not in that little room anymore, the door is open. He must have taken our Nicky with him to see Mam.

Mrs Downing is asking us to follow her, but I have to find Dad. She takes us into a room that's bigger than any I've ever seen in a house. Dad's not in here either. It's full of kids, some as little as Nicky, some my size, some bigger than Arthur. They're all sitting on high stools round a huge green furry table with round holes at the corners and little nets hanging down from them. All around the edge of this table are mugs and plates with huge thick slices of soft white springy bread slathered with butter and jam. I can see our little Nicky sitting in a high-chair with a plate and mug and a half-eaten doorstep, but Dad's not there. There's red jam all around the baby's mouth, eyebrow and hair, making it look pink. I sit in the next place and stroke the soft blond hair.

'Our Sue,' I hear and I get a big smile.

'Where's Dad, Nicky?'

There's no answer. I smile again and help the baby with a drink. I swallow my frightenedness down till it's like a big lug, the sort I get in my hair that's hard to get out. It's stuck there, in my throat. I pick up the nearest drink to my stool because I want the lug to go away. She said come in for supper and all the other kids are drinking one and Arthur's got one so this must be mine. It's hot and sweet and milky, a bit like those malt biscuits with the animals on but different and really, really lovely. We never have this at home.

I pick up the bread and jam doorstep and open my mouth as wide as it goes but I can't fit it in. I lean it upwards so I can take a bite of the best bit and I get jam on my nose. I pull faces at Nicky, showing how hard it is to get the bread and jam in my mouth and we both laugh. I hope they've saved some supper for Dad. He must be seeing Mam on his own and we aren't allowed. But what are all these other kids doing here?

When everybody's eaten their doorsteps and drunk their drink that somebody says is Ovaltine, like in the advert on telly, Mrs Downing shows us where to go to the toilet. I've never seen a toilet inside before, even at school. There's one side for girls and one side for boys and washbasins in the middle. After we've all been, she takes us to the bottom of a big wide staircase.

'Come on now, off we go to bed,' she says.

I know she doesn't mean us, we have to go home. 'Dad will wonder where we are – he won't be able to find us when he's ready,' I tell her.

'Your Dad has gone home love and you will be staying with us here for a while.'

A big tear squeezes itself out of my eye and wets my cheek. I want to be at home. I don't even mind if it's that smelly damp cottage and not the farm, or even if Mam's not there, I just want to go home. I grab my little Nicky's hand but my legs follow her up the stairs because they don't know what else to do. Arthur is messing about with some lads higher up the stairs so he must think it's all right.

When we get to the landing, Mrs Downing opens a cupboard and warm comes out. She pulls out a big box full of clothes and rummages through it until she finds some pyjamas for Nicky and then gives me a flannelette nightie.

'That's not my nightie. I want my nightie,' I stamp my foot and fold my arms; tears are falling down my cheeks and heavy sobs come from right down inside me. The lug is still there. It's getting bigger.

'Look, it has little blue flowers on it, isn't that pretty?' says Mrs Downing. 'You can tell your mam about it when you go home.' I go quiet and think about telling Mam but the tears are still dripping. She takes us along a landing and stops at a door. Inside there's a big room with five beds, each with a little cupboard next to it. She takes me to one with nothing on its cupboard.

'Now you get ready for bed and I'll be back in a minute,' says Mrs Downing, smiling. I see her walking down the corridor with Nicky and Arthur before I go in.

The other girls in the bedroom look at me and then turn away and talk to each other. I take my dress off and put on the nightie over my vest and pants and get into the little bed. When Mrs Downing comes back, she tucks me into bed. 'Now, don't forget to say your prayers before you go to sleep, all of you,' she says as she walks to the door, then it all goes dark.

'Why you cryin'?' says the girl in the next bed.

'I want my Mam or Dad.'

'It's all right, you'll soon get used to it.'

'I'm not stopping,' I say. 'I'm just here till Mam gets better and then we're going to a new house.'

When I wake up in the morning the bed's wet. All my tears must have come out of the other end. Mrs Downing comes into our room.

'Come on girls, up you get.' She comes over to me. 'Oh dear, what's happened, Susan? Well, make sure you don't do that again,' she says. 'If you need to go in the night there's a potty under your bed.'

* * *

The Home is called Fartown Grange, and it's nice here. We're allowed to wander around and play when it's not school or Sunday school or meal times. I sit in the playroom reading or I play with the metal humming top. Sometimes I play jacks or allies with the other kids my age. We go to school just across the road, and on Saturdays we get sixpence to spend at the corner shop. I take Nicky. I've collected lots of beautiful little coloured stamps of Jesus in my blue Sunday school booklet, one for each time we go. The glue tastes sweet but not nice.

The things I like most about the Home are the doorsteps for supper and the books. I love one book so much that I want to be able to find more books just as good. So I look for what's special about this book. It has the name of the person who wrote it on the top of the pages on one side and the name of the book on the opposite pages. I decide that if I look for more books like that, I'll always be able to find the best books.

Today we're having a party. There's music from a radio-gram. I soon learn the words and sing *Last Train to San Fernando* by Lonnie Donegan, Perry Como's *Catch a Falling Star* and Bing Crosby's *Swinging on a Star*. I imagine flying through the sky or putting a tiny sparkle in a matchbox. When they play *The Dambusters' March* we all zoom around pretending our arms are plane wings. We make vroom-vroom noises and, at the end of the record, we fall over as if we've been shot down. I like sliding along the polished parquet floor and doing the splits. If you win at musical chairs you get a chewy square of jelly straight out of the packet from Mrs Downing. It's nice living here, even though I really want to be with Mam and Dad.

* * *

'Take your coat off and go and play, your Daddy won't be here for a long time yet.' Mrs Downing shoos me out of the hall. I go and find Linda. She's outside on the back lawn.

'Linda, will you please come in and play with me in the playroom so I can watch the front door for my dad? He's coming to pick us up in his van.'

'Only if we can play jacks. You're lucky that your dad is coming. You've only been here for four Sunday schools. My dad hasn't been since I've been here and I've been here a whole year.'

I find the jacks and we get as far as double bounces and caves. I can see the front door with its glass porch from where we're playing. When we get fed up we do cat's cradle for a bit and then it's teatime. I don't even taste the bangers and mash. The apples in the crumble burn my mouth as I shove spoonfuls in as quick as I can. I can't wait to get back and keep watch.

Back in the playroom I try to read a book, holding it so my eyes can still see the door. Just one more page but no, my arms ache too much. I have to put it down and just watch the door instead.

At last! He looks just the same – big, tall, dimple. Brylcreemed hair and special motor oil and cig smell, his checked work shirt and a-bit-shiny navy-blue trousers. I run to my daddy and he picks me up and swings me round and then gives me a chin rub with his whiskers and it's even better than floaters and books and doorsteps and parties, winning a jelly square and doing the splits all at the same time.

'Let's see if I can still pick thee up,' he says and I turn around and bend my arms. I know I have to keep them stiff. He puts his hands under my elbows and whoosh, I'm in the air really high. My daddy is really strong and I'm smiling right down to my tummy.

Mrs Downing is in the hall now with Nicky. I don't want to wait for Arthur to wash his black knees. He's been playing football. Dad has his works' van. We all sit in the front next to him. Nicky wants to touch everything in the van but soon starts to fall asleep. I look down happily at the little blond head on my knee. Dad's taking us to see Mam at Grandma Swift's and we're sleeping there. It's a long, long way but I don't care how long it takes, because I'm with my daddy. I don't even care when Arthur pokes me and says, 'Shove up.'

*   *   *

Fifty years after we were taken to Fartown Grange, my older cousin Pat tells me that when her dad, Uncle John, came over from Conisbrough and took Mam back with him, he told Dad that I could live with him and my auntie and cousin. Arthur and Nicky could live at Grandma's, less than a mile away from where I would be. But Dad told Uncle John he wanted to keep us together, and of course in the Children's Home we were nearer to him, not 60 miles away in South Yorkshire. I'll never know if that was the real reason or if he was afraid that he would never get us back. Grandma had form. She had not given back grandchildren before. But if Dad had accepted these offers, we would all have been very near to our Mam in her final year and I might have been able to remember her a bit more.

THE NEW DRESS

It's dark when we get to Grandma Swift's. I wake Nicky who looks at me with sleepy eyes. We all tumble out of the van into the house. I run up the passage into the living room and Mam's there, sitting by the fire in her nightie with a blanket round her. Nicky tries to climb onto her knee and she helps but really carefully, as if there's an invisible kitten already there. Arthur sits on the sofa and watches the telly. I stand next to Mam with my arm around her looking at her lovely face.

It's warm by the fire. Someone makes tea and pours it into cups for us. Dad toasts Grandma's barm cakes on the fire with the toasting fork that you can pull out to make longer and we eat these for supper, dripping with best butter and jam. I tell Mam about the doorsteps at the Home and how I've got friends who sleep in the same big bedroom. Mam smiles a lot and strokes my hair but doesn't move very much.

'How are you doing at school, Arthur?' Mam asks my big brother.

'All right,' he mumbles.

'And what games do you like playing, love?'

'They're called sports, Mam.'

'Well, what's your favourite sport, love?' Mam says this in a nice way even though Arthur wasn't nice to her, 'Do you like football?'

'I like cricket and rugby, and where we're staying in the Home there's Fartown Rugby Club right next door and on Saturdays we climb up and sit on the wall so we can watch them play.'

Grandma is sitting in her chair next to the fire, opposite Mam. 'Now have you all got a kiss for your old Grandma?' she says. Grandma never wears her false teeth, except for weddings and funerals. She has dry, craggy, hollow cheeks. When I go over, she pulls me in and holds me fast and her lips make a trumping noise as she sucks my face. The baby isn't leaving Mam, so Grandma gets up and leans over and says, 'Ah, me likkle babby,' and does another trumpy kiss. Arthur stays on the sofa.

I don't want to leave Mam but my eyes are closing. The baby has fallen asleep already.

'It's all right love,' she says, looking at me, 'I'll be here in the morning when you wake up, now go to bed nicely for Grandma.'

Nicky makes a little moany noise when lifted from Mam's knee to go up to the cot. Mam gets up out of the chair, she's going to bed too. I have to go up the yard to the toilet. It's cold and you can just see the way by the light from the kitchen. There are squares of newspaper threaded on a piece of string hanging on a nail. Then Arthur goes and we have to wash our hands and face with a flannel at the kitchen sink.

I'm sleeping in Grandma's room, in the chair that folds down into a bed but still has arms at the sides. I can hear the telly from the living room and I think about Mam and Dad. I don't make a wish because I know that we're going back to the Home and I don't want to waste it.

In the morning I get up as soon as I'm awake. It's cold and I've only got my knickers and vest on. I go into the living room and find Dad making up the fire. He puts a winceyette blanket round me that smells of Mam and I sit all cuddled up in the chair she was in last night. I pretend she's still there and I'm on her knee. I watch Dad doing the fire then he goes to make some tea and after it's brewed and he's poured us some, he puts the pot on the hearth to keep warm. Then the fire's ready to make some toast. I'm allowed to hold the toasting fork. It's nice to have a family again. I want us to be together forever, even if it's not on the farm.

Arthur comes down and asks, 'Can I go and see the pigs?'

My uncles have got allotments where they keep pigs and hens and pigeons.

'I expect thi Uncle Arnold will take thi down there when he goes down to feed 'em later,' Dad says.

Mam comes down wearing a black dress with a collar of black and white and a white pinny at the front. She's wearing a brooch. I wonder if we're going out.

'Mam, Mam!' I call, dropping the toast and toasting fork on the hearth and run up to her and grab her hand.

She looks down at me, smiling. 'Come on, let's get you dressed, I've got a surprise for you,' she says.

I remember the toast and pick up the long fork and give it to Dad. I look at his eyes and he's not cross.

Mam takes me into Grandma's front room, where we never go, and there's a smell of lavender polish and it feels cold. She opens a bag and takes out a beautiful blue dress with darker blue flowers on it and a little collar. I step into it and she does up the buttons at the back. I rub my hands together so I don't get crumbs on my new dress, then I touch its smoothness. It's really soft, brushed cotton, Mam says. I'm a gypsy princess. Then she brushes my hair and puts a ribbon in to hold the front part to the side, and I put on some new white socks and blue sandals from a different bag.

'Mam, can I leave my dress here so I can wear it when I come to stay with you?'

'Don't you want your new friends to see it, love?'

'Well, in the Home we all have to share our clothes. They put them in a big box and anybody can have them. You can keep your shoes but the clothes all come from the big box in the cupboard.'

'Oh, I see. Well I'll talk to Dad about that and see what he says.'

Arthur comes into the front room. He's dressed in his playing-out clothes and wellies.

'When are you coming back so we can go home?' he says.

'Soon love, soon,' says Mam, 'I just have to get a bit better first. You know what I told you when we first moved to the Leeds Road cottage, that we wouldn't be here for long, that we were going to live in a beautiful new house, but we had to wait for it to be built? Well, soon we'll all be in the brand new house together and you'll all have a new school, right next to the house, now won't that be nice, eh? Dad's going to get it all ready while you are away so that it's all lovely for when I'm better.'

Arthur doesn't say anything but I smile up at Mam and put my hand in hers, I think that will be really nice.

Arthur goes down the gardens (which is what everyone calls the allotments) with Dad and our two uncles who live with Grandma. I don't want to leave Mam so I help her with looking after the baby. Uncle Ernie and Auntie Grace come from across the road with my cousin Corrine who's the same age as me. Uncle Ernie wants to take a picture of us on the rec at the back of the house. Mam, me, Nicky and Auntie Grace and Corrine sit on the hills for the photo. Uncle Ernie says we are sitting where there were shelters for people to go during the war but I can't see any doors where they could get in. I forgot to wipe Nicky's face and it looks a bit mucky. After the photo, Auntie Grace and Mam have a cup of tea and I play with Corrine. Nicky is our little baby who pretends to cry to get arrowroot biscuits and dandelion and burdock pop from us.

After Sunday dinner the next day, I think as hard as I can of the doorsteps and the books and the tops and my friends, and of Sunday school stamps and spending money, but I still cry. I can't think of enough good things that will make it better than being with Mam and Dad, but Dad says we have to go back to Fartown Grange. I give Mam a great big love and then we have to be kissed by Grandma – again.

We get back in time for doorsteps and cocoa but I don't want Dad to go. I want to be back in our life with just our family. He says he has to talk to Mrs Downing.

'Can't I stay with you while you talk to her, please Dad?'

'Well, I need to talk about grown up stuff wi' 'er lass. Let's see if tha's grown over't weekend.' And he turns me round and lifts me up by my elbows and it feels so nice going up to the sky. 'Now, tha gan an' help Nicky wi' t' supper cos babby's too little to manage and I need thee ta tec over from thi mam while she's getting better.'

Arthur is already at the billiard table. I find a place where I can sit with Nicky. I stuff my doorstep into my sadness until I can't feel it any more. I burn my tongue drinking my cocoa as fast as I can but Dad's not there when I come out.

* * *

The photo from that day, with the five of us on the rec, sitting on top of what had been air raid shelters, is the last one that was ever taken of my mother. Perhaps looking at it would have been a comfort to her in those last months when we were so far away.

UNWANTED

Grandpa Swift died the year before our mother, he was 71. Given the smart black clothes and brooch that my mother is wearing in the photo, it is possible that this was the day of her father's funeral and Auntie Grace, also in the photo, had come round to take care of us while the rest of the extended family had gone to chapel.

SHAMED

It's hair washing day. I'm standing in a long queue while Mrs Downing washes each child's hair in the big white pot sink that Christopher was sick in. He was choking on a marble. Mr Downing ran the taps and held him upside down over the sink and thumped his back till the marble came out and then Christopher was sick. We all thought it was the best thing ever! I'm near the back of the line, there are only four kids behind me.

When I get to the front I know what to do. I bend my head over the sink and Mrs Downing pours water that's still just warm from the big enamel jug over my head, rubs in shampoo then rinses it off. She's being a bit rough. She hasn't said anything. Now she's taking a towel off the pile and wrapping the towel round my head. Something's wrong. She's looking at me in a funny way. I feel uncomfortable and start to shuffle about. Then it happens. She says, 'Now Susan, why did you say that you didn't want to bring your new dress back here with you?'

Oh, my lovely new blue dress that my mam gave me that I don't want to go in the clothes box because it's so special I want to keep it for myself. Mrs Downing's face has changed from her usual kind one. This one looks hard and mean. She's standing with her hands on her hips and leaning forward over me. I can't make any words come out. It's like there's only me and her in the whole world. The kids behind me have become invisible there's no noise from anybody or anywhere else, just Mrs Downing and me. I'm shaking inside.

'So you're happy to be given clothes to wear from the clothes box but you want to keep your own nice clothes for yourself, do you? Well come on, speak up.'

I shrink up like one of the silver balls I make from the paper inside Dad's empty fag packets.

'How would it be if everybody was like you?' she demands. 'There would be nothing for you to wear, would there? You're very selfish, Susan.'

My cheeks are hot. Tears mix with the water dripping down from my hair. She rubs my hair a bit, takes the towel off and throws it into the wash basket. I shuffle off into the playroom, sit by my books and cry. I bet she'll take my dress off me now. The dress that my mam gave me. I'll have nothing that's mine. I wish Mam was here, or Dad. I wish we were back on the farm where everything was nice and everyone was kind.

*　*　*

'If you wet your knickers again,' Mrs Downing says, 'you will have to put them on your head and walk round this room carrying a sign saying, "I WET MY KNICKERS".

You will be with the children with a sheet on their head carrying their signs that say, "I WET MY BED". Now is that what you want, Susan?'

We're in the room where we have parties and they play those lovely records with the sing-a-long songs. I don't want to parade with my knickers on my head and a sign round my neck. 'No, Mrs Downing.'

'Well, that's what will happen if you do it again.'

I can't help it. I don't know how I wet my pants, it just happens. Except the time when that lad with the thick glasses came into the toilets and made me lay down. He pulled my knickers down and poured a glass of water on my fanny. They got wet then. I never go in the lav on my own now. I get my friend Shirley to go with me.

I'm running around outside with Shirley and when it's time to go in for tea I go to the lav with all the others and see that my pants are wet. I take them off and shove them behind the fat silver pipes. They dry all stiff but I can put them on again before Mrs Downing finds out.

FORGOTTEN

I don't want to be here for Christmas even if they are having a party and even if their parties are good here. I want to be at home with Dad and Mam and just us kids. Mr Downing puts up a Christmas tree in the party room and he stands on a stepladder to fix the paper chains that we've made with Mrs Downing. They go from the corners to the light in the middle of the room. Everything looks special.

It's the day before Christmas and I'm sure that Dad or one of my uncles will come in their van and take us to Grandma Swift's so we can be with Mam. I'm not asking Mrs Downing, though. I don't want her to tell me that we're staying here, and if we do have to stay how will Father Christmas know where to bring our presents? I want to snuggle up in bed with Mam. I want my daddy to stir his tea and put the back of the hot spoon on the back of my hand so I pull it away and squeal. Best of all would be if we could all go back to the farm to stay with Grandma Cooke and Rhonda the dog.

I stay in the playroom reading the books and playing with the tops so I can keep looking in the hall. I see grown ups arriving. The cold comes in with them, clinging to their coats and scarves and hats. When they leave, they take one of the boys or girls, or even two or three, and Mrs Downing wraps them up so that they match their grown ups. They'll have a lovely Christmas with their mam or dad or somebody who's special for them.

Each time I hear the big front door opening I ask Jesus to make it Dad, but nobody comes for us. When we're all going in for our tea I give in and ask Arthur. 'Nah, we're staying in this dump so you'd better get used to it,' he says. But how can he know?

Even though I smile at our little one while we are eating tea and even though the food is hot, inside I feel just like it looks outside the windows, cold and dark.

After tea, the few of us that are left go into the room where we have parties and hang our pillowcases around the hearth of the big fireplace. There's only me and one other girl, my friend, Diane, left in our bedroom.

When I wake up on Christmas morning Diane is already awake. We hold hands and creep down the wide staircase in our nighties, trying not to make it creak. The girls from the other bedroom are already there. We get really excited when we see that our pillowcases are now a bit fatter and lumpy. Father Christmas must have come down the chimney in the night. We don't dare look in them or stay downstairs, so we run back up and get washed and dressed as quick as we can.

In the dining room there's hardly any of us. I sit next to Nicky for breakfast at one of the big tables. Milk and Frosties have slopped out of the bowl. 'What did you ask for from Father Christmas?' I say.

'Farm animals,' I just make out, between eager slurps.

We have to go to the toilet and wash our hands and then it's time to go into the party room. We open our pillowcases. I've got a little doll, a set of jacks, some nuts, a tangerine, a chocolate smoking set, a selection box and some socks and pants. Nicky, who is now three, is very happy and lays tummy-down on the parquet floor and, with chocolate pipe in mouth, starts playing with the wished-for toy farm animals. I ask if I should peel a tangerine.

When everybody has emptied their pillowcases, Mrs Downing says that Santa has left some big presents under the stairs. Big presents...wow! Have I got some roller skates or even a big girl's bike? I had to leave my tricycle with its three big wheels at Grandma Cooke's, Mam said it would be dangerous to ride it at the cottage but we could get it when we moved to the new house. My three-wheeler was Arthur's till he got too big for it.

Mr Downing goes to the cupboard and we all follow him like the hens used to follow me and Mam when we took their corn out. He brings out a present, it's a red two-wheeler that's too big for me. It could be for Arthur though. There's a label on the handlebars. He calls out the name, it's for Brian. It's shiny and the tyres are really black. Brian pings its bell straight away. It's brand new.

The next big present is a blue scooter. That's brand new as well. I go all wobbly inside and I've nearly forgotten about being with Mam or Dad or at the farm. Whatever mine is it's bound to be brand new, because all the others are. I don't think I've ever had anything brand new, except my lovely blue dress of course. All I can think about now is what big present I'll get.

I like all those that have already gone. Somebody else gets a three-wheeler and I won't mind if I do get one but Santa must know that I'm nearly six so ready for a big girl's bike, but maybe girls aren't allowed two wheelers.

Mr Downing is bringing out a shiny blue and silver doll's carriage pram that hangs on leather straps and buckles so you can waggle the pram and the dolly will be rocked to sleep. Oh yes, this must be for me. It's like the one Mam had for me and Nicky. I will be so proud pushing that around. He gives it to Linda. Everyone else has had one now so it must be just ours left. I'm nearly bursting with excitement when Mr Downing goes back to the cupboard. He shuts the door.

'Please Sir, Mr Downing,' I say, 'I haven't had my big present yet, or Nicky or Arthur.'

'I'm sorry Susan, but that's all the presents finished now.'

I must've been naughty. I know I keep wetting my pants but I don't think anybody knows. Maybe Santa's like God and sees everything or maybe God told Santa and that's why I didn't get a big present. It's because of the dress and being selfish. Yes, it must be that. But Nicky couldn't have been naughty because babies are too little. Arthur could though. Did Santa not give us three a big present because of something he did? 'Mr Downing, why isn't there a big present for us?' I ask.

'Father Christmas just didn't leave one for you Susan, I'm sorry.' Mr Downing looks as sad as me.

I'd made Santa a card and everything. I won't bother next time! Now all I can think about is not being at home with Mam and Dad. I wonder what they're doing and why they don't want us. I try to play with the things I did get but I can't. The lug is back in my throat. I try to make it go away with a chocolate cigar and the chocolate pipe and then some sweet cigarettes while I snivel to myself.

* * *

Mam was only three months away from death that Christmas. The Home's policy on presents would have been controlled by the local authority, not the house parents, and it was probably complete orphans or just long-term residents that got the more expensive presents. But back then, all I knew was that we'd been forgotten.

Letting Go, 1958

I'm back at Grandma's house, in Mam's bedroom, with our Mam. We don't come to see her very often, just a weekend at Grandma's now and again. I don't know it, but it's the last time I'll see her. She isn't getting out of bed. Dad says she's not feeling very well today. Just today.

She's not moving except for her eyes sometimes, looking at us – from one to the other as if she's forgotten who we are. She's shrunk. Our mam looks like a big doll on the feather bed and bolster. She's got rouge on her cheeks. She used to put it on mine when we played dressing up. There's a dried line of silvery slaver going from one side of her lips to half way down her chin, as if a slug climbed out of her mouth and fell off on the bed. I look at her face then I feel on the covers for the slug. The room smells of Dettol. There's a full cup of cold tea on the bedside table and a medicine bottle with measures up the side and a dried sugary line near the top.

Arthur's eight now. He climbs onto the big bed and begins jumping. Nicky can't manage to get up there with him. I help Nicky and climb up myself, managing to avoid Arthur's scrawny knees with the coal dust scars just below where his trousers stop.

We jump up and down on the bed and laugh, trying to push each other off and into the sharks in the water. Arthur gives me a shove; I shriek and fall on Mam. She groans, her grey face twists but she still tries to make a smile. Dad must have heard us making a noise. He comes into the room and orders us off the bed and says we have to go back downstairs.

'It was him, he got on first and then he shoved me onto Mam.'

'No, it wasn't me it was her; she fell on Mam.'

At the door, I look back at Mam. She's lying still again, her eyes make it seem as if she's looking far away but her head is turned towards us and I'm sure, yes really sure that she's looking at me. And she smiled, I know she did, and she lifted up her hand, just a bit. I keep my eyes on her until we're out of the room. I can see her mouth moving, but no words come out.

* * *

Betty is lying in bed in her mother's house. She tries to fix the faces of her four children in her mind, though she is delirious from the drugs that distance her from the pain as the cells in her bones and brain are replaced by cancerous breast tissue. In her mind's eye, two of the bairns seem the same age. When she said goodbye to her first-born, Norman, he was three, just like her little blond Nicky is now. She can't try to think what Norman must look like at 16, it's too hard. She sees Susan, her lovely little lass. She must have had a birthday in the Home and be six now. Oh, what will become of them? How will Arthur manage on his own?

She comforts herself. Norman has a good family to care for him. Young Arthur will be all right, he's already confident and independent, but what of her little girl and the baby? Her big, strong Arthur will look after the little ones, she's sure of that. At least she had some good years with them. She struggles in her mind to count them. Yes, eight good years with young Arthur. She treasured every day with the children.

'How can I bear to leave them when they need me so much?' she thinks. 'Why would God do something like this? But no, I shouldn't think like that. But what will become of them without a mam? Arthur is a good man, he'll take care of them and Mam will still be here. They both promised to look after them for me, though they keep telling me I'll get better. I know I won't. I'm too tired, I can't keep going.'

Her eyes open for a moment and she sees her husband, Arthur, beside her, dozing in the chair, a full ashtray and a cold cup of tea on the little round table next to him. The next time she opens them it's her mam. She comes and goes trying to get her to eat or drink something and rourin' her eyes out at the least little thing. Betty doesn't want anything, just the medicine, and even half of that seems to end up on the sheets. It's hard to move.

Her brothers come in but don't stay long, except for the eldest one, John. Even though he now has a family and no longer lives here, he has come in from work every day and stayed with her, keeping watch every night. She knows they have all left money for her, for the new house that must be nearly ready by now. They put the money in her black patent bag for her. The lads just sit a while in the chair and when she looks again the chair's empty or Arthur's there. She's seen them crying, too. She's sorry for them. She's past caring about herself, there's just the pain now, and the bairns, her poor little bairns.

Sometimes she wakes and Arthur is holding her hand. It's swollen but she can't help that, not now. She must look a sight. She's sorry for letting him down. He's a good man, he'll take care of the bairns, he promised. She tries to see if he's there now, but her eyes won't work. Is she making a smile? She's trying to just in case he is there, but she's not sure whether it shows on the outside. It's getting harder to breathe. Yes, she can just make out Arthur and her mam and John. She can't keep her eyes open any longer. She tries to make words, 'Arthur, you will look after the bairns, won't you?' She can't hear them. Did they come out?

THE STRANGER

The tin top hums in my teeth. I push down harder on the handle so it goes faster and keeps going and humming, humming and going. I control the top.

'Susan, can you leave that for a minute love and come with me? There's somebody who wants to talk to you,' says Mrs Downing, standing in the doorway of the playroom.

I stop the top and follow her. She takes me to the door of the biggest room, the one with the parquet floor where we have our parties. She says I should go in by myself. I can see a man in the room. A man I've never seen before. He's wearing a suit. I look up at Mrs Downing. She tells me again to go in and closes the door behind me. The room is silent. There is no noise from the other children or the kitchen but there's a lovely smell of dinner that's nearly ready.

The man is standing in front of the big stone fireplace. His suit is navy blue, like the one Dad wears for special. The man's shoes are shiny. He's looking down at me. I look up at him, but not right up to his eyes. There's a little suitcase on the floor next to him. It's open and I can see papers inside it. He's looking at the paper in his hands. I look at the fireplace. His voice floats down. His shoes smell like Dad's. The fireplace goes up a long way but it's not as high as him. It's made of stone blocks and there's thin lines between the stones. I want to run my hand over the smooth stones, but I daren't. The room seems much bigger than when it's full of us kids. The man's saying who he is. I'm not listening. Then it goes quiet and this time I hear.

'I'm sorry to have to tell you, that your mother is dead.' Then it's quiet again. 'Do you understand?'

What? Who is 'mother'? It can't be our mam. Mams don't die. We're just in this Home until Mam gets better, then we'll all be back together again, in the new house, Mam says so, Dad says so, and Grandma. The man's feet make a squeak on the polished floor.

'It's very sad but that means that you will never see her again.' He makes a noise in his throat. 'She's gone to heaven.'

The suit man is still talking, shifting his feet, rustling his papers and picking up his little black suitcase, but I can't listen anymore. I put my hand on the cool stone and move it down across the thin gap and onto the next smooth part. Then I look at the man properly for the first time and say, 'Can *I* be the one to tell our little Nicky about Mam please?'

GRANDMA COOKE
AND THE WISH

Why can't I fall asleep? Is it the voice? I can hear somebody moaning, whining, but like when you blow through a comb with a paper over it. Oh no, it must be me. The itching won't stop. I want to scratch and scrape until my arms and legs and body bleed. The sickly smelling calamine lotion that Grandma Swift put all over me with lint hasn't made it any better. I want Mam. Every minute's like a week. I hate just lying here. They wouldn't make me lie here by myself in the dark all night if Mam was here. It feels like we can't manage now Mam's gone. We just all get poorly without her.

After a long time, the itching and spots go away and my Auntie Grace takes me to a lovely school with my cousin Corrine. It's much better than the two other schools I've been to at the cottage and the Home. We sing songs like *The Big Rock Candy Mountain*, and there's stilts and big hoops in the playground and new tables in the classroom. I love it... but then Dad says I have to leave.

After Mam's death, the council gave Dad a month to take

us out of the Home. They felt we had family enough to care for us. Perhaps they thought we should stay with Grandma Swift but this solution was not acceptable to Dad. He was angry about being given notice and told me that he said to the woman from the authorities, 'How's tha expect me ta find mesen a wife so fast, will tha marry me?' Then we all contracted the chicken pox on a weekend visit to Grandma Swift's and the Home refused to have us back.

It's hard for Dad. Auntie Dorothy lives in Huddersfield but she can't help him with us because she has her life and her cafe to run. Grandma Cooke and Grandma Swift live too far away to be able to help, and Dad has to work as much as he can because he had lots of time off to be with Mam.

I'm happy to be at Grandma's. I love my school. I love spending time with Auntie Grace and being able to play with my cousins Corrine, who is just a few months younger than me, and Cynthia who is a bit younger than her. But Dad says I can't stay. Even though I don't want to leave my lovely school I know I have to do what Dad says, because he knows what's best and he will make everything better in the end.

Auntie Dorothy's husband, Uncle Jimmy, has found me a foster family in Huddersfield. He's a rent collector and these people need some extra money to pay their rent. Arthur's nine so he's old enough to live with Dad. Nicky is only three so too young and has to stay with Grandma

Swift. I think Mam wants Nicky to be with her in heaven or he wants to be with Mam.

* * *

The foster family's dog's got worms, loads of them, they wriggle around by her bum in her bed. They've got four kids and we all sleep together. We play in the woods but one day a man is there and we think he's nice because he wants to give us piggy back rides but he puts his hands under the bit between your legs when he bounces you along and it doesn't feel nice, so we don't go again.

Arthur comes to see me for a bit every Sunday. I wait with him at the bus stop when he has to go back because I don't want him to go, but I don't cry till he's gone.

Then one day Dad comes for me with Arthur and we go to see Grandma Cooke. *'We're off, we're off, we're off in a motor car, a dozen bobbies are after us and we don't know where we are.'* Dad starts off the song but I sing the loudest. I'm so happy and I think Dad is, too.

'Reet, which one a thi's gonna be first ta see t'sea?' Dad says.

Arthur usually wins but he's doing the *I Spy on the Road* book and after a bit I shout, 'Me, me, me, I can see the sea!' and Dad smiles and I smile all the way down to my tummy because we're coming home, back to where I was born and where we lived before Mam got poorly, back to my favourite place in the whole world.

'Now, tha behave thi sens fa thi Grandma,' Dad says.

I run in to see Grandma Cooke. Her cottage still smells of baking downstairs and talcum powder upstairs. She's so different to Grandma Swift – tall and slim and soft and gentle, like Dad's sister Auntie Dorothy. She has long grey hair done up in a bun like a ballet dancer and keeps her teeth in all the time. There's a white embroidered tablecloth on the round table with Grandma's special pots laid out for tea and a coffee and walnut cake, Dad's favourite. I do a big sigh. I want to go running to the orchards to pick apples. I want to play in the barn where Dad put up the tyre swing for us. I want to smell the hay and jump in the straw bales. I want to feed the hens and the turkeys. I want to see my best aunties who Dad says are really my great aunties. I want to look at all Grandma's old lovely things and listen to her play the organ. I want to lie on the floor with Rhonda, her Welsh spaniel and I do and we roll around and Rhonda licks me and we giggle.

After tea and cake my best aunties, Renee and Anna, who live in a nearby cottage, come around to take me to feed the hens. They pick me up and hold me like they used to when they took me to the beach when we lived here.

'Come on chuck, chuck, chuck,' we call and the hens come running as if they're clowns in hooped trousers.

When we get back the aunties go home and Dad says to wash my hands for dinner. Now the round table is laid with big plates and knives and forks and dishes with covers on.

Dad brings out a chicken with roasties round it, in a big dish all sizzling, and puts it down in front of his chair. Rhonda is drooling and I'm drooling on the inside as Dad rubs the big knife against the round sharpener and then picks up the big fork and says, 'Now, who wants breast and who wants leg?'

When we've finished, Dad says that Arthur and me can pull the wishbone. I win. I never win anything so this must be really special, like magic. I close my eyes tight and make a wish. 'Please can my Mam come back,' I plead to the fairy godmother.

'Na tha munt tell nubdy what tha wished lass,' Dad says, 'else it'll not come true.'

'OK, I promise, I won't tell anyone.' I think that's an easy thing to do if it will make my wish come true. After a lovely day at Grandma Cooke's I have to go back to the foster family on the council estate. 'Why can't I come home with you and Arthur, Dad?' I ask.

'I'm sorry lass, I want thi to come wi' us but t'new 'ouse in't properly ready and I want it to be really nice for thi.' But before I can tell him that I don't care what the house looks like, I just want to be back with them, he says, 'And tha's a bit young yet to be leaving thi by thi sen after school so tha'll atta stay wi' them folk a bit longer. I'll be comin' to collect thi soon, for good, and we'll all be together.'

So, it would come true then, we would *all* be together in the new house. 'Dad,' I ask, 'will Arthur still come to see me this week even though we've been to Grandma's?'

'Nay lass, he has ta go ta school. 'E'll come and si thi next Sunday though.'

Although the farm and Grandma Cooke's was my favourite place in the world, I knew I couldn't live there because Dad wouldn't be there. I understood that he needed to work at his job in Huddersfield, and wherever it was that we lived didn't really matter as much as being with Dad did.

* * *

Grandma Cooke would have been in her seventies by this time and could no longer manage to live at home on her own, let alone take care of a six-year-old. Dad's visit that day must have been to arrange for Grandma to come and live with us, so we kids could be at home with him again. We had been happy enough in the home so he probably thought I would manage with foster parents for a while longer, and I did.

The New House, 1959

Grandad Swift had given up work at 35 to dedicate himself to his hobbies: drinking and backing horses. Grandma did anything to make ends meet, including taking in washing. Her eldest son, John, was the first one to bring in a wage. As the other sons became old enough to work, as was the custom in this working-class culture, the lads would 'tip up' their wage packets to her and she kept them all in food and clothes until she got the opportunity to buy a fish and chip shop.

Grandma saw to it that all her 10 children (including the two grandchildren she brought up as her own) were able to buy their own houses, and at least three of them set up their own business. Grandma had promised that there would be enough money to pay for the deposit on our new house, but when Mam died she was no longer keen on handing over the money that she and Mam's brothers had given our Mam. She said this was because Mam wasn't going to get to live in her dream house and that, 'Arthur made our Betty live in hovels.' Why should she stump up for a new house for him when Betty wouldn't get any benefit from it?

Grandma didn't trust banks, so the money that she and Mam's many brothers had given to Mam while she was poorly was kept in Mam's fake patent handbag. After Mam died, Dad asked for the handbag. He said it was for me. Grandma said no. Dad asked Mam's eldest brother, John, to intervene.

Uncle John had taken on responsibility for the family along with Grandma, once Grandad had decided to retire to the sofa. It was John who persuaded Grandma that the new house had not just been for Betty but was for 'Betty's bairns as well', and that giving Arthur the money would be what Betty would want. According to our cousin Pat, John's daughter, if Grandma had not stumped up the funds put aside for the deposit for the house in the black handbag then Uncle John would have provided the money himself. By now Uncle John had his own fish and chip shop in Denaby near the colliery as well as working part-time in a paid job. Uncle John always did the right thing and he was Grandma's rock. Whatever the problem was, 'Our John' would always be sent for.

That black, fake patent 1940s handbag is the only thing I have of Mam's.

* * *

After a really long time and lots of visits from Arthur, Dad comes to collect me from the foster parents and takes me to the new house. This is the house that we had all dreamed about since we moved to this town before everything went wrong with

Mam getting poorly. Mam was supposed to have this lovely new house to live in after she got better, but they said she died, so I suppose she won't come now and I just have to accept it, no matter how much I want her back and even though I used up a wish on the only ever time I have won the wishbone. Why do they say you can make a wish if it isn't going to come true? Did I know when I made the wish, was it just a message to Mam to tell her how much I missed her? I don't know but I'm starting to believe that she is not coming back.

Our brand new house is on a beautiful wide open street on a hill. Eighty-six Moor Lane, Netherton, Huddersfield, will be our new address and, even if Mam can't come, the rest of us will all live here together. Well, as soon as Nicky is old enough and can come from Grandma's.

There's only one other house joined onto ours, not like the little ones across the road that are all joined together with pretty gardens at the front. Ours has big windows at the front, upstairs and downstairs. Arthur says we are the first people to live in it and that it's much better than that slum in Leeds Road. There's a little lawn and rose bushes at the front and the same at the back and over the fence there are playing fields. And, just like Mam said, our new school is just up the road, about one minute's walk. It's near Dad's work at the tractor factory too, he says.

In the living room and passageway and all up the stairs there's a red carpet that goes right to the sides. I look in all the bedrooms to see if Mam is there poorly in bed. She's not but

Grandma Cooke and Rhonda are in the living room sitting on a beautiful sofa. There's a special room just for eating in, with a round table and some doors that are really windows that Dad says are called French windows, out onto the garden. It's so nice living with Dad and my family again and Grandma and Rhonda. I've got my own little room over the stairs. It's tiny but there are no other kids in it like there was at the foster family and the Children's Home. It's like we have landed in heaven.

I love my school. I love being with my family again. Soon it's Mischief Night, the last night of October when kids can play tricks on grown-ups or we can play tricks on each other. When we get up and try to get dressed, dad has tied knots in the sleeves of our clothes and taken the tea out of the tea caddy. There's just the tea-caddy spoon left in there. It's great fun. He must have done the mischief after we had gone to bed or before he went to work.

We are all happy here and Dad gives us the best Bonfire night. He makes a little bonfire in the garden and sets off the fireworks while we watch through the French windows. There are Catherine wheels and Roman candles and golden rains and Mount Vesuvius ones and we are allowed to hold sparklers and then we have parkin and potatoes that dad has baked in the fire. Our dad is just the best dad ever, but I wish Mam was here as well.

Then one day, just after bonfire night, Rhonda isn't there anymore. Dad says he ran away because of the bangs but I don't believe him. I know Dad used to shoot rabbits with Rhonda in the fields at the farm so he wouldn't have been afraid of bangs. I think Dad might have shot Rhonda, because just after that Grandma goes to live with Auntie Dorothy and Auntie Dorothy wouldn't want Rhonda to live with her, but I would have looked after him and loved him here.

Now, instead of Grandma Cooke and Rhonda we have Auntie Pat coming to see us on Wednesdays after school and on Saturdays or Sundays at teatime. She looks after us and I help her make tea for us and wash up.

I feel sad that Grandma has gone, so I ask, 'Why doesn't Grandma come back to stay with us, Dad?' Dad never says much, but this time he says, 'Well, she was very old love; she broke 'er hip at Aunt Dorothy's and then she went to t'hospital and she died, so that's why she can't come back. But if she could she would still love thi.'

'What does it mean when you die, Dad?' I ask. 'What happens to you?'

'It's like going to sleep forever, lass.'

'Well if you are only asleep you could just wake up one day,' I say. 'You could just open your eyes and be alive again.'

'It's not like that, lass, you really are asleep forever.'

This makes me feel very sad. If it's true what Dad says, then it means that Mam will be asleep forever as well. But I still don't tell anybody about the wish I made at Grandma Cooke's that Sunday in her cottage by the seaside, before she moved here, when I got the wishbone, and asked for Mam to come back. I can't ask Dad how long I should give the wish fairy because he might tell me that if it was going to come true then it would have by now. But Mam never does come back. Then I imagine opening her coffin to see her, to be close to her, to know what she looked like. I can't remember. My Auntie Grace said once that, 'If you opened up a coffin then the body will still be perfect but if you look away for a second, then it will all turn to dust.'

And I said, 'But what if you don't look away?' I want to say goodbye to her, to say 'I'm sorry I gave you those flowers. I didn't want you to die.'

* * *

Even though I miss Mam and Grandma and Rhonda, I am really excited when it's Christmas. Dad says there is a works do for us kids to go to. He takes us in his van and when we get out we're at David Browns Tractors and we go into a big hall. It's decorated with trimmings and there are three really long trestle tables covered with paper and little paper plates and coloured hats.

The plates are piled high with little triangle sandwiches. Some ladies ask what we would like. 'One of everything please,' I say, because I want to see if I like them all. There's mashed up egg, fish paste, sandwich spread, brawn and cheese spread. We all get lemonade as well and it's fizzy and it goes up my nose. I tell Nicky and we both laugh at the bubbles. I put on our little hats and then reach sandwiches for us both. When everybody has had enough sandwiches, the ladies take them away and come back with pretty little waxed paper trifle bowls with Christmas pudding in them and white sauce on top. I don't really like mine and Nicky just eats the white sauce. But the ladies come back with mince pies and Christmas cake so we have a bit of both of those.

After everybody has finished eating, we have to go to sit on the floor by the Christmas tree because someone special is coming to visit us. Then Santa comes in ringing a school bell and he's got a big sack and I'm sure it's our dad but I don't say anything to Nicky. Santa sits on a chair by the tree and puts his hand in his sack and there's a present for everybody, all wrapped in Christmas paper. When Santa goes, the ladies ask us if we want to go to the toilet so I go and take Nicky. When we get out Dad's there and he finds our coats and takes us to the van and I fall asleep on the way home and I can feel my Daddy lift me up and carry me up to my little bed in my room.

It's Christmas day. I wake up in my own little room in our beautiful new house and go straight into Dad's room. He's buzzing his face with his razor then blowing the bits out into his bin.

'Go and get our Nicky dressed and then it will be time for Christmas,' he tells me.

I pad off, on the lovely carpet that goes all the way to the walls, into the other bedroom. It has a big bed and the window looks out onto the garden. I jump on the bed. Nicky is wide awake and pulling stuff out of a Christmas stocking. I'm saving mine for later when we are all together downstairs. As well as nuts and tangerines, Arthur has toy soldiers and a little gun that he says fires proper matches.

'Sue, Sue' – our Nicky is really excited – 'Father Christmas came in my bedroom in the night, but I peeped because I was trying to keep awake and I think it was Daddy Christmas.' I smile to myself and help Nicky to go to the toilet and then get dressed. Arthur is already playing with his soldiers.

When I'm dressed and Nicky and Arthur are playing soldiers, I go back to Dad's room. 'Na then lass. Let's see what Santa's left thee on this shelf up 'ere.' Dad reaches up to take down a big, long box and I sit on his bed to open it. Inside is the most beautiful doll I have ever seen. She is a grown up lady and has golden hair and a pink and green dress and matching hat with a jewelled brooch on both of them. She has lipstick on and when you move her legs as if she is walking, her head turns from side to side. I love her. I love Dad. I'm so happy. I give Dad a big hug and he takes my hand and we go downstairs. I've got my dolly in the other hand so I can't get my stocking but I can come back up for that later. I want to go down with my Daddy. He makes a fire in the front room and I play with my beautiful lady doll walking her along the carpet while her head turns to look all around. When the fire catches Dad goes to put our Christmas dinner on, so I go up to get my Christmas stocking. Arthur and Nicky are too busy playing to come down yet.

'Do you want me to lay the table Dad?' I ask.

'Aye, that'd be grand lass,' says Dad. So that's what I do.

We all have toast and tea round the fire in the living room then Dad gives us our presents one at a time in age order: 'One for Arthur, one for Susan, one for Nicky.' I've got some roller skates that go over your shoes and Dad adjusts them for me so they fit and I've got a little piano from Grandma Swift and I learn to play 'Jingle Bells' by following the book – 333 333 35123 for the first line – and we've got some presents to share. One is a compendium of games which contains lots of different games like chess and drafts and ludo and snakes and ladders and loads more. We play with our presents while the smells from the kitchen get better and better and soon we sit down to a fantastic Christmas dinner in the dining room.

After I've helped Dad with the washing up, he sets up games from the compendium and we play Ludo and draughts and blow football and we are all happy and cosy by the fire. For tea we just have pork pie and piccalilli, and then for afters there's tinned mandarins with Carnation milk and we have to have bread and marg with it because you can't have just fruit by itself. Then there's Christmas cake and some white cheese that crumbles everywhere.

After tea, the three of us swap sweets from our selection boxes. I like Caramac and Bounty, but Nicky doesn't like coconut so I can have those. I swop for my Turkish Delight. Arthur likes all of his so he's not swapping. Then we play card games that Auntie Pat has taught us and Take Two that Arthur learnt at school. We bet with monkey nuts – peanuts in their shells – when we play cards. I like playing Newmarket and pontoon because you can bet more than once, so you can win lots of peanuts. Then it's sad because it's time for supper and bed, but I've still got my beautiful doll to take to bed, so that's a bit less sad.

With no nice grandma and no Mam and no Rhonda, we only have Dad to love. I love little Nicky as much as I can as well.

* * *

We have been in the house for just two terms at school when one day Dad says we have to leave because we're wrecking it. That's not fair, because it was Arthur who pushed Nicky down the stairs. It wasn't my bum that went through the window. I didn't do anything.

Later Arthur told me that we left the house because we couldn't afford it any more. With Grandma not living with us, Dad had to give up his job travelling around the country fixing newly delivered tractors that had teething problems and go to work in quality control on the production line instead. He also had to pay Auntie Pat to come in twice a week to help look after us. And he was a 60 a day man. Perhaps the bus fares for Arthur to go to grammar school in town cost a lot as well. Perhaps he thought he would get some money when Grandma died, but he didn't.

*　*　*

Do children become more beautiful the more loved they feel? The two children shining out from the black and white picture were dressed with love, in warm clothes against the autumn weather. The four-year-old girl is wearing a blue woollen coat with a velvet collar and matching pocket cuffs. I remember that they were blue, too. My big brother, aged seven, looks smart in a corduroy jerkin with matching pants. We're both wearing socks and smart sandals, like nice school shoes, the ones with cut out diamonds on top. Someone took pride in us. We were loved. We're on the farm, Arthur's jerkin is full of scrumped apples and I'm his accomplice. This was one of the many photos taken of us when Mam was alive. It sings out the pride she took in us.

Then there's the photo from the Children's Home. I'm wearing the blue dress that Mam gave me, that I didn't want to share. Someone who cared has put a ribbon in my hair. The house parents at the Home were kind.

The final photo we have from our childhood screams out the absence of our mother, who by this time is being cared for in Conisbrough. Perhaps Uncle John or Dad took it so mam could have the most recent photo of us. If that was the case she would have had a fright. The three of us are standing in front of Dad's van and we look like Victorian urchins, scruffy and poor. I am wearing a small white apron with a bib, Arthur and I have wellies on. We all have bare legs. But though we may have been poorly turned out when there was just Dad, we were loved. In the seven years after Mam's death, we managed. Dad was good at the dad things: work, overtime, food, paying the mortgage, fixing things, day trips and love. But he was no good at the Mam things: teeth, we never had toothbrushes or visited the dentist, nice clothes, shoes that fitted.

Moving Again, 1960

I'm eight when we move to the eighth house I have lived in, including the Children's Home, living at Grandma Swift's and the foster parents.

Our new house at Tunnacliffe Road, Newsome, is only three miles away, but it could be in another world. It's nearer to town. It feels rougher here and more exposed. It also seems duller — less green, less space. The house is made of stone; it is old and dark, not new and light. It's just one in a row that goes up and down the whole road, not like the lovely house we left that was only joined to one other. There were fields at the back of that house. At the back of this one there's a council estate like the one I lived on with the foster family. This tiny square kitchen has a flagstone floor, not like our long, light, clean kitchen at the beautiful house. There we had a proper dining room and French doors into the garden. That house smelt of paint and polish and new carpets and when you went outside there were trees and roses in the garden that smelt so nice that I tried to make perfume with the petals. This house doesn't smell of anything. I had a best friend next door at the lovely house and our school was just a few doors up the hill. Here I have to take Nicky with me on a long boring walk to school and I don't have any friends.

In this house, the living room and dining room are the same room. We've got all Grandma Cooke's furniture, her huge sideboard and her lovely little organ with lots of white stops with words on. In the kitchen there is a stone sink in one corner and a marble-topped table, a washing machine with a wringer over it and a gas cooker. In the living room there is a little table with a yellow Formica top and Grandma's old chairs. Dad hammers hardboard underneath each one. Now you don't fall through when you sit down but the springs stick up your bum. There's a pine chest of drawers with two food cupboards on top of it and a telly, a Yorkshire range fireplace and a dark green plasticky three piece. There's just lino and an almost threadbare mat on this floor.

In this house the front room is just for best, which is Christmas, but you have to walk through it to get to the stairs. Dad's bureau with the fold-down front is in there. He keeps important papers like our birth certificates, bills and photos in it. There's a tall round lamp on top of it. It has a special brown smell. It's never lit because that would be *a waste of electricity*, but once Dad turned it on to show me that the heat of the lamp makes the horses and hounds ride through the fields after a fox. The lamp and the bureau, like Dad's blue suit, are from a life that we don't live in. There might have been a chance at the new house but not now we live here.

Mam hasn't come back from being dead like I'd asked for in the wish. I have to stop expecting her to come now. It hurts too much when she doesn't. In my mind I can see Grandma Cooke taking down her bun at night before bed into that lovely long, thick grey plait, but I can't remember Mam – except from photos.

I like to be with Dad as much as I can when he's not at work. I watch him while he builds a wall and a door in the big bedroom at the back of the house. The hardboard smells nice. Dad will have one of these little bedrooms, with a single bed. Mine's at the front next to the bathroom. It's loads bigger than the others, but I still want to be back in my tiny room at the lovely house. To cheer me up, Dad takes me to town to choose the wallpaper for my new room. I watch him do the papering while I weave concertinas from the long edges that he's taken off.

There's a back-to-back next door, down the hill from us and two Polish nurses who work at Stores Hall mental hospital live in the back. I don't know who lives in the front. The nurses have a mongrel called Peggy. Dad says he had to drown her puppies. I don't know why he told me that, because it made me very sad. Perhaps he doesn't have anyone else to tell. Perhaps sometimes he thinks I'm Mam. Everybody says I look just like her.

One night, Peggy must have been coming through the hedge into our garden when I threw out the old tea from the teapot onto the rhubarb patch before making a fresh pot. We heard a yelp from the dark and then, 'Has some buggar thrown tea grounds all over you Peggy?' We all laughed (quietly). The daughter of the family in the house next to them goes to the high school and people say that she got herself *into trouble*. Getting into trouble is the worst thing a girl can do.

Every Friday, after our fish and chip supper, Dad puts the immersion heater on for an hour and adds a scoop of Omo or Daz to the bath water. I have to get in first when it's really boiling, then Nicky, and Arthur last. I'm not sure when Dad goes in. The only heating in the whole house is from the coal fire in the living room range, so in winter, on bath night, Dad lights the paraffin stove in the bathroom and tells us, 'Na, tha munt touch that or get watter [this rhymes with 'matter'] on it 'cos it's dangerous.' I don't care. I flick water at the heater so I can hear it sizzle.

I went to Sunday school when we were at the lovely house in Netherton and I'm still allowed to go. Barbara Smith is my Sunday school teacher. She is 21 when I first meet her – tall, slim, very smartly dressed and clever. She has short blonde hair in a tidy, curly style cut into her neck and says love in a special way, pronouncing the 'o' like in 'lost'. She has taken me under her wing and every week after Sunday school she invites me to her house for tea and we sometimes go on picnic trips with her little dog Hamish (a white Scottish terrier) or on local walks with her friends. She is a secretary at David Brown's Tractors where Dad works.

Barbara is a bright star in a dull world. Although I only see her on Sundays, I take her with me all week, somewhere inside. She is part mum and part big sister. I stayed over at her house when it was my birthday and in the morning she played *She Loves You* by the Beatles on her Dansette to wake me up. It was a birthday present from her. Then she took me shopping to buy some shoes. I love listening to the LP she has of *South Pacific*. We know all the songs off by heart. She took me to visit an uncle of hers who lives in a different world to ours: he had a conservatory and had brown sugar cubes with his tea or maybe it was even coffee. She has a friend called Sue who lets me plink plonk on her piano and another one called Rhoda who got engaged and showed us her opal and diamond ring. More than anything, Barbara is kind.

PIG SWILL AND THE PEE BUCKET

Since Mam died, we've spent every school holiday at Grandma Swift's. Arthur takes us on three buses and as soon as we arrive, Arthur and Nicky change into their playing out clothes and the wellies that grandma buys for us every year and go down my uncles' allotments to play around with the dogs, pigs, hens and pigeons. When we came out of the Children's Home Nicky slept in a cot in the tiny room next to where Mam died. Now that room's used to keep crates of Babysham and other stuff from the wholesalers that Grandma can shop at because of the chip shop. I sleep in the back bedroom on my own. There's a bath in it, a sink and a tallboy, but no toilet.

Up the uncarpeted staircase to the second floor there are two large attic rooms with bare floorboards and treasure. Here we found a *National Geographic* magazine with pictures of dark-skinned women with eyes painted on their naked breasts. I asked Grandma about the piano accordion up here and she said it was Dad's. He'd left it with her as a deposit for a loan. I wonder what the loan was for and if he could play the accordion and if he ever paid the money back? The accordion seemed to belong to the world of the hunting lamp and the bureau and Dad's blue suit, a world that we just missed somehow, perhaps because Mam died.

Our favourite thing up here is the wind-up gramophone and pile of old 78s. When we put in a new stylus, we can just hear George Formby distantly singing about Granddad's flannelette night shirt or leaning on the lamp post.

Downstairs there are three big rooms – the living room with the range and dinner table, the front best room which also has a fireplace, and the middle bedroom where Grandma sleeps. Tacked onto the back of the house is a little kitchen whose sink runs into a drain in the yard. Grandma, squats at this drain when she can't make the few extra feet up the yard to the lav. Her overall pinny makes sure you can't see her bum. I don't think she wears drawers 'cos she never pulls anything down before she goes and when she's been sitting down her pinny gets stuck in what she calls, the 'nick of her bum'.

Grandma Swift is almost square shaped and would feel undressed without her overall floral pinny, the sort you put on over your head. She has scant grey candyfloss for hair, probably from all the home perming, and only wears her teeth and corsets for weddings and funerals. Her 90-denier American tan stockings come to just below her knees and need to be regularly re-knotted with a deft twist of her equally knotted but fully dexterous fingers.

The Co-op is just opposite Grandma's and outside it there's a bubble gum machine. By turning the knob really carefully not quite all the way round each time, I discover I can empty it with one penny. I share my booty with all the kids that play out. I do this a few holidays until the manager's penny drops and he realises that the machine is only cleared out when we're there. He wouldn't dare question Grandma, nobody would, so it's always out of order when we visit after that.

'I think Arthur should give me the Family Allowance when you're staying here.' This is the only time I ever heard Grandma say anything that could be taken as a complaint about having to look after us.

I used to go out and play in the allotments. I collected the eggs and helped Uncle Arnold put potato peelings into a boiler to make the pigs' dinner. The steam curled up and joined onto the clouds in the sky. I wondered if clouds were just steam that had gone a long way up. The pigs squealed when we put the boiled potato peelings mixed with meal into the metal trough. Their mouths were like shovels digging up the food. But now I'm bigger I'm not allowed to go down the gardens any more, I have to help Grandma. She puts me to work while Arthur and Nicky play out. It's not fair.

On Mondays I fill up the copper boiler with a pan from the sink tap, go round the bedrooms with Grandma to collect the washing, peg it out, bring it in and help fold it. On Tuesdays I'm not allowed near the iron, I just fetch and carry the laundry. On baking day I have to take the barm cakes to and from the range to be turned while they rise.

'Don't brush your hair near me bread, the lads'll gip if they get that in their throat.'

Her lads are more important than me. What about me? Don't I matter? I don't care about the hair, what I care about is the difference in what she thinks about 'the lads' and what she thinks about me. It's like when Arthur tells us that Auntie Dorothy has given him 10 bob for getting a good school report. She never even asks about how I'm doing in school and I know Dad doesn't care because he said I don't need to bother – but he is very proud of Arthur's school work.

But when the first of the bread cakes are ready and still warm, I'm allowed to have one. They smell of yeast and drip with best butter. Though even that doesn't make up for not being out having fun down the gardens with the dogs. I'm bored, bored, bored.

It was Uncle Cyril who taught me to tell the time. He used to be a miner but Grandma says he's badly with his heart. Now he spends his time between the sofa, the bookies and his pigeons down the gardens. If he's not well he stays in bed and I have to take him cups of tea and empty his pee bucket. It stinks.

I'm sure the only reason they don't get me to clean the front step and run over its edge with the donkey stone is because Grandma doesn't want the neighbours to know they are using me as a slave. One day, at home, a neighbour said to me that my hands 'look like an old woman's'. That was when I was 10.

We get free coal because Uncle Cyril was down the pit. I have to keep refilling the coal bucket from the coal 'ole, right up the end of the yard, all day and once, when there was a delivery, I had to shovel the heap of coal from the cinder path behind the house into the coal 'ole with the big shovel. My other daily jobs are feeding the dogs their tinned food mixed with sliced white bread – 'And don't cut your fingers on the tin.' I make lots of cups of tea for Grandma – 'Be careful! That's hot and don't break that' – between tidying, dusting and sweeping.

The worst and most boring thing I had to do, just once, was to use the eyer, the pointy bit on the end of a potato peeler, to remove the eyes (the bits where the sprouts would grow from) out of all the potatoes for the night's chips. The water I took them from and put them back into was freezing, my hands were red raw when I'd finished. I have to go and help in the chip shop most nights it's open, but I'm not allowed to do anything except stand around and fetch more peeled spuds when they're needed.

'Keep away from that chipper, you might cut your fingers off.'

'Don't go near that hot pan or you might burn yourself or get a hair on the chips.'

'No, you can't take the money, you might give the wrong change.'

But Uncle Albert trusts me. He lets me serve behind the counter in his hardware shop in the village. I know where things are and how to take the money and give change – that's fun.

The chip shop is really boring and sometimes the customers talk about me.

'Is that your Betty's lass? Oooh, she's the image of her.' They always say that. I hate it. I don't want to look like Mam. I don't want to die when I'm 33.

'Aye,' Grandma once replied to one of these comments, 'but our Betty's legs weren't so hefty.'

On the evenings when we're not at the chip shop, Grandma gets me to brush her hair while she cries for her dead children. She'd lost five of them already.

'Why did He have to take me bairns, why couldn't He have taken me?'

Why's she telling me, over and over, the same words? I don't want to know. She tells me other things that I'm too young to hear, like what she said to Grandad when he had a stroke – 'Ah tha'll not lift that hand na more ta strike me.' But I have to keep on brushing and pray that *Coronation Street* will soon be on so she'll watch that and I can stop doing jobs for half an hour.

About twice a week, when I've been working for Grandma all day, I dare to ask to go across the road to my aunt's house. Grandma usually lets me go but she expects me to spy on her daughter-in-law. Auntie Grace gives me and my two cousins, Corrine and Cynthia, lovely homemade meals and is the only person to ever buy me an ice cream from the van.

I'm only six months older than Corrine but I'm twice her height. That might be why people treat me like a grown up.

The kind women in my life, like Auntie Grace and my Sunday school teacher Barbara, treat me like a child who still needs a mum. I wish I could just come and stay with Auntie Grace for the whole holiday or, if I have to stay at Grandma's, go down the allotments to mess around with the others. It's like I have to earn all our keep.

My three uncles who still live with Grandma – Arnold, Cyril and Georgie (who we have to call uncle but, rumour has it, is really our cousin) – have their meals sitting at the table. Us kids have to stand. At dinner time I shift the trammel on the table onto the other half and put newspapers down to protect the table protector. I get money from Grandma to go to the Co-op to buy a quarter of potted beef or brawn, or I have to heat up a small tin of soup between the three of us kids, rinsing it out with water to make it go further. We fill up on Grandma's bread cakes and best butter. The only sweet stuff around is arrowroot biscuits. When I'm on my own I make an arrowroot sandwich with butter between the two tasteless biscuits.

I like chips in a barm cake, and best of all if there's a left-over fish for us to share. If not, I put bits on the chips. Bits are the escaped squiggles of batter that get fried along with the fish and chips. Sometimes people ask for them specially if they can't afford a fish. 'Chips wi bits on please.' The heat of the fish or chips melts the butter and as you bite into it the creamy butter mixes with the tomato sauce and, if it's a Saturday dinner time, mushy peas. After your teeth get through the soft buttery bread there's the perfect crispness of the batter then the softness of the chips and the fish... it's heaven. Eating a fish and chip butty can make me forget how unfair everything is.

On Sundays eight of us sit at the table, even us kids. We have Yorkshire puddings with the fat crozzled on the bottom and thick gravy on top, then meat, spuds and peas and more gravy. I have to help make it all, serve it, then clear away. The worst bit is the washing up. Every surface, including the gas rings and the fold-down door of the tall kitchen cupboard, is covered with greasy plates, pans and the big roasting tin. They wouldn't dare do this to me if Mam was alive.

In one of the big pans there's still some of the potato and swede I'd mashed with butter and milk. I pick up one of the great big serving spoons, dig it into the mash and shove it in my mouth. It's like baby food. I smooth the mash on the spoon with my top teeth as I pull the spoon out again just leaving a little pile on my tongue. I'm like Cinderella. I hate them for making me do all this work. Why don't the others have to do it? Why can't I go out and play down the allotments with the animals? Why do I have to stay here and help Grandma?

I put the spoon back in my mouth upside down and lick the mash off it. I'm already really full so I have to force it down. It's the only thing I can give myself. I do it in secret so it's like stealing. I want to steal something from them as payback for all the slavery. It's not just Grandma, Uncle Arnold is really mean and makes me do all the washing up. Its only Uncle Cyril and Georgie that don't say anything mean. There's no way out of my life but the feel of the mash in my mouth, just for that moment, makes it better.

My tummy screams at me to stop. I can't. I roll my tongue over another spoonful of mash. Then I push it through my teeth while I take the kettle off the gas and pour the boiling water into the sink. It's hard to force it down but I have to. I force it down because I don't go to a good school like Arthur, because I'm always bored at home, because all I do here is housework and because my life is wasting away. I want to read or even just play, but there are no books and no one to play with.

* * *

The doorbell rings and I'm sent to open it. It's Lillian, the daughter of Mam's older sister, Aunt Alice. They live in the next street. She's six months older than me. She tells Grandma her mam is very poorly. Aunt Alice is always poorly with her asthma so this must be really bad. The family think she needs to go to hospital. She is due to go in the next day anyway. I'm sent to the doctor with a note. The doctor won't go to see her, he just gives me some medicine.

I run down the street to Aunt Alice's house. She's leaning over the open bureau, failing to get her breath. She thanks me between hungry gasps and manages a thin smile. I fetch her some water from the little back kitchen and open the pills for her then go back to tell Grandma.

Aunt Alice dies in the night. She's 51. They send for the doctor again and this time he comes to sign the death certificate. Her husband grabs the doctor by the throat and shakes him. 'Ah, tha'll bloody come now won't tha, nar it's too late!' he says, as the neighbours send for the bobby.

*   *   *

Aunt Alice's death certificate cited congestive cardiac failure but, as I was to learn later, the poor woman's life had been as tragic as my mother's. It was not good to be born female and poor at that time, in that place.

Though I angrily resented those visits to Grandma's, I absorbed several important lessons from them. I grew up eschewing boredom. I knew I was different to the people who lived in that South Yorkshire pit village. I knew I was yearning for something bigger and these stays at Grandma's when Nicky and Arthur had the freedom to run and play with my uncles' animals and I was forced to clean and work for my grandmother served to stoke a desire to *do* something with my life. Back then, suffering from boredom and physical, social and mental confinement, I had no idea what that meant. I just knew I wanted out of this kind of life as soon as possible. Perhaps that's what my mother had been seeking when she left home for Filey.

Scrap Heap for Scruffs, 1963

When we had been in Netherton and Grandma Cooke had left to live with Auntie Dorothy, Dad had found Auntie Pat to help look after us. She still comes to us on Wednesday teatime and Saturdays. She is about 60, not much over five foot, has fluffy dyed hair, wears face powder and draws her eyebrows on. She is married to a man she calls 'the Spaceman' and she is Dad's sort-of girlfriend.

She helped me to knit my very first thing (a dishcloth) for school in Netherton, when I was seven; navigated me through the terror and shock of my first period at 12, showing me how to sling what felt like a board rubber between my legs; teaches us card games and how to cha-cha and eat soup like posh people do. She even takes us to the flicks to see Cliff Richard in *Summer Holiday* and comes with us all to see *Ben-Hur*. Sometimes, when we're getting tea ready together, she links my arm and we march around the room singing, 'We're silly old maids, we walk along, want a chap and we can't get one.' When I get to 13 she comes into my room to say goodnight and tells me to dream of teddy bears, not teddy boys. She is with us for six years and I love her.

When Auntie Pat isn't here, I make beef burger and chips, sausage and mash or egg and chips for tea for all of us. Once a week we have domestic science (DS) at school and whatever I make for tea, I bring home and we eat it together. When we kids are home alone in the daytime, I make our own version of Welsh rarebit – bread toasted one side and then marged on the other and put back under the grill till it's crozzled. None of us had ever had Welsh rarebit or even proper cheese, except with Christmas cake at Christmas, just spread cheese triangles. We also make sandwiches with tomato sauce or crisps or golden syrup or jam (always Bramble seedless because of Dad's false teeth. He had all his removed as a birthday present when he was 21).

On Friday nights, we have fish and chips that Arthur or I have to fetch. On Saturdays we have a treat tea. Well, Dad thinks it's a treat but I don't like the cold sliced pale meat that he sometimes asks me to get in town from the barbecue chicken place. I'd rather have a pork pie, but not if it's hot and the jelly has melted. I do like the buns we have though. Dad and Arthur have a favourite. Arthur's is meringue with cream in the middle; Dad really likes date and walnut cake. I have a different one each time so I don't really have a favourite and Nicky likes whatever I get. Dad always watches the wrestling on a Saturday. On Sundays I help Dad with our special Sunday dinner before I go off to Sunday school and tea at Barbara's. If I need any extra food for us in the week, I just get it on tick at the corner shop and Dad pays it off when he gets his wages.

Once I got a packet of special biscuits and kept them for myself. I thought I deserved it. I got away with that but another time, when I was 13, I got five Woodbine and the shopkeeper told Dad. I got told off but he didn't hit me like he would have done if it had been Arthur. But Arthur would never have done that.

Every day I walk Nicky to our new school. I follow the other kids and find a little shortcut through a wood where the dry-stone walls are broken at either end. If we've got any pocket money left, we call in at the sweetshop where we have to cross the main road with the lollipop lady. Nicky goes to the infants' side and I go to the juniors. After I've been here a few days the secretary gives me a big bag of her clothes. They're too old and too posh for me even though I'm big enough for them. One of the skirts has permanent pleats.

At break, in the teachers' kitchen, I take the milk off the gas just as it's about to get to the top of the pan. When I've made their coffee, I go down to the school hall, which is also the dining room, and I get all the packets of biscuits out for the other children to buy one or two to have at break time. A friend helps me and we sing Cliff Richard songs while we're setting up the Lincoln biscuits, which have dots on, and malted milks that have pictures of cows feeding their babies. Afterwards I give the money to the teachers. Sometimes they send me to the infants' side to help with the little ones.

My big brother Arthur just managed to pass his 11-plus at South Crosland Juniors, the school next to the lovely house.

Dad and Dad's sister Auntie Dorothy are really pleased with him. I really want to go to grammar school as well but Dad doesn't want me to.

'Tha's a lass, tha dunt need to go ta t'high school. When tha' finishes school tha can stop 'ere and look after me. It's bad enough 'aving to keep up wi' uniforms an books for one wiout 'aving ta do it for thee an' all.'

At the end of the year I don't come top at anything and you only get a prize if you come top. But because I was so helpful and clever in other ways, the teachers feel I should have got a prize, so they invent a new school prize for me, for 'initiative', and I get presented with a book. They all expect me to pass the 11-plus so I suppose I must be good at some things, but maths frightens me and I can't spell, and I miss lots of lesson time helping the teachers because they think I am so grown up and helpful.

When it's time for me to sit the exam I'm really worried. Some of the questions are easy and obvious but in none of the six schools I've been to has anyone taught me how to work out about how long it takes men to dig holes, so I have to guess. And anyway, everyone says that girls can't do maths.

I know that if you're going to the high school you get a fat envelope. I pray to Jesus for one. When the envelope with the council stamp on it arrives, it's thin. I want to cry. I feel angry. They've cheated me. Everything nice happens to everybody else. Nothing nice happens to me. I can't help it if I'm a girl.

The teachers are really surprised and sad. They can't understand why I'm not going to the high school. I can. It's obvious. I'm scruffy and it's only the kids with smart clothes who are going to the high schools. The rest of us scruffs are being shoved on the scrap heap of the secondary modern. The rest of us, except me and a few others, live on the council estate.

* * *

It was clear to me even then that the system was there to maintain the separation of proles and posh. Better off kids got caught in the colander of grammar school while the ones in cheap slippery nylon anoraks fell through into the sink school. As an adult, my smouldering resentment at being sent to a secondary modern was re-ignited to full flames when I discovered that girls had to score 10 per cent higher than boys on the 11-plus exam in order to keep the number of each sex equal at high schools. Although Arthur only scraped a pass in the 11-plus, he was soon brilliant at maths. That's what going to a good school can do.

Was it the 10 per cent differential responsible for my failure, my nomadic early years in six primary schools, or the powerful discouragement at home? The other possibility is unthinkable, that I did pass but Dad declined a place for me at high school because of my sex and the expense involved.

When I was an infant, I never felt angry at whatever happened to us, just helpless and bereft. My only attempt at rescue and retaliation had been the wish for the return of our mother. But now, aged 11, here was something that I felt was a grave injustice. I had been put on the wrong train, the one that goes nowhere.

I could have learnt so much and shone at grammar school like my big brother and perhaps followed my dream of being a vet. Instead I wasted seven years bored out of my wits, first at school, then doing mindless menial jobs, before I began the process of getting *myself* educated.

Secondary modern school was little more than a vehicle for lowering self-esteem and ambition and training us for the more lowly positions in society. While my contemporaries at the high schools could contemplate A-levels, university applications and consider career options, the best we could hope for was to become wives, work in the local mill or go for cannon fodder in the army.

MADEMOISELLE, AN
EPIDIASCOPE AND MR WOOD

At least the five of us who, in my 11-year-old's opinion, should have gone to the grammar were all put in the A stream. It's our first day at the new school. I choose two of my friends for our class representatives. The teacher opens up the pieces of paper and announces, 'Susan Cooke, you have the most votes.' What? That can't be right. Why would my classmates pick me? But they did. Wow! I can't wait to tell Dad and Auntie Pat. I skip home.

Auntie Pat is there when I get in. She's getting our tea ready.

'I got picked as class representative at school,' I tell her.

'Well, it's probably just because you're the biggest one,' she says.

I don't bother to tell Dad.

The art teacher is gorgeous, just like Dave Berry the pop star, and I'm really good at writing sketches for drama. Everything else is boring. Then the A stream starts French lessons taught by Mademoiselle, a teaching assistant. She has a big poster covered in all kinds of activities and tells us in French what's happening in each part of the scene. I walk around school saying *le pneu crevé,* the French for punctured tyre, because I love the special sounds. Mademoiselle says my accent is perfect. I can't spell in English but, because she teaches us how, I can spell all the French words. I'm top of the class. Then, after just one term the lessons stop.

'Why can't we do French any more, Miss?' I ask Miss Whittle, the deputy head, when I'm helping her with the Freedom from Hunger charity display.

'The council has decided that pupils at our school don't need to learn French, Susan.'

'That's a shame Miss, I really liked those lessons.'

Miss Whittle teaches us art appreciation. She puts pictures inside an epidiascope – a huge machine with a light in it which projects a large image of the picture onto a screen on the wall. We learn to appreciate the old masters, Gainsborough's portraiture, Stubbs' horses, Constable's landscapes and the dramatic style of Turner. She shines a light into a world that is more than smoke-blackened cottages, mill chimneys, low expectations and housework.

Mr Wood, our new music teacher, is pure honey. He infects us with his passion for Gilbert and Sullivan; we thrill to Benjamin Britten's *The Little Sweep* and are indulged in any number of silly songs that make music fun. I go from being ashamed to sing, after my primary school experience of being told to keep quiet because I put the others off, to joining the new school choir and singing solo in *From Out of a Wood Did a*

Cuckoo Fly, as part of the Christmas service. I feel really warm inside, even though there's nobody in the audience that's there to watch me.

I never forget my swimming costume, rubber swimming cap, towel and Oxo cube every Thursday. We walk the half-mile from school to Cambridge Road baths to train for our certificates. When we're dressed and dry we put our Oxo cube in a cup and the teacher adds hot water.

One week a girl pipes up, 'Miss, Miss, my mum forgot to pack my Oxo cube.'

And for the first time I realise that other children not only get their food made by their mums, and their clothes washed and ironed and their beds changed – all things that I do at home for all of us – but they don't even have to pack their own swimming stuff or Oxo cubes. I don't usually notice I don't have a mum to look after me but hearing about the Oxo cube gives me a big, heavy, sad feeling.

* * *

It's a grey day with a chill wind. Maggie and I lark about as we walk around the back of the hall building, past where the ice cream van parks and the hundred yards out to the cricket pavilion on the playing fields. I look around to see if I can see John, the young groundsman with the Beatles haircut, long lashes and long legs in narrow jeans. Apart from his big nose, he's gorgeous. He's as gorgeous as George Harrison.

When we're both on the field at the same time I look at him longingly and he hides under his fringe. He's not there today. I ask the little old groundsman about him and he says John is always in college on Thursdays – the day we have PE.

'Leave your coats hanging up in the pavilion girls, the weather is fine.'

'Yes, Miss.' I hang my thin bri-nylon anorak on the peg besides Anne Longley's and Linda Bright's well-padded ones.

I'm quite good at rounders. I can usually whack the ball. The previous week I'd been picked for the school rounders team. I was really excited. I knew that being in the team would change my dreary life and make it more like my big brother's, as Arthur is always playing in some team or other. But then in the first practice game I whacked the ball well past the farthest fielder then set off running. I realised I'd forgotten to drop my bat so I threw it behind me for the next batter and ran as fast as I could round the posts. I did a full rounder before I realised that there was a commotion around the backstop. It seems that she was hit with the bat. I was banished from the field in shame and that was the end of my plans for sporting glory.

Today I'm careful to drop the bat straight down and we have a great game. Back at the pavilion where we've left our stuff, I pull on my anorak and shove my red-with-cold hands into my pockets to try and warm them up. As feeling returns, I notice something very strange in there.

'Ann,' I say, 'there's something in my pocket that wasn't there before the game and it doesn't feel very nice.' I fish it out. We all look in shock and then horror as I drop it.

'Yeuck,' says Linda.

'Ugh, what is it?' says Ann.

Somehow some of us know what it is without having seen anything like it before.

'It's a rubber Johnny filled with spunk,' says Maggie, matter-of-factly.

'You have to tell someone,' says one of the Gillians, the daughter of the local bobby. She and I sometimes go in the caravan at the top of their long back garden and, for some reason, at her suggestion, we drip hot wax on each other's bare bellies.

'I'm not telling Miss,' I say, thinking of the new sports teacher who makes me go in the shower with the others even though I am the only one who is *developed*, 'and I can't tell the head or our form teacher, Mr Stevens.'

'Well, tell Miss Whittle then, you're her pet,' suggests Ann.

I think of the time when Miss Whittle caught a group of us smoking down the field and told me that if it hadn't been for that I would have been a prefect. I'm sure she was secretly pleased, because they don't really want prefects with scruffy clothes and laddered stockings.

I go to the toilets in the pavilion and get some of the Izal toilet paper while the others stand guard over the thing, then I carefully pick it up in the paper and, once it's wrapped, I hold the very edge so I don't have to feel the disgusting squidgy bit. It's break time now and I don't want to keep it with me so I go to the staff room, knock at the door and ask for the deputy head.

'What is it Susan?' she says when she appears. 'You look upset.'

'Miss,' I say, stretching out the vowel, 'someone put this in my pocket while we were playing rounders.'

It seems easier to pass her the thing because it's in the tissue now and she won't see it at first. 'Careful, Miss, it's not nice,' I say.

'Oh, Susan, how awful for you,' she says after opening enough of the paper. 'Do you have any idea who it might be?'

I feel so relieved that she cares, that she isn't angry with me, or suspicious that I was to blame in some way, and that she's taking it so seriously.

I think it might be the old groundsman with a hunch back and a limp because he's always leering at me but I don't dare to tell her this. I'm frightened that he'll know I told her and do something worse to me.

'No, Miss,' I say, 'but there was only us and one groundsman there.'

'You leave this with me Susan and I'll make sure that nothing like this ever happens again.'

It doesn't, but the old man still leers.

BULLYING AND BLACKMAIL, 1965

It's my turn in the rope, they're calling me in: 'So come in my Susan dear, Susan dear, Susan dear while Jane goes out to tea...' A big rough girl from the B stream in the next year up is watching us and, after my turn is finished, she comes up to me, pokes me in the chest and says, 'Hey you, you're trying to steal my boyfriend.'

Our game stops, my friends move to be close to me. Eventually I twig – she must mean the scrawny older lad from the council estate that hangs about the rec. He's talked to me a couple of times. It's nice that somebody bothers with me but I definitely don't fancy him, he's ugly.

'I'm going to bash you for trying to steal him,' she says, 'I'll get you on Friday after school so you can't go whinging to the teachers.'

She's built like a bulldozer and more scary than any lad but I'm with my mates so before I can stop myself I say, 'I'm not interested in your bloody boyfriend. It was him who talked to *me*.'

'Don't try and get out of it, he would never talk to another girl when he's got me, I'll get you on Friday.'

'Right, let's go to the bogs,' says Maggie.

When we get there, we check there's no spies from the enemy camp. My mates decide that the best thing to do is to spread the word that I'm a good fighter and I've never lost a fight. The last bit is true, because I've never had one. When I was little, I remember fighting with my arms rotating like a windmill but forwards, but I'm not little any more. We all leave the school together on Friday, just in case, but the rumours have worked. The bulldozer isn't there.

Then the following Monday she's on at me again. 'You're a thief, you are,' she says, wagging her finger at me.

I just glare at her, trying to look as hard as my mates have said I am, but inside I'm shaking.

'I know you nicked those stockings,' she says, looking at my legs. 'If you don't nick some for me, I'll tell on you.'

My lovely thick dark stockings aren't the usual cheap ones I can afford with my spendo. At 13, I'm taller than anybody else in our class and because of my long legs the cheap stockings are so stretched that they ladder after a day and I have to stop the ladder with the nail varnish I nick from Boots. The rubber buttons on my jumble sale suspender belt snap off and I use farthings or a sixpence instead. Dad doesn't give me money for stockings because he wants me to stay in long socks and freeze because stockings are too expensive and, according to him, I'm too young for them. So the bulldozer bully is right: I did nick this thick comfy pair from the indoor market. When Dad saw them he said, 'They look like good stockings, where did they come from?'

'They were on sale in the market Dad, only a shilling a pair,' I lied.

'Well here's another bob so tha' can get thi sen another pair.'

They're at least five bob and I have no intention of stealing some for this bully.

* * *

Arthur reads (and I devour any books he brings home). Arthur goes to Scouts (I stood outside the Guides' hut longing to be inside but I have no money for a uniform or subs). Arthur does sport (I got chucked off the rounders team on my first game). Arthur learns interesting things at school (we don't get taught anything useful or interesting).

All I have is nicking.

Every Saturday I go either shopping (window- or -lifting) or swimming. If I don't nick stuff, I'll have no hair lacquer, make up or presents for birthdays and Christmas. My best places are Boots and Woolies but I also do the indoor market. I've been doing it for ages and I've never been caught.

Then one Saturday just before Dad's birthday I call in at Woolies. I pull open one of the big heavy doors under the red sign and visit a few stalls helping myself to a small sachet of hair lacquer for me and, at a different counter, a large jar of Brylcreem for Dad's birthday. It's dead easy. Then I pick up a pad of Basildon Bond for Dad and I know that someone has seen me. I head straight for the side door.

A floor-walker stops me and sends for the coppers. I'm so embarrassed. My cheeks burn while I wait in a room with nothing on the walls and no seats, just a table. When the two policemen come one says, 'Now give me your duffel bag,' and as he starts unpacking the contents onto the table he asks, 'Well, what's all this for?'

'I'm going swimming,' I tell him.

He unrolls my cossie from my towel and handles the lacquer and then the jar of Brylcreem, 'And the Brylcreem?'

I know I'm for it now.

'That's for my Dad,' I say, telling the barefaced truth. He then puts the towel, cossie, the small amount of money I have for the baths and the bus home and the lacquer and Brylcreem back in my bag. 'Now come along let's take you back home, we need to have a word with your mum and dad.'

'I haven't got a mum, only a dad.'

If it wasn't for the embarrassment, I could have been excited to ride in a proper police car with a red stripe and a blue light on top. All the time I'm sitting in the car, my mind's racing around the obstacle course of Dad and what he'll say. When the car stops, I say, 'Can I go in first please so that I can tell Dad what's happened? He might be too upset if he sees you straight away.'

I know it will be better for me to tell Dad myself. He won't hit me on my own but he might clip me in front of the coppers, just to show them he's disciplining me.

'All right then, but we can only give you five minutes,' says the one who'd looked in my bag.

I get out of the car and go down the ginnel and along the back of next door's house, across the flags to our house and every step feels harder and my legs heavier. Dad is sat in his chair watching football. Poor Dad. All he ever asks for is a quiet life and I've brought trouble home.

'Dad, there's two policemen in a car outside. I got caught shop-lifting and they brought me back,' I say as quick as I can.

'Tha what?' Dad says, getting up and turning down the telly. 'What's tha done?'

The two policemen must have thought better of their offer once they'd seen me disappear down the passageway because the next minute one of them is braying on the back door. He looks relieved when he sees me through the window. Dad lets them in.

'Is this your daughter?' he asks Dad.

'Aye, that's reet,' Dad replies to the coppers. 'What's ta do?'

'Has your daughter explained that she was caught shop-lifting?'

'Aye, she 'as that,' says Dad. 'Can we get thee a cup a tea?'

'No thank you,' says the tallest, and the other looks disappointed.

'Well, will thi sit down for a minute?' Dad says. 'I used to be in the specials mesen during the war, so I know a bit about it. I hope tha won't be too hard on t'lass, they have no mam and I manage on me own, but that'll change soon so we'll be able to keep more of an eye on 'em.'

I stay nearby looking at my shoes.

'Well, we can't say what will happen, but it's likely that she'll get a formal caution and no record as she's under age and it's a first offence, but I can't promise owt.'

'What did she pinch?' asks Dad.

'A pad of writing paper, best quality, Basildon Bond.'

After the policemen leave, I make a cup of tea for us all while Dad rolls one of his fags.

'Ah,' Dad says when he has his tea and has lit up, 'that pad a Basildon Bond woulda come in reet 'andy.' Dad would never encourage us to steal, but he has found something to say to make me feel better and it works. I wonder what he meant about things changing though, it's not like Dad to tell lies.

A week later I go in to the sergeant. No adult ever accompanies us for anything. If it concerns Nicky then I go with him, and if it's me then I go alone.

The officer at the station is much more serious than the two that had taken me home. He speaks to me very sternly about what I've done and then says, 'Now you have any other offences that you want to be taken into account?'

'What does that mean?' I ask.

'Well, if you have done any more shoplifting or anything else that is against the law and you tell us about it now, then you can't get into trouble for it later, we will wipe the slate clean.'

I think about all the make-up and other stuff I nick almost every week that they can't possibly know about and I'm sure I'm OK on the lacquer and Brylcreem.

'Well I did steal a pair of stockings from the market. A girl at school said I had to steal some for her and I don't want to. She said if I didn't, she would tell on me.'

'Oh, did she?' says the officer, making a note of the bulldozer's name. 'Well, we'll be having a word with her.'

My smile is only on the inside.

I'm given an official warning and no criminal record like the other bobby had said and I never have any bother from that girl again.

Running Away with Toffee

Some Saturdays I go to the pictures. I use my spending money, along with the odd bob and tanner that I nick from the change that Dad collects in one of Grandma's bowls. There are two matching silver bowls held between two angels that stand on her huge sideboard. I buy a Mivi ice lolly from the machine outside before I go in because it's cheaper than from the usherette in the interval.

'Hello, you on yer own?' says a lad, and when I nod, scared to speak because he's so gorgeous, he sits down next to me. He's got dark hair that comes over his forehead like a pop star and I feel really shy. In the interval he tells me he's got a motorbike. He holds my hand in the film and I feel all warm inside.

'Do you fancy meeting up next Saturday and I'll take you for a ride on my bike?' he says when the film finishes.

His name is Steve and we meet in town the following Saturday and we go across the tops on his Norton. It's near bonfire night and we stop at a bonfire to watch the fireworks and hold hands watching the sparks and flames crackling before they disappear into the black sky. We snog and cuddle and he takes me straight home after the fireworks. I tell Arthur about him.

'Where's tha off ta?' Dad asks the following week, when I'm all dressed up, my hair backcombed and lacquered. 'Tha dunt need that muck on thi face, a lovely young lass like thee. Is tha goin' to meet a lad?'

'Yes Dad.'

'What's 'is name?'

'Steve.'

'And where did tha meet him?'

'At the pictures.'

'And how old is he?'

'He's 21.'

''E's what? Thas only 13! Well, tha's not meetin' 'im and tha's not seein' 'im again and that's that.'

'Why not? He's nice. I can't not go. He'll think I've stood him up, can't I just meet him to tell him I can't see him again Dad, please Dad?'

'Tha's not goin' an' that's final.'

Dad doesn't say why I can't meet Steve. He's the best lad I've ever met. The ones my age at school seem really young and I'm taller than all the ones in my year. I go to my room and sulk. He'll be hanging around waiting for me and thinking I've stood him up. If I could tell him then maybe we could wait until I'm old enough to go out with him. I moan the lyrics to *A World Without Love* by Peter and Gordon.

My sulks, moans and sobs turn to anger and I hatch a plan. Next day I pack my duffel bag for school with some spare clothes. We're making toffee in DS today. I've got the ingredients ready. I can take the toffee with me when I run away.

After school I set off. I don't know where to go. I just walk at the side of the road and walk and walk till it's getting dark. I'm frozen inside as well as outside and most of all I need a wee. I know I'm beat. I'm in Dewsbury. I see a police station's blue light and I remember the time we lost Mam at the market in Doncaster and the milk and biscuits and warm fire.

'I've run away from home and I need the toilet,' I say when I get in.

There's no milk or biscuits, not even a cup of tea or a fire, just hard mean faces and snide looks. The policewoman goes through my duffle bag and picks up the toffee that I should have simmered for longer – it looks more like fudge.

'What's this?' she asks with a mean voice, looking at me with her currant eyes.

What's wrong with her? 'It's toffee,' I say. 'We made it at school.'

'And why do you have it in your bag?'

Is she thick or what?

'Where do you live? Where are your parents?'

'I've just got a dad. He's working nights at David Browns Tractors.'

Still no milk, or biscuits, or even a cup of tea and definitely no kindness.

Dad arrives and speaks to the policewoman then tells me to get in his painted-with-a-brush dusky pink, more-filler-than-car Hillman Minx. There is no prodigal daughter reunion or fatted fish and chip supper on the way home because I've missed tea.

'Now what the bloody 'ell does tha' think tha's playing at?' he says once the car's going. 'Police dragging me outta work in t'middle a' t'night.' (It is about 9 o'clock.)

Dad is never angry with me. Even more of me closes up. I don't know myself what I'm playing at, and I can't think of anything to say that won't make him more angry. He drives on towards Huddersfield.

'If tha' dun't say summat sharpish I'll stop t'car, tek thee out and gi' thee a good hidin'.'

I've heard him hit Arthur for doing stuff.

'I...I don't know what to say,' I sob out my terror and all the emptiness of my whole life comes rushing out with it.

Dad drives on and just like usual he finds something softer to say to take the edge off things. 'Tha's got me missin' me tea break.'

He drops me home and goes back to work. I make some tea and our version of Welsh rarebit and when I get upstairs, I feel happier than I ever have to be in this house in my own room and bed. I try not to think about Steve and how lovely it was leaning up against his back with my arms round him on his bike.

PART TWO

MURIEL

Despite the odd problem created by me – running away, being attractive to boys much older than me because I was 'developed', the nicking incident and the occasional mishap with Arthur and Nicky, usually involving an injury to Nicky – we are a family. I deeply resent being made to work at Grandma's and having to go to the secondary modern but, otherwise, our family works. We love each other and have a strong bond and sense of security at home. We have survived the loss of our mother because Dad has kept our little family together. We manage. We have Auntie Pat and I have my Sunday school teacher, Barbara.

Then, suddenly, Auntie Pat tells us that 'the spaceman' is now very poorly and she has to look after him all the time so she won't be able to come to us for a while. I am old enough now, I can manage to look after us, just like I do on the days that Auntie Pat is not here. I think we'll manage very well. Dad has always said that I will look after him when I leave school, so I expect our lives to continue much as they had up until now.

But I was wrong, so very wrong. Being so keen on his 'quiet

life' Dad never went out, so I thought our family was enough for him. We were happy with how things were, with Auntie Pat. I never imagined that anything would change, that he would want to meet someone nearer his own age. I had always thought of Dad as just our dad, I didn't know that he was also a man. I was to have a very rude awakening.

When I tell Barbara that Auntie Pat can't come any more because she has to nurse her husband full-time now, she shows me a Valentine's card with Dad's initials – J.A.C. – inside in his beautiful cursive script. The card had been received years before, when we first moved to Netherton. Dad was about 33 then and Barbara was 21.

Barbara is really kind and sweet and gentle and she has Hamish the dog and she makes the most fantastic cakes and biscuits and puddings, but she also has her elderly mum who she lives with and has to look after. 'What happened?' I ask, so excited at the thought of how perfect it would have been if the two of them had got together. Two of my favourite people to love us. I loved Auntie Pat but it would be even better with Barbara.

'Well, one day, while I was sitting in the works car park having my lunch, Pat Sykes [Auntie Pat] came up to me. She lives near to the offices you know. She said, "I want a word with you. Keep your hands off Arthur Cooke, he's mine." That was when you lived in Netherton and you first started coming to Sunday school. So it would have been about five years ago.'

Poor Dad, did he just think Barbara wasn't interested when there was no response to his Valentine's gesture? Were both of them too shy to take things further? Was Barbara put off by that encounter with Auntie Pat, or at the thought of three near-feral children? I feel so sad hearing this because I love Barbara and she isn't married. I have no idea what it would be like if she and Dad got married, what it would be like to have a stepmother – probably a bit like when Auntie Pat comes over but with her being there all the time, doing fun things and teaching us stuff and taking us to the pictures. It would have been more than perfect if Barbara had come to live with us.

Dad is six foot two, dark, broad, handsome, with a full head of hair and that lovely dimple in his chin. He is about 39 now and almost always in overalls or old work clothes. He does lots of overtime and the only time he goes out is when he takes us on day trips in the summer.

Arthur says that Auntie Dorothy, Dad's sister, told Dad he should try the lonely hearts ads to find himself someone else, and he does.

'Well, she was no good,' he says after he has been to meet one of them. He rolls up a cig in the tiny hammock in his little box, then closes the lid and a ready-made fag pops out through the slot.

'Why Dad, what was wrong with her?' I ask, eager to know more.

'We met up at t'Wellington and I asked her what she wanted ta drink and she asked for a short! Well, I wouldn't be able ta afford ta keep '*er*.'

Dad doesn't tell me about any more of his dates, but one day he says he's going to see a woman called Muriel, and he's going to take us with him. Arthur says she's 40.

We get out of Dad's car in Primrose Hill at the bottom end of Newsome. The house is an old stone terraced cottage, blackened, like most of the older buildings in our town, by a century of grime from the mill chimneys. Dad's new girlfriend is quite tall and dresses like a granny. She's wearing a blue and white frock, white cardy and a bibbed pinny. She's got a cauliflower hairdo, like most of the old women who go to our chapel. Even Auntie Pat, who's 20 years older, is more modern than Muriel. Her cauliflower looks greasy and smells. She's got a limp; one of her legs is fatter than the other. She tells us it's because she had polio as a child.

She gives us tea and iced buns. The buns are really boring and as dry as sawdust but there are three days to go before Sunday school and my lovely tea at Barbara's. Dad and the boys have never tasted Barbara's eclairs or butterfly buns and the only way we use eggs at home is to fry them to eat with chips, so we all tuck in.

When we get home, Dad says Muriel is a widow with no children. She owns her own house and works at the mill two miles away in Armitage Bridge. I wonder if Dad's thinking that now that she's his girlfriend, there'll be no need to pay Auntie

Pat to help us any more. There'd also be two wage packets, so less need for him to do overtime. Muriel isn't married, like Auntie Pat, so she could come over and look after him every day and make him dry buns. Maybe we'd be able to buy clothes and shoes if she's his new girlfriend. We only ever get the odd thing from Grandma, though Barbara once bought me shoes and Auntie Dorothy got me some trews for my birthday when Dad asked me to go to where she works, at the furniture shop in town, and ask her for them.

The next Saturday, Dad invites Muriel to our house. We all have to stay in. He fetches her in the car. I mash a pot of tea. We don't have any buns. Dad tells us all to sit by the range on our pretend leather suite and when we're settled, he says, 'We want to tell thi that we've decided ta get married.'

What? Why? Shouldn't he have asked us, or warned us? I thought it was going to be like the Auntie Pat arrangement – helping me with the housework and food and a bit of a fumble with Dad upstairs. I saw them once, Dad rolling over on the bed and Auntie Pat leaning forwards over the edge when I went into his bedroom that time to complain about Arthur taking up all the fire with his long legs.

'I've looked in the bible,' Muriel is saying, even though no one asked, 'to find out who I will be with in heaven and I'm satisfied with the answers I've found.'

Oh my God! Why does Dad want to marry a nutcase? Why does this stranger think we care what the bible tells her?

She keeps prattling on. Why does she think we're interested in hearing that her husband died of a heart attack? It was probably from eating her stone buns. And now she's saying, 'And we've decided you should call me Mum.'

What! We don't even know you, you old bag! How dare you say that to us. I feel like one of the characters in the *Beano* when a one-ton weight drops on them. It's crushing me, I can't breathe. How did this happen? How did we get from dry buns in her front room to 'Mum' by our range? She's a frump, religious, hard-faced. We've still got Mam inside us, all wrapped up and special because she died when we were so young. Auntie Pat, yes, or Barbara, because they're lovely. But not her, not when she's forcing us, like she's controlling us. Why would you even want to know anyone who *makes* you call her mum? We've only met her once and I already know she's not a nice person.

Then she says, to me, just to me: 'I won't be one of those wicked stepmothers that you read about in fairy stories. It will be nice having a daughter, we can do each other's hair.'

I want a mum more than anything else in the world. Someone to teach me things that Dad can't, about hair and clothes and cooking, Barbara would have been perfect, but not her, not like this. I won't do it. I'll call her other things. I daren't call her Muriel but I'll try mumsy and mummy and mums to make it different from it being properly our mum.

A knot inside me is getting tighter and bigger. Of all the sad and bad things that have happened to us, nothing has felt like this. Those things were about losing something, or having to do things I didn't want to but I knew I had to for our family. This is about being controlled. It feels like when I got told off in the hair-washing queue at the Children's Home. It's about someone using their power over you because they can.

Dad takes her home and when he comes back things are just like normal again. The knot must still be there but I can't feel any tightness. It feels like we were in prison while she was here, and now we're free again. The atmosphere has changed. We've got our Dad back. He talks to us like he always does, like we're friends but we still know who's boss. He says, 'I've been thi mam and thi dad up till now, but now tha's grown up it's time fa me to do summat for me sen.'

What! Yes, he has been a widower for seven years, but haven't I been the mum in this family? And how can he say we're grown up – we're not, except for Arthur, he's 15. I might look on the outside like I'm older but I'm only 13 and Nicky's only 10.

THE WEDDING

Perhaps because Dad has no living parents, after taking his new belle to see his big sister Dorothy, they make the trip to Mam's mam, Grandma Swift, in Conisbrough, perhaps naively intending to gain her blessing. Grandma, about 72 by now, is still the matriarch of her large extended family. Her dominant personality and determination are probably how all her children, including the adopted ones, survived childhood and are now financially solvent. She inspires respect, devotion and probably a little fear from her brood, most of whom do not get on with each other. They speak about each other, rather than to each other, even when they're in the same room. Grandma has never said a nice thing about Dad, but Dad is utterly dependent on her for childcare in the holidays.

During their visit, while Muriel is out scouting in the back yard for the little girls' room and subsequently enjoying the delights of dabbing torn pages of the *Racing Times* against her nether regions, Dad confides to Grandma Swift that Muriel has 'a bit a money on 'er own', as she has 'an owse ta sell an' a job'. A statement which Grandma gleefully repeats whenever she wants to belittle our dad who she calls 'that long dog from mucky 'Uddersfield.'

Did Grandma, in some way, blame our dad for Mam's death? She often repeated that phrase the doctor had used, that Mam's condition of advanced cancer was due to 'sheer neglect'. And Grandma hadn't forgiven Dad for making Mam live in what she called 'hovels'. This was certainly an accurate description for the cottage at Leeds Road but may also have been true for one or other of the farm cottages that we had lived in in North Yorkshire that I was too young to remember. I couldn't recall the buildings and anyway, as a child, it was only the love they were filled with that made a lasting impression.

*   *   *

They say I'm going to be a bridesmaid but I have nothing to wear and there's no offer from Dad or Muriel.

Mrs Wressle was my first teacher when we moved to the house in Newsome and I started at Stile Common Junior school. She is old and gruff, with a stubbly chin and 'tache. She paints beautiful pictures in watercolours. Because she could see how useful I was at school – doing the coffee for the teachers, helping with the infants and doing the biscuit shop – she asked me to go to her house and help her with the cleaning and changing the bed one evening every week. She gives me my tea in return. Sometimes she asks me to do some shopping for her on a Saturday when I'm in town anyway and then bring it on the day when I go to help her. She never gives me any money but a couple of times I take a bit from her change.

On one of my cleaning visits to Mrs Wressle, I mention that Dad is getting married and that I have nothing to wear to be a bridesmaid. She takes me to an old lady dress shop in town and buys me a hideous pastel pink two-piece suit in an open weave fabric as well as an awful green old-lady dress. I usually wear cast offs or jumble-sale clothes, or stuff I make at school from jumble-sale clothes I've unpicked, but I'll be embarrassed to wear these granny clothes.

On the day of the wedding I'm sent to have my hair done at Muriel's hairdresser. I'm so excited – I've never been to the hairdressers before. Even if my clothes are frumpy at least my hair will look like a princess's. I've been looking in magazines and I know just how I want it – backcombed and done in a French pleat. It will look lovely and my Dad will be so proud of me.

I skip down our street, over the wall into the shortcut through the little wood, down to the main road, cross over, walk down the other side and I'm there. It has never been such a short walk. I'll have to go the long way round on the way back, as I won't risk spoiling the lovely hair-do I'll have by then by going through the wood. I look through the window of the hairdressers at all the grown-up women sitting under dryers or having rollers put in. I'm only 13 and I'm getting my hair done properly. I'll look like a pop star.

I open the door and step out of my awful boring scruffy world into one where women can have their hair done by someone else, just like they want it. I breathe in the special women smells – shampoo, lacquer, perm solution all fighting with each other. It's a special world just for women and I'm a part of it for the first time ever.

I find a woman wearing an overall who isn't doing someone's hair. I tell her who I am and she sits me down in a chair in front of a mirror.

'Right, love, how would you like your hair done?' she asks me.

I can hardly speak. It's like being offered a whole sweet shop.

'Can you put it up please, in a French pleat?'

All the smart girls in my *Bunty* comic have their hair done up when they're going for an interview for a job. So do the ballet dancers, though they have buns.

'Oh, we can't do that,' says the hairdresser, 'your mum said you would look too grown up with it up.'

What? What! How dare she! 'Your mum!' The only time I get to go to a hairdresser in my whole life and she's even told them how I can have my hair done. She has to control everything. There's something about her that isn't right. I already know she is two faced.

My mouth drops, my excitement all drained away. What can I do? I'm being forced to have something done to me that I don't want. She's not even here and she's doing this.

She's spoiling my one chance to look special. She is so very different from Barbara and Auntie Pat and even from Grandma, who everyone is scared of. None of them would ever do anything like this. But what can I do? I don't want to spoil it for Dad. I look at the hairdresser and at the women under the dryers reading magazines and I feel like I did when I realised, what seems now like many years ago, that Mam wasn't coming back, ever.

The hairdresser does my hair. It doesn't make me look different or special or someone to be proud of. It makes me look how she wants me to look, like the suit makes me look, like an old bag, just like her.

When I get home she doesn't say anything, so I say, 'The hairdresser said I couldn't have my hair done up because you said it would make me look too grown up.'

'Well I never said any such thing,' she says, looking straight at me, and I know who to believe.

In a photo taken at the chapel, of me, her, Dad and her other bridesmaid, I'm wearing the vile two piece and a matching hairstyle but my fingers are interwoven through those of my dad and, for that moment, everything is all right. I feel safe. We have come through a lot. I had to grow up very quickly and learn to take care of all of us, but our dad has always been there for us. He kept us together when other dads might have left us in care or had Grandma bring us up. He could have abandoned us but instead he worked and did his best for us, always. My dad had made even the very worst things all right, but this time, just this moment, would be the last time. Then time moved on and I was back to the reality of what was happening to us.

On the night of the wedding us kids have to be out of the house. Arthur's friends from grammar school have different families to ours; families where it's OK to have a friend stay over. Nicky has to go to the house of the best man, Dad's work mate. I have nowhere to go but I tell them that I can go to my friend Maggie's house. It's all I can think of. There is no 'do' after the wedding, everyone just goes home.

They take me to Maggie's in Dad's car. Dad says he'll wait to make sure they're home. They aren't, but I pretend they are because I don't want to spoil his day by waiting about, and I know I can't go home with them. So I wave and they drive off.

I hang about in the rain looking a fright in the ridiculous pink suit but there's no way to get around the back and I'll look even more stupid walking up and down the streets, so I wait outside Maggie's. A man comes past. He's talked to me and Maggie before. He says I can wait in his place a bit further up the road, out of the rain, and he'll make me a cup of tea. I don't want to go, but I need someone to be kind to me. I need someone to pay attention to me and to look after me. At least he cares that I am in the rain, no one usually does.

When we get there, he goes over to the little kitchenette to put the kettle on. Then he says that there's no money for the meter. So there's no tea. When I say I don't want to do what he wants me to do because I might get into trouble, he says I'll be all right as long as I go for a wee afterwards. I shut my eyes and wait till he's finished. It's horrible. But at least it doesn't hurt too much, and anyway, I feel like a zombie. I pray to Jesus to forgive me and not to let me 'get into trouble' because I know that's the worst thing that a girl can do, and it wasn't even me that did it. I didn't want him to do it.

After he's finished, I go to the toilet like he said. When I come out, he says, 'You'd better get off now, your mate will probably be back.'

I look at him and I know I have to go. I walk down the stairs from the bedsit as slowly as I can. I want to cry but I can't – someone might see and it's my fault anyway – I went up there with him. I let him, so it's my fault. I wanted somebody to be kind to me but I didn't want him to do that. I shouldn't have gone with him. I shouldn't have believed him when he said it was for a cup of tea. I'm 13 now, I should have known what would happen. Why couldn't he just have been kind and given me a cup of tea? Why couldn't he just let me leave when he couldn't make me one? I wanted someone to hold me, to care about me. It will be my fault if I get into trouble.

My hair's gone flat in the rain. The pink suit is all damp now. I'm shivering. I walk down to Maggie's but she's not back yet. I have to walk up and down the street now just to keep warm. I make sure I don't look at anybody. Everything that happened in that little bedsit goes around and around in my mind but I can't make it any different.

After ages, Maggie and her mum come back from town. Her mum is kind and she does give me tea and sits me by the fire to dry out. Before we go to bed, we have supper. Maggie lends me one of her nighties and we do top and tail for the night. I lie awake in the dark. I can't even curl myself up around the empty dead feeling inside me because I don't want to disturb Maggie. I hate who I am. Worst of all I wonder if I'll be *in trouble*. Each time I think about it I start to cry, but then stop myself or Maggie will ask why, so the lug in my throat just gets bigger. I can't tell her or anybody else what happened because I know everybody will say it was my fault.

Padlocks, Silence and Betrayal

I am big, too big – lumpen they say. Feet too big, breasts too big, hair that stands out in two thick curtains, like those on the school stage, and a fringe, cut across the top where the third curtain would have been. Who I am inside, a little girl who is managing, doesn't belong in this body and my body and who I am on the inside no longer belong in this house. I'm unwelcome, unwanted. This house is not ours anymore, it's hers.

I'm sitting on the sofa, in our living room, and she says, 'Don't sit with your legs crossed in the house. Your dad can see right up your skirt.'

Why would my dad want to look up my skirt? Anyway, he'd have to get on the floor. It's her. She's the reason I've started to feel wrong, awkward, conscious of my body, bad, wicked just for being there when she is – and she always is. Wherever I am downstairs she's there – watching, judging, waiting. I have to be alert, on edge, to stop myself every time my body wants to cross its legs. What will I do wrong next?

'Wear trousers when you're in this house, you're disgusting showing all your legs like that.'

I hate her, I hate my legs, I hate being a girl and being in this house with her. Everything was all right before she came. Why does she have to be here? What's happened to our lives?

* * *

I've just come into the living room where we used to watch telly, where we used to sit by the fire. It's morning, my eyes are full of sleep but yes, there's something different. There's some big change. Inside I know what it is because my belly folds over onto itself, but the rest of me is not sure yet. The shock when the penny drops is sharp and deep, like the only time Dad clouted me.

Our neighbour – the only one we talked to and we don't any more – had come around to complain about me doing chalk drawings on their flagstones. The shock of the jarring of my head was nothing to my hurt feelings, the sense of betrayal. My dad hitting me, no that doesn't happen, but it just did. I thought we were a team. He did it just to show he was doing something about the complaint. He didn't even ask me about it first. I didn't get a chance to say I was showing some little girls how to draw eyes with eye lashes on the heads they had drawn.

But now there is no feeling of betrayal; my body is reacting but my mind feels nothing. To feel betrayed there needs to be trust, like I had back then. Now, after all that's happened, this new thing is just another of the ways that Muriel is mean to us.

We lived in this house for five years before she came. I did the shopping, cooking, washing up, ironing, changing the beds. Dad did the washing, because he didn't want me to get my fingers crushed in the electric mangle, and I hung it out. Auntie Pat helped us. We kept the food in the two wooden cupboards that stand on the chest of drawers here in the living/dining room. We still keep the food there, but now, this morning, the thing that is causing my stomach to churn is that there are padlocks on both of the food cupboard doors. Nobody says anything. We've learnt never to say anything, to each other, or to Dad.

Muriel has gotten rid of the furniture we got from Grandma Cooke, the furniture that Dad grew up with in their farmhouse. Even the beautiful little chapel organ that we were never allowed to play because it was so precious is smashed up with an axe in the back yard and burnt. Dad's bureau and the lamp with the hunting scene escapes. As does the table with the yellow Formica top.

The bureau stays but not its contents. The sound of each rip cuts through me as *Mum* tears apart our family photos. She throws out the only photos we have of Mam and us as children. Fragments of black and white faces look out from the potato peelings and lamb chop bones. I get a glimpse of the one of me and Dad at the wedding before it joins the other waste.

'Can't I keep these?' I plead, nearly crying, pointing to a final picture of Mam and another of when I was a bridesmaid for my uncle.

'You can't live in the past,' Muriel replies, replacing our precious pictures with some of herself and her dead first husband on boating holidays on the Norfolk Broads.

The *atmosphere* that oozes out of Muriel is constant. It's her real weapon of terror. It's alive; it follows you everywhere, even when you're in the toilet or in bed, at school or on the streets. It's not easy or quick, but somehow I work out how not to exist when I'm at home so I can't be her target. There's plenty of room to hide inside my cringing fear.

There's now an unspoken rule of non-communication between me and my siblings and between me and anyone else in the house – unless it's her and she has asked something. This is part of my drift into non-existence. I knew nothing then about coercive control – society didn't even know about it back then – but I experienced it as one personality, Muriel's, utterly crushing another, mine. I internalised her rules and requirements, one of these was to know my place, and a big part of that was not doing anything that confirmed my existence.

It doesn't enter my head to whisper. I know what is expected of me and I am so utterly crushed that there is no question of rebellion, disobedience or insubordination. I know there is no one there, in that house, on my side any more. There is also never any question of taking my problems to anyone else. The control is too all pervasive for that, but on some level I must know that there is no one who can help me anyway. The only time that anyone tries to intervene is when Muriel has made someone in authority aware of what she is doing. And even then, I am the one who pays the price.

I become a rubbed-out cartoon character, knowing she is always waiting to pounce on my every breath, my every move.

I don't know why she bothered with the padlocks. I wouldn't dare move my face in a way she might disapprove of, let alone open a drawer or a cupboard anywhere except in my room. But at least this way she can't accuse us of 'stealing' food.

The padlocks are just the physical manifestation of what has been happening ever since Muriel moved into our house. The most important change was invisible, something that started small and wispy, like a smell floating through the air in a Tom and Jerry cartoon. The wisp soon became a thick, heaving, menacing, invisible fog. It began to cling to me until it got so strong that it squeezed the spirit out of me. Now I don't know what it would feel like to be really here any more. The fog is in every room in the house and it's inside you when you leave. The fog means that I know I can only talk to her and only if she's spoken to me first, or to ask to leave the table. I used to be a happy-go-lucky kid, now I'm alert, on edge, an anxious wraith. It wouldn't enter my mind to catch Nicky's eye, even when she's out of the room. When we are at home there's no one else in my world anymore – just her.

And yet Arthur escapes all this. He is not really part of our world. He goes off on his paper round before Nicky and me have breakfast. Sometimes he is there for tea. Why isn't anything different for him? He behaves just the same as before, talks to them as if our life is normal. Is it because he's older and a lad and earning money for them, so she doesn't mind him, or doesn't she have the same effect on him because he goes to the grammar and Scouts, does sports, has a bike, has friends with nice houses and normal families?

I know it's not Dad's fault. It's her, it's all her, she controls all of us, including Dad. So I never think about who must have put the padlocks on the food cupboards for her.

*　　*　　*

It's the holidays, so Nicky and me have been packed off to Grandma Swift's. Arthur is sitting at the table doing some homework and the only person in when there's a knock at the door. It's Auntie Pat.

'Hello love, is your Dad in? My husband has died now so I can come back.'

Arthur doesn't like Auntie Pat. She used to hit him with a long cane when he did naughty things, until one day he took the cane off her and broke it over his knee. Dad gave him a good hiding when he got home but Auntie Pat never hit Arthur again.

'Dad's got married,' Arthur says, and Auntie Pat leaves.

Poor old Auntie Pat, the comforting occasional but consistent presence in our family for six of our motherless years, callously and casually dumped without a word from Dad. We never see her again. Perhaps she was one of the people who might have saved us, might have changed how things were at home. Or perhaps she would have had to stand by, just like everyone else.

UNWANTED

Many years later, as I put flowers in the stone vase on her grave, I say a silent 'thank you' to Pat for bringing a little sunshine and softness to a bleak childhood and feel a sense of regret that I'd left it too late to try and find her again. I hope she knew how important her kindness had been to us.

The Miracle Mother, 1966

She's stopped work and our pocket money, which had doubled when she moved in, has gone back to half a crown. It doesn't matter, it didn't make up for having her living with us. She's been strutting around the house singing old Jim Reeves songs and crowing about the doctor calling her his 'Miracle Mother' because she's 42. She was married to her first husband for ages but they never had kids.

When the time comes, Dad takes her to the hospital for her confinement. When he gets back it's the first time we've been alone with him since they got married. He speaks to us like he used to, like he cares about us, and we can speak to him. The TV isn't working. He fixes it so we can watch it that evening while he's at the hospital. He's our dad again. From that moment, on that day, I know that my lovely dad, the one that still loves us, is just tucked away somewhere inside the person he has to be when *she's here*.

We lived for seven years with just Dad, so I know that there'll be a time when she's not here any more, I just have to wait and we'll get our real dad back and we'll have lovely day trips and nice food again. That dad is the one that brought a

Caramac or Bounty back with him when he had to work away because he knew they were my favourites; he's the one that gets the paper shop to deliver our *Bunty*, *Beano* and *Dandy* comics; the dad who gave us fantastic Christmases, played card games, Monopoly and snooker with us and bought me the best doll ever the Christmas I came home from the foster family. My real, hidden away dad is the one that bought me a transistor radio when I was 12 and made sure we had great bonfire nights and once, when we just got together in the new house, after Mam died, tied knots in our sleeves on Mischief Night. He's the one who let me twirl round his finger, lifted me in the air by my elbows, smelt my face when I asked him to because I'd left soap on it like ballet dancers do so they can have soft skin.

I cling to the dad who made us lovely Sunday dinners that we ate at the yellow Formica table listening to *A Walk in the Black Forest*, *the Singing Nun* and *Stranger on the Shore* on Two-Way Family Favourites. He's the dad that took us to Blackpool and Bellevue Zoo and Bridlington and Scarborough for days out and sung songs with us on the way. Those were the best days, when we had our dad all to ourselves the whole day, doing nice things.

That was the dad that made up for leaving the farm, for having no mam, for living in so many different places, for the Children's Home, chicken pox, foster care, Grandma Cooke and her dog Rhonda dying, and having to leave that lovely new house. That dad was still there, that was my real dad. He just had to hide away when she was here.

'This'll be t'last bairn, there wain't be na more, tha can bank on that,' Dad tells me that evening when he gets back from the hospital.

Is he saying that he didn't mean for this to happen? And why's he telling me? Is he sorry for what he's done to all of us by marrying her? It feels to me that he is sorry that she is having a baby. It's not what he had planned when he told Grandma Swift about the two wages and her house that they would be selling. Then he was thinking of a brighter future, of a step away from the breadline. A new baby will bring him, and us, back there. Instead of two wages he now has two extra mouths to feed from his one wage.

It's hard to know exactly why he is saying this but he is speaking to me, and that in itself is something wonderful, but more than that, he is speaking to me like an adult, an equal, reassuring me, or perhaps because he wants my forgiveness in some way. What does matter in this moment, what really, really matters, is that Muriel's absence has created an oasis of love. We have our little family back.

Somehow this scene cements in my mind a conviction that because our dad is different when she is not here, that he is as much a victim of Muriel as we are. Whatever the motivation behind the words of this man of so very few words, I know, in his clumsy hopeless way, he's trying to make it all right. But even as I realise his intention I know that we are in far too deep now for anything to be all right ever again.

THE PRESSURE COOKER

When she came home, nobody said, 'You've got a new brother.' It's something that happened for them, not us. The new baby is off limits. How could someone who has no right even to exist communicate with anyone, let alone someone as precious as Muriel's baby? There is an invisible barbed wire fence around the pram and highchair. Two separate families live here now and there can be no cross-contamination from the three inconvenient step-kids, who have to be fed and housed, to the new pampered treasured one. However, my non-existence doesn't stop her crowing at me.

'I change his bedding every day,' she says while I'm at the table, 'because it's so nice to go to bed in clean sheets.' And, 'I want him to experience as many tastes as possible.'

She feeds him honey and other things from the padlocked food cupboards, things that we've never tasted. She shows me a gadget that she has bought called a Mouli Baby. It's like a mincer in a bowl made of metal. When he's old enough she will use it to mince up their food so he can eat it.

'His name is Edward and if one of his mates comes to the door and asks for Eddie, I'll just say, "Eddie's not in."'

THE PRESSURE COOKER

The new family – Muriel, Dad and Edward (in his highchair) – sit close together at one long side of our small yellow Formica-topped dinner table while we three left-over kids have the other sides, one on each.

Now we stepkids have workhouse food. We no longer have Frosties or Sugar Puffs for breakfast but a plop of grey porridge. At first, the golden syrup tin is left on the table for us to help ourselves. I see the look on her face when she sees me making drizzling patterns onto my bowl of warm sludge. What does she hate about that? Does it slow me down getting out of her house? Is it proof that I exist or is it because I am having a tiny pleasure? Maybe everything I do irritates her. After that day the tin of Tate and Lyle's is gone. There's a spoonful of syrup pre-dolloped into the bowl. Nobody says anything. She's decided, so that's it.

When he's old enough, Edward is given coddled (whatever that is) eggy and soldiers or scrambled egg or poached egg or something else for breakfast, always with best butter. Whatever it is, it's always better than what we're having. If she's not in the room I look across in envy as I force down more of the slimy sickly muck.

At teatime, us stepkids get oxtail slurry or thick stodgy split pea soup with specks of ham. She brews everything up in her scary pressure-cooker which, for me, is her. The knob at the top bobs about, sizzling and whistling. I know it's going to explode one day, showering scalding slime all across the kitchen and me. Even worse than her slimy concoctions are the fritters: thick slices of spud, battered and deep fried. Because she keeps the chip pan temperature low, the grease stays in the batter and oozes out when you bite into them. It's like biting into greasy sick, but there's nothing else. Sundays are even worse than fritters day. We kids get breast of lamb which is so full of grease that one bite sends fountains of fat cascading down your throat and chin.

The new family on the other side of the table has steak, mushrooms and chips, or bursting shiny sausage and chips, or liver and bacon and onions, or lamb chops and creamy smooth mash, all with thick rich Heinz tomato sauce, as we struggle through our sludge, slurry or sickly grease. Edward shares in their luxury thanks to the Mouli Baby. On Sundays they have chicken or a joint of lamb with mint sauce or pork with crackling.

Muriel says, 'This is just for us because you have your school dinners.'

* * *

She's standing outside their bedroom when I'm on the way to the toilet. She never does that. Why doesn't she move? She doesn't want to see me; I don't want to see her. I have to pass her. She hands me something in a paper bag. 'Auntie Dorothy sent this for you,' she says.

Since Muriel arrived, I no longer see Dorothy at all. And yet she still buys all of us fireworks, Christmas and birthday presents and a gift from her travels each year, even though my big brother is very clearly her favourite.

This year, Dorothy's holiday must have been to Spain. Inside the paper bag is a pair of red painted wooden clackers. I look up from the bag. Through the open door behind Muriel – a door that is never left open – on a shelf in the bedroom that was mine before she came, I can see a Spanish doll in a plastic tube wearing a beautiful flamenco dress.

'Oh yes, she brought that back for me,' Muriel tells me.

Around this time, the new family go to visit Aunt Dorothy and her now husband, Jimmy, to ask for a loan for the deposit on a car. Aunt Dorothy is 10 years older than my dad, and when they were children she'd doted on her beautiful brother with his mass of blond curls. She had always helped him out. He had followed her to Huddersfield from the farm; she had found the cottage for us. Uncle Jimmy had found the foster family for me. She would be prepared to help out again, regardless of what she thought of his new wife. Dad asks about the loan.

'Well yes, we might be able to help, how much do you think it will be?'

'Well it shouldn't be much, we're only getting a Reliant Robin.'

'But Arthur, that's not a family car. I can't lend you money for a little three-wheeler. You have four children, you need one big enough for all of you.'

'Well you can keep your money then,' pipes up Muriel. 'Come on Arthur, we're not having interfering busybodies telling us what to do.'

Teen Idols

I'm in love with Dave Berry and George Harrison and their fringes and loads of other lads in pop groups. Except for sweets, stockings and the occasional flicks, I spend my pocket money on pop magazines from the indoor market on a Saturday and keep the centrefold posters of my favourites.

Muriel says, 'You've got far too many posters in your room, you need to get rid of some of them. Put your favourites in one pile and the others in another and I'll throw those away.'

How will I live without my dreamboats? I can't think of parting with even one. She's making me do this because it's the only thing I have in my life. She's taken Dad and my family and my life and now she's taking my posters. They're not bothering her, they're not in the living room, they're in my bedroom so why should she care? She's doing it to get at me, taking me apart bit by bit, day by day. I feel like one of our ripped-up photos from in the bureau. Why does she do it? I used to have a pen pal in America but I haven't had a reply to my last letter. Did she not write back or did her letter end up in the bin or on the back of the fire?

Next morning, I hand over a pile of centrefolds.

'These are the ones for throwing out,' I tell her.

'Put them there, next to the telly,' she instructs while feeding Edward what smells like minced sausage and tomato with scrambled egg. I force down my wodge of porridge then leave for school.

When I return at teatime, I go up to change into my 'playing out' clothes and my pile of best posters is gone. I check under the bed, on top of the wardrobe, in the drawers. Where's she put them? They're nowhere. I go downstairs. Before I can stop myself, dismay overwhelming the suffocating fear, I hear myself speaking. It sounds wrong. I know it's wrong but once I've started, it's too late.

'Have you moved my posters?'

'Yes, I threw them out like I said I would.'

The bitch. How could she? Stupid question. Easily! I hate her so much. I turn to go back upstairs and I notice that on the chest of drawers, next to the TV, the pile of posters I put there that morning is still there. 'These were the ones for throwing out,' I say, my heart clinging to the shred of hope that the bin men don't come till tomorrow.

'Well it's too late now,' she says, 'I put them on the fire. You should have told me which ones you wanted to keep.'

I used to be the mother in this family, looking after Dad and my siblings, and I used to be a sister. We kids used to play ping-pong across the Formica table with blocks of lard and marg instead of a net; touch and pass rugby or French cricket on the rec or our own game, servee – Arthur's version of hide and seek where you get whacked with a yellow plastic sword when you're found till you say 'servee master servee', just like when Mick McManus bangs his hand three times on the wrestling ring floor to submit. We used to watch the wrestling with Dad. Now there's no games, no Christmases, no day trips, no nice Sunday dinners and certainly no telly. Nothing nice at all, there's not even crisp sandwiches.

When she burned my special pop star posters, I wanted her to fall on the fire and burn her sticky Vitapointe hair and her full-length pinny and the way she walks; burn her singing all those Jim Reeves love songs and the way she shoves all the special things she does for Edward in my face. But nothing's changed except I'm even more full of hardness and hate.

I'm not allowed in the kitchen now and I'm not allowed to do the washing. I have to leave my dirty clothes in the wash basket. I don't have many. I've never dared to shoplift clothes. I get cast-offs from my older cousin at Grandma's, make things at school and I once bought a striped shirt, now much repaired, from a friend's mum's catalogue, paying it off with my pocket money. I love the trews I got from Auntie Dorothy but my very favourite thing is a woollen cricket jumper I bought at a street jumble sale at Grandma's for a few pence. Having this jumper is like sharing in a different world where people have special clothes for sports. It's massive. I disappear in it, feel cuddled by it.

It's teatime and, just like every day after school, my stomach churns as soon as I come out of the passage at the back of our house. It's not because I'm hungry. Long before I get to the kitchen I feel anxious because I know that I'll have to walk through that door and she'll be there despising me, wishing I didn't exist, slowly devouring my soul. Just like every other day I want to run the other way, but where could I go? I have to do exactly what's expected.

As I'm taking the gut-wrenching final steps to the back door, I notice something out of the corner of my eye. Oh no, no, please. It's as if she has punched me in my already knotted up stomach. A wave of shock and weakness passes through me. I steady myself on the door knob. Can that really be my beloved cricket jumper on the line? The bloody bitch has shrunk it to half its size and then she's hung it up as if there's nothing wrong. I push my hatred and anger away somewhere deep inside the fear – I have to. Better to just keep feeling dead so she can't touch me any more. But she's won, like she always does. I won't cry, even though I will never be able to wear it again. Never be able to feel it smothering me with its too-long arms and its comforting warmth, its specialness.

I still have to go in. I still have to sit there and have my tea with her hovering round like a prison warder. I still have to force down the muck and behave as if nothing has happened. There's no explanation, no apology. Ha! As if. The shrunken, deformed thing is just returned to me with my pants and skirt and blouse and cardie. It's shrunk until it's useless, just like my life. When I hug it to me and cry silently in my bedroom, it's not just about the jumper, it's not because I don't have a mum to love me. Mam had no choice about leaving us, Dad did.

SHOES

My feet always hurt. Dad never gets us new shoes, just plastic sandals in the summer from Woolies and Grandma gets us wellies from the warehouse. The bits of cardboard from cereal packets that I put in my shoes don't last long. A few steps and my soles are rubbing on the flagstones again. The school health visitor sends me to the foot clinic in town. I do exercises every week with her, they don't work. My toes get more bent over, my feet more deformed. The woman in the white coat tells me that I have to wear bigger shoes, shoes that fit, but she doesn't give me any.

One day, just after we've had our tea and I've been upstairs to get changed out of my school clothes, Muriel calls me over to the range where she's sitting with Dad. There's a box. Fear spreads out through my belly like a raw egg dropped on the floor.

'Your mum has got you some new shoes,' says Dad, who never says anything.

Barbara bought me a new pair once, in the sales. We chose them together. Can this really be true, that *she's* done something kind like Barbara did and actually got me some new shoes that fit? How could she if I didn't try them on? She opens the box, eyes glued to my face. I look down. I look at the box. She lifts the tissue and takes out a pair of black lace up prison-warder shoes, the ugliest ones I've ever seen. She probably asked for the ugliest ones in the shop. All my mates wear sling backs or slip-ons, nobody wears policewoman's shoes. The shoes Barbara bought me were soft brown flat slip-ons, not men's clodhoppers. I know, without doubt, that she has done it on purpose.

I save my spendo and the five bob we get from each of our uncles when we have to stay at Grandma's until I've got enough money to buy a pair of shoes in the sale – proper posh shoes, not plastic sandals or wellies or prison-warder shoes. The shoes I buy are shiny patent with low heels and pointy toes. I know that these shoes will change my life completely. They will lead me to that other life, the one where Dad would have worn his suit and played the piano accordion, the one that the bureau and hunting lamp have leaked out of into our life. When I'm wearing these shoes, I'll feel special and hold my head up and people will think I look smart and they'll be nice to me. I'll be posh like the people who live in semis on the main road. They go on proper holidays and buy school uniform for their kids. I'll be like the girls on *Top of the Pops* with their trendy miniskirts and perfect hair dos.

It's a Saturday and I put on my new posh shoes ready to go out though the back door into my new posh people's life.

'Arthur,' she says as I pass them in the living room. Sometimes she says stuff straight at me and at other times when Dad's there she does it through him but it's meant for me. 'Look at the shoes she's going out in. You can't let her go out in those shoes. What does she look like?'

Her words stop me dead. The bitch. She means they're like prozzie's shoes. Just because she goes to church and wears old lady shoes and these are smart and shiny. Her tongue's like the bacon slicer at the corner shop. My new posh life and my weeks of saving drain away. I know I can't go out so I stand there in the kitchen shaking inside until I'm sure she's finished, then I drag myself back upstairs and put on the prison-warder shoes.

When I go past them again, she says, 'You just treat your father with contempt.' He says nothing, as usual, just sits there letting her cut slices off me. 'You should have some respect for your father, because he gave you life.'

That's the slicer on the widest setting. I love my dad more than anything else in the world. I would do anything for him. Is it easier for Dad to believe what she says than face up to what he's letting her do to me?

THE WORM TURNS,
THEN SHRIVELS

I'm upstairs lying on my bed out of her way, bored, bored, bored. The baby is in his pram and Muriel and Dad are sitting by the fire when our dead, grey, menacing, controlled life explodes into full colour. I hear the back door open and some kerfuffle and then Muriel screaming, 'LET ME IN ARTHUR, ARTHUR, LET ME IN ARTHUR!' as she hammers on the door with her powerful fist. I can't believe it – he's actually chucked her out. Ha, ha, ha! Brilliant! It's too good to be true. At last we'll be free. A massive thrill goes from my stomach right up to my mouth. Thank you, God! I'm on tenterhooks.

I want to scream out to Dad, *Don't Dad, please don't let her back in,* but I daren't. Once he would have listened to me but now he is a different dad. He's hers. Silently I beg him to let her stay out and never come back, let her die in the cold and shrivel up to nothing like vampires do on the telly.

But her caterwauling is enough to disturb the neighbours on both sides and Dad is a very private man. Then the baby starts screaming. After what seems like ages, I hear Dad's chair squeak on the stone floor and his hobnail boots heading for the kitchen.

Each step crushes the life out of our family. Then I hear the sound of the bolt being drawn back and the latch lifting. He's left it too late. There's a baby. Her house is sold. They're religious. He's made his bed... and we all have to lie in it.

Because of the communication controls in our house it's 50 years before I get to find out what precipitated Muriel's screaming and banging. I hadn't known that Nicky was sitting downstairs at the Formica table and witnessed the whole event.

'I'm fed up with it, Arthur, you've brought me here to this hovel, skivvying after these kids, it's not what I expected,' Muriel had thrown at Dad.

Dad, who hadn't expected a baby, nappies, broken sleep and two extra mouths to feed, had exploded with, 'Well tha can buggar off then if tha thinks tha can do better,' and frogmarched her to the back door, shoved her outside and bolted the door.

Not long after the 'Let me in' incident, Muriel tells me, 'You can go out after your tea and be back by 9.30. We will all be in bed so you can lock up.' She doesn't say in so many words that I *have* to be out, but I know what she means. If a neighbour – or the authorities – ask why a 14-year-old girl is roaming the streets at night even in the dark she can answer that she didn't tell me to stay out. 'Well I didn't say they had to go out, I just told them they can,' she could say to anyone who would care to enquire, though unfortunately no one did.

Such was our fragmented family, its members totally isolated from one another, and this was another step into oblivion. I wander the streets taking shelter where I can. My anorak is cheap, thin and old. When it rains the hood sticks to my head. My face and shoulders get wet and my skirt and legs are soaked from the rain that runs down it. I sometimes sit in a bus shelter at the top of Newsome, or there's a covered seat in the rec – not the one nearest us, that was a danger zone – the one at the top of Newsome that was much nicer. I learnt when I was 13 that our local rec isn't a good place for a girl, a big girl, a girl who 'didn't get those tits from sitting by the fire', to hang around alone.

I am isolated, lonely and bored to tears. However, although it is desolate walking the streets in the cold or even in summer, perhaps the worst bit is actually coming home. Everyone is in bed so there's no one to say goodnight to, no one to even see me.

I come home to a house where we had laughed and played and had such lovely, special times. I have to lock up, walk through the house in the dark, into the living room with its padlocked food cupboards, through the front room, up the stairs past their bedroom to the toilet, then down the step through another room in to my bedroom. There was never a sound from anywhere, just emptiness – an emptiness that reflected what I was feeling on the inside, completely alone in a house full of people.

Arthur is out a lot with his mates anyway. He has a different life to us, a full life – hockey, paper rounds and cashing up at the supermarket – and she doesn't seem to mind him so much anyway. And every school holiday they get rid of us to Grandma

Swift's for the cost of the bus fares. With us out of the way she can play happy families.

Breakfast and tea are always on the table ready for us. Get up, eat and get out. In from school, eat, out again. This imposed regime means I hardly ever get to see Dad but at least she can't say nasty things to me or look at me in that way she has, except at mealtimes.

'Well, you've worked for them all your life Arthur, and what have they done in return? Just thrown it in your face by causing trouble and upset for you. Why should you have to put up with that now when you should be having a bit of comfort in your life? At least they behave better now and you don't have so much worry or trouble to contend with. Here, have another chop love.' Is this how she dripped poison into Dad's ear?

Muriel vs School

In Domestic Science – 'DS' – we've learnt how to iron a shirt and wash woollens, but most weeks we make something to eat. After each DS lesson, we get the list of ingredients for the following week. Before the padlocks, before her, I used to take what I needed from the food cupboard and get any extra bits the recipe required – like a quarter pound of Cheddar, or a tomato – on tick at the corner shop. Back then, I'd bring home whatever I made and we would all eat it for tea. 'Ee, that looks grand lass,' Dad would say, as I opened the lid on my latest creation. Not any more. Now I hand over the list to Muriel when I get in after school, along with the cake tin containing whatever we made in the lesson. I never see it again. She must bin it. She would certainly never give it to Dad. So, if it's something that won't be noticed, I start to nibble bits off it on the way home, like when it was butterfly buns. I lifted off the wings and ate some of the butter cream, then rearranged them to hide what I'd done.

Today is DS day. I get dressed for school and the wall of menace and hatred hits me as soon as I step into the living room. I swallow the maggots of fear and sit at my place at the yellow table. My DS cake tin is usually next to my place, with the ingredients already in it. It's not there. That means I'll have to talk to her. I try not to panic.

She's busy spreading things we never get on Edward's soldiers. I can feel the tangy saltiness of butter in my nose and mouth as I watch it soak into his toast. I absent-mindedly stir my own grim breakfast as I imagine my teeth are biting through the crisp outer edge of the toast, into the softness beneath, all swathed in the richness of the sweet butter. There are lots of jars and spoons on their side of the Formica table, near to Edward's highchair tray. She dips one of the spoons into a pot to fish out a fat juicy strawberry and spreads it onto one of the soldiers. A wave of saliva hits the underneath of my tongue. Then she spoons out a luscious dollop from the jar of lemon cheese. It's like torture.

My own bowl of gruel has somehow become empty while my mind flitted between Edward's feast and my absent cake tin. I'll have to say something, but she can't have forgotten. It's bound to be something worse than that. I'm so unused to speaking in the house and I'm frightened to use the wrong words. I know I have to get what I say just right, not sound cheeky or demanding or expectant or complaining. My mouth's as dry as a bird's nest and I don't want to ask her what I have to, because I know she's feeding off it. She's enjoying me squirming.

'Where are my ingredients for DS, please Mum?' I have no choice but to use the hated word. She looks up from Edward's ranged troops and I catch a sickly waft of Vitapointe hair gel as she turns to look at me for the first time since I came in.

'You won't be making anything at school any more,' she says, as she dips one of the unused spoons into the jar which says acacia honey. 'We can't afford it.'

Her words crash through my mind like a wrecking ball. What can I say? She'll have won, whatever it is. She always wins. I can't risk sounding as if I'm talking back to her.

'Please may I leave the table?' I ask.

'Yes, you may,' she replies, and walks off into the kitchen leaving Edward in his highchair with his luxury artillery lined up in front of him.

I force myself up from the table. I still have to pass her to get out of the door. I pick up my anorak and duffel bag with the big black stitches around the plastic piping at the bottom where I had to sew the seam together. I want to make for the door and get away from her but I have to say it because I know how mad Miss gets with us if we don't have just one of our ingredients.

'What will I tell the teacher?'

There's no reply. Is it because I didn't say 'Mum' or 'please' or because she has already finished talking to me? Whatever it is I don't dare say anything more. She goes back to Edward, leaving the kitchen clear. I move slowly, making each step take longer, to see if she might say something else. She doesn't. As I get to the back door, she starts singing one of her Jim Reeves songs: *'I love you because you understand dear, every single thing I try to do...'*

All the way to the end of the street I feel hot and it's like the turning drums on a one-armed bandit running through my mind. What will Miss say? What will the class think? What will happen? I can see them all staring at me. I'll be ashamed, a laughing stock. I wait at the bus stop.

The bus comes, I sit down. 'Half to town please.' It all goes through me again. I'm not thinking it, it's thinking me. What she said. What Miss will say? Can I find a way round it? Could I nick the ingredients from shops? Where could I put them if I did? All the class laughing at me behind their hands and calling me poor... and that blasted flaming song. Has she told Dad? Does he even care? All the way on the bus, 20 minutes of stopping and starting and Jim Reeves' words in her voice, so smug and satisfied and not a care.

I get off the bus and try to buck myself up, setting off up New North Road in the black prison-warder shoes, the loop still playing in my head. I'd like to scrape the top of the shoes against the wall as hard as I can, because she got them and I hate them and I hate her, but I daren't. I walk past the penny bun shop without even looking in the window.

When I get to school I stand around with my mates in the playground. The empty space where my DS tin should be screams at me from inside my duffel bag. They're talking about the weekend. I'm not listening, my face is a fixed half smile, my head's fuzzy as if I've had to get up really early. There's registration, then assembly, then it's DS for the first double period, then break.

'Here, Sir.' Registration's over.

I mouth the hymn and prayer in assembly and ask God to help me, to free me from her.

I cross the yard to the DS room, fear rising, heart sinking, every step bringing the moment nearer. I never bunk off, my gang doesn't do things like that. Every single girl has her cake tin, even the B and C streams who join us to do DS. Even the poor girl from the slum area that everybody bullies and calls Spider because of her long skinny arms and legs and greasy black hair. I bet even she has a mum who cares about her.

Miss is small and she bustles around. She's got short efficient hair and rolled up sleeves and is wearing her white pinny. She demonstrates to the whole class how to make a marble cake: weigh out, blend the sugar and margarine with a wooden spoon and change to a metal one after the egg, divide into three... chocolate powder, cochineal... fold in the flour... dropping consistency... a little milk. I hear the sounds but I'm not listening. All I can hear are Muriel's words, over and over.

Then Miss is saying we can use some of the little bottle of school milk that we get at break time. I clutch onto her words: that's one ingredient I will have, and Miss always lets us use her cochineal so we aren't all running around school with red dye, so I'll have two. Oh don't be stupid, two's not enough, two's nothing.

She's going to be finished in a minute and I'm going to have to tell her. She'll tell me off in front of all the girls in our year and they'll all stare and they'll talk about me behind their hands and they'll tell their parents, who'll look at me funny if they see me in the street, and the teachers will all gossip about me in the staff room and think I'm poor, and my classmates will hiss at me like they do with Spider...

'Now, does everyone have everything you need? The list is on the board to remind you,' Miss says.

I could bluff my way through, pretend I've forgotten my ingredients or left them on the bus, but what would I do next week, and the week after that? I've got to tell her. God steps in to save me.

'Please Miss, I haven't got any self-raising flour, we only had plain,' one girl says.

'Please Miss,' pipes up another, 'my mum forgot the cocoa powder.'

'All right you two, come up here. You've had all week to get these things, why don't you check the list on Saturday to make sure you have everything? Hmm? Come on now, speak up girl!'

'Sorry Miss,' is the only response.

'And it's your responsibility, not your mum's.'

No answer is expected. She tells us this every week. I've never forgotten anything. She gives them the small amounts of cocoa powder and flour that they need. 'Now, don't let me see you up here again.'

'No Miss, thank you Miss.'

The girls blend back into the sea of cookers. Miss is looking at me with her hands on her hips. I'm looking at the floor.

'Now Susan, why are you standing there like a wet weekend?'

I freeze over inside, crawling with shame and embarrassment, but there's nowhere to go, no ground to swallow me up, no guardian angel to come and save me. No words come. It's all gone quiet. The room has 20 cookers, each with their own work surface and chopping board; two girls stand at each one. I daren't look up but I know that there must be 40 sets of eyes on me. The sour tang of disinfectant and acid green washing up liquid hits me and I feel sick. No cupboards being opened, no clatter or natter. I imagine everybody moving in slow motion, I know all their ears must be tuned to what Miss is saying and they're waiting for me to speak.

I'm waiting for Miss to say something mean like, *Come on, out with it girl, where are your ingredients?* Instead, she says to the class, 'Get on with it now, do your weighing out. I'll be round to see you all in a minute.'

Then there's the faint sounds of cupboards being opened, bowls being brought out, the dull thud of the wooden spoons and the plastic click of weighing scales being assembled, but the sounds are miles away, around me and Miss there's just a thick fog of silence that's keeping the words in my mouth.

Instead of Miss, I see Muriel's pressure cooker ready to explode, her bacon slicer of a mouth spinning, ready to push me through. I force out some words.

'Please Miss I, er... I'm not allowed to do Domestic Science any more,' I say as quietly as I can. There's a low murmur from the sea of cookers and I can still feel their eyes on my back. I'd be looking and listening if it was anybody else getting told off.

'You what?' Miss thunders at me, folding her arms under her small bosom. Her voice is mean and so loud that the whole class can hear. 'You can't do Domestic Science any more? What do you mean by that? Where are your ingredients?'

She hasn't got it. I try again. 'Please, Miss, I can do it if I don't need ingredients, I mean I just can't bring ingredients anymore because we can't afford it, Miss.' My voice tails off as I say the last bit, the bit that Muriel said because she needs to justify what she's doing. She isn't doing it out of hatred for me and a desire to destroy me, or because she is jealous of what I bring home, or because she needs me not to exist – she is doing it because we *can't afford* the ingredients. Even the poorest kids from the C stream can afford the ingredients.

'*You can't afford it!*' Miss bellows my whispered words as if she's an amplifier. She isn't a nasty teacher, just an ordinary one trying to get on with a lesson that I am interrupting and taking her away from. She's cross.

'Well, what am I supposed to do with you all lesson, I'd like to know? I can't be giving you ingredients every week. You can't afford it? I've never heard the like. The rest of these girls manage. Now you come with me young lady and you can explain yourself to the head.' She turns away from me for a moment and I can feel my face burning.

'And the rest of you get on with your cakes. I want to see the mixture ready to go into the cake tin when I get back. Don't forget to grease your cake tins but don't put any mixture into the tin until I've seen it. Right you, come with me.'

I can't stop the tears, they're just there. It's not fair, it's not my fault, why is she shouting at me? Does she think I can get the money from somewhere if they won't give it me at home? I want to do DS. I like it. I wipe my sleeve across my face. It takes away the tears but spreads the snot. I try again with the other sleeve. I keep my head down. It's hard to keep up with Miss. She's almost running across the yard and up the steps. We're both in our pinnies but everyone's in class so there's no one to see.

As we pass the gym, I can hear the echoing shouts and squeak of pumps on the varnished wooden floor. I hate gym but I wish I was in there now, anywhere but where we're going. I've never been sent to the head before. Only the bad kids get sent there and I'm good. I was nearly a prefect. It isn't my fault so he won't be angry with me, will he? Well, Miss is and she must know it's not my fault.

There are two boys in the corridor outside the head's office standing away from each other, facing the wall. Will I have to do that?

'Now you stand there, young lady, and wait until the head is ready to see you,' Miss says, leaving me in the secretary's office. She doesn't say anything about the wall. She speaks to the secretary in a low voice then leaves. The secretary picks up the phone and says something into it and then she goes to the head's door, knocks and goes in. While she's out of the room I quickly wipe my nose really well on my cardigan sleeve. My cardie is maroon so I have to wipe my sleeve on my pinny so the white smear of snot isn't so obvious. All the girls in DS will be talking about me and sniggering while Miss isn't there. I can still feel the humiliation of being frogmarched up to the office.

The gentle voice of the secretary cuts through my shame and pain, 'The head will see you now Susan, can you go in please.'

Her kindness brings back the tears. I push them down into a hard lump in my throat. I know that if I have to say anything to Mr Heap I'll start to cry again. He gives the boys the cane when they've been naughty, but I know that he's a kind man really. Once, in an assembly, he said that he knew some of us children had already come through dark tunnels in our lives and I knew he meant kids like me, because Mam had died and I'd been in care. I don't know if he knows anything about how things are at home now. Though I've never told anybody anything about the poisonous world of home I just hope that people will know by a kind of osmosis. My world is so bleak, it must surely ooze out of me at school or Sunday school into the unpolluted world. The only person I have ever complained to is Grandma Swift, because she is so far away and because she is so keen to be critical of the woman who has replaced her daughter. I go to the door and open it. I've forgotten to knock.

'Now then Susan, come and sit down and tell me what this is all about.'

Oh no, he's being kind, the tears come back and I feel empty inside, like I haven't eaten or don't want to struggle any more. I have to stop myself crying because there are lots of papers on his desk, and if I start I'll never stop and he's too busy to have time for me.

I force out the words, 'Please Sir...' but my lip trembles and my throat blocks up and only a great shuddering sound comes out of my mouth even though I didn't mean it to and tears push themselves out of my eyes, because there's no room for them inside any more.

'It's all right Susan,' – Mr Heap sounds more like a nice dinner lady than a head – 'your teacher explained what you said about not being able to do DS anymore because your family say that they can't afford it. I'm going to write a letter home to your dad and ask for an explanation.'

Panic, terror... if her name isn't on the letter, she'll get me for it and I can't let him think Dad would stop me doing DS. I make the words come out: 'Please Sir, it's not just Dad any more, he got married.'

The snot is flowing again. I daren't use my sleeve. Mr Heap passes me a tissue. 'It's all right Susan, it's not your fault. They've no business sending you to school without your ingredients and leaving it up to you to explain. They could at least send a note with you. Now go back for the rest of your class and see how the others make their cakes and everything will be all right for next week. Come back at home time and collect your letter from my secretary. Here, take some more tissues with you.'

I can't go back and face the others. What will my friends think? But my legs keep walking – out of the office, past the gym, down the steps and across the yard. Then I freeze outside the double doors of the DS classroom. Gillian sees me through the glass top half of the door. She smiles at me. I have to go in now. As I open the door a delicious waft of baking cakes hits me, and I think of Barbara, my lovely Sunday school teacher, and of what it must be like to have a mum and of love and kindness and this whole horrible mess of my life.

Miss seems to have calmed down. She pairs me up with my mate, Maggie, and we get on with the rest of the lesson together. After ages, the silent sobs, gulps and sighs fade away. Maggie doesn't have a dad. But I bet that when she sits down with her mum for tea, they eat what she makes. Maggie's cake is flat on top, just right, not pointed or dropped in the middle like some of the others.

Maggie comes to the head's secretary with me when I collect the letter at home time. It's OK, it's addressed to Mr *and* Mrs Cooke. Maggie must have cut up her cake with one of the dining room knives at lunch time, because as we walk down New North Road together to our different bus stops, she gives me a piece and takes one herself. It's lovely, soft and moist in the middle, just perfect.

'Won't your mum mind?'

'Course not,' she says as she puts her cake tin under her arm, holding it flat with the lid upwards like all the other girls in our year, except for me. But we don't talk about that. We chatter about everything except the DS class. Sometimes I ask her what they will be having for tea and I imagine I'm going home with her and sitting with her and her mum having a lovely tea and not feeling frightened at all.

Mr Heap was on my side so he will have made everything OK, but she'll still be there judging, boring right through me with her look so I'll still feel wrong all over.

In the early days, when they first got married, she used to let me help in the kitchen. She put a raw egg yolk into the mashed potato and said it would be our secret. I liked that. Why couldn't it have stayed like that? Why couldn't she just have been nice like Auntie Pat or Barbara? Another time, in the early days, she said I could make a blackberry and apple pie with the blackberries I'd collected and brought home. I did, but when it was finished I was so scared that I dropped it on the stone floor.

Because of the letter I have to do something different. The safety of doing the same thing I do every day is gone. I have to hand something over to them. I have to say, 'The head teacher sent this.' It won't be like usual. I won't just go in, eat the slop or grease that's on the table waiting for me, get changed and go out without speaking to anyone except to ask to leave the table.

Doing something different means danger.

I walk up our passage and my insides freeze over just like they always do, knowing she'll be there. And she is always there. I open the back door into the kitchen. Her pressure cooker's hissing on the gas stove; I walk past it quickly before it gets me, down the stone step into the living room and sit down in my place. I'd rather be anywhere than here at this yellow Formica table. My eyes dart around, now the freezing has turned to a stone in my stomach and it's getting heavier. She puts a bowl of slop in front of me.

Dad's back from work and he's sitting with her and Edward on their side of the table. They're having lamb chops, smooth creamy mash and shiny peas. The minty tang of the peas hits me and I can feel the texture of the mash on the roof of my mouth and the taste of it on my tongue. I imagine the satisfying ooze of the fat on the outside of the chops bursting as I bite into it. My slimy slop has bits of tails floating in it. There's a marged slice of bread next to it. She must put the marg on and scrape it off again.

Edward has some mash in his bowl and some Moulied chop – no peas because, as she told the room in the early days, *babies can choke on peas.* She feels quite free to talk at us whenever she wants, it's that we can't speak. The words are filling me up. I have to get them out before I can force any of the brown slurry in.

'The head has sent a letter about me not doing DS,' I say, putting the envelope as near to their side of the table as I dare. I know I can't give it to Dad and I won't give it to her. So even if Dad didn't know about me not being allowed to do DS any more, he does now. I like to think he didn't know.

The letter sits on the table like an unexploded bomb. The slop smells like just what it is, cows bums, but I eat every scrap because there's nothing else.

'Please may I leave the table?' I say, not to either one of them.

'Yes, you may,' says Muriel.

I go up to the toilet and get changed out of my school clothes into even more scruffy ones for going out. I drag it out as long as possible because I don't want to go out into the cold. I can't hear her singing. They must still be eating. When I get downstairs Dad is still sitting at the table, his plate still in front of him. I go towards the kitchen to leave by the back door.

'Just you wait there a minute young lady,' she says.

I freeze with one foot still in the living room and one on the stone step to the kitchen. No further instruction, so I turn.

Edward's highchair, with its surrounding invisible electric fence, is empty. He must have been put in his cot for a nap.

'Now just you sit down over there,' she continues, in a really mean voice, pointing at a chair the other side of the table. I notice from my cast-down eyes that Dad's eyes are searching the bones on his plate as if he might have missed a speck of meat. I sit where she said, opposite both of them. It's got to be about the letter. That's the only thing that's different from when I left the table.

As soon as I'm sat down, the 'pressure cooker' valve bursts open spraying me with burning fat.

'You're a lying little bitch,' my stepmother screams.

Did I see Dad flinch? Oh yes, please, he must have.

All her previous attacks have been underhand, sly, controlled, calculated – this openly vicious attack is a shock. What have I done wrong? It's *her* that has stopped *me* doing something, got me into trouble at school, but now it's *my* fault. What have I lied about? I must have got it wrong, but how? I was so careful with what I said to Miss.

Dad's eyes continue to examine his plate.

'I told you that we *can't afford* for you to do cookery anymore,' she yells in my face. 'But no, you couldn't pass on a simple message, you had to lie. You told the school that you're not *allowed* to do cookery anymore.'

Yet again she has twisted the truth to make it look like it is me in the wrong. I did tell them we couldn't afford it. I did, didn't I? She makes me doubt what happened, what I said. I thought Mr Heap had rescued me but he hasn't, he's made it worse. The head was kind, but kindness is no good. He tried to help but nobody can help. He's done this. It's his fault. Oh God please let me not be here. Tears squeeze out of my eyes and run down my cheeks.

'And don't turn on the water taps for your father' – she blasts another sheet of scalding poison at me – 'he's not affected by them.'

These words slice deeper than *lying* and *bitch*. I'm crying because she's screaming at me and because my life is so horrible and she's shaming me for it, saying that I am doing it to make my dad care. Is that because she thinks he might care? Is this how she has been brainwashing him, making him believe that my feelings are just 'put on'?

How can Dad just sit there and let her be so cruel? Doesn't he love me any more? Isn't he my Dad anymore? Does he believe her? Does he think that I've been really bad and told lies? Has he forgotten all those years before she came and how I looked after all of us? Is it because he wants a quiet life? She is still fuming at me, *bitch, nasty, lying, evil.* I try stopping my tears coming out so she'll stop shouting at me, but I can't, it just makes more come.

Finally she says, 'Right, go on then, get out you nasty, lying little bitch, I'm sick of the sight of you.'

I get up, walk round my dead-eyed dad and his seething wife and slouch towards the back door, pulling my thin anorak tight to my body for comfort that doesn't come. The empty evening stretching ahead like a night when you can't get to sleep.

I set off to walk to Maggie's. It's a long way but it's the only place I can think of. I walk the half mile to the bottom of our road then I turn to walk alongside the river, trying to keep under the gas lamps as long as possible and running in the dark bits between them. I feel very sad and sorry for myself but I don't fear that anyone outside the house will harm me, not here anyway. I would never walk around Lockwood where that man offered me five pounds and I knew what he meant and I never go up to our rec alone. If Maggie isn't in, I'll leave straight away and go up by Newsome Church where its light and there are people around going for chips. Some of my mates might be out.

As I walk, I mouth the words to Pet Clarke's song, *Downtown*. It's meant for people like me: '*When you're alone and life is making you lonely…*' I want to be where all the lights are bright, but there's just the dim light of the lamps reflected in the cold wet York stone pavements. The sound of the weir in the river gets louder then quieter as I pass it.

Just another 10 minutes and I'll be at Maggie's. It'll be even darker before I get back for half nine. I'll have to walk along this long, deserted road by the river again. I hope she'll be in, but even if she isn't, I'll have killed an hour walking there and back.

* * *

I never thought about putting an end to my awful life. I had Barbara, my lovely Sunday school teacher, to keep me from losing myself completely, but mostly – in my young mind – I had my dad. But there was a stronger reason than all of these for not wanting to jump into the cold water of the Colne river. Suicide, perversely, is about taking control and indicates a certain freedom to think and make a decision. I could do none of this. I was utterly passive in the face of Muriel's destructive cruelty. There was no fight in me, just subdued black hatred, all of it focused on her.

That day, for the first time, Muriel accidentally shone a light into our home life. She got a shock when the school challenged her behaviour, but the authorities had no authority in our house and, on this occasion at least, were no match for my stepmother.

I still went to DS lessons. The teacher just paired me up with one of my mates and we worked together to produce whatever it was that we were making that week. The only difference was that I never took any ingredients in and I never had anything to take home.

It can be hard to love an adolescent stepchild, perhaps because of expectations on both sides, or maybe the solipsism of youth. It seems all too easy for the children from the first family to be edged out of the consciousness of their blood parent for whom it becomes convenient to believe the practised narrative of their new spouse. Fairy tales warn us about the potential failures of stepmothers, but it was Hansel and Gretel's father that took them into the woods. Our father continued to keep a roof over our heads and food on the Formica table, but there were much more important duties that he failed on. He failed to protect us, all of us – even Edward as it turned out – from serious, calculated, devastating harm.

At the time, I never stopped to think that Dad could have stepped in and stopped me being banished into a twilight of non-existence and slop food. Perhaps he found it convenient to believe her version of the truth. Muriel did an excellent job of managing him, ensuring he could have his sacrosanct quiet life. Something he certainly didn't have before she came to control us. She fed him well and managed his wages better, so there would have been more money for things that made his life easier. With her, he could have a decent car and holiday money and meals that he relished.

One thing was certain, while Muriel was in our house, the man who lived with us was no longer our father. Fathers love and protect, fathers care. I know these truths now. But back then, had I allowed these thoughts to creep in and question Dad's love, then I may not have survived. My life would not have been worth living unless I was certain that our dad was still there – somewhere underneath.

Tea and Kindness

I'd been in love with John, the young groundsman, at our school since I first saw him. I've been making it obvious for ages that I'm interested but he just hides under his fringe. He's got long legs and when he walks in his drain-pipe jeans it's as if he doesn't bend his legs at all, he just swings from his hips. Then one day he asks me if I want to go to the flicks. Soon after that he invites me to have tea with his parents and see his rabbits. Dad isn't interested any more in whether I'm meeting boys, even though I'm still only 14.

John and his dad breed and show rabbits. They live just round the corner from Barbara and our Sunday school. Their house is tiny with a little yard at the front. Inside there's just one room downstairs with three arm chairs round an open fire and a table at the back of the room where there's a pot sink and a bit of a kitchenette. I've never seen upstairs.

John's dad's head looks too big for his body, his face is pasty white with big open pores and he has nicotine stains on his long first two fingers, just like Dad. He's too tall for the ceiling of their tiny living room and has to bend over like the Honey

Monster to miss the beams. He's much older than my dad and has yellowish white hair that, just like Dad's, is slapped down with Brylcreem. He worries that I might be put off John because he spends so much time with the rabbits. I don't mind, we even go to rabbit shows together.

His mum is soft and gentle and looks after both of them. We've been talking about the Netherton village show and she says she used to do embroidery, so we look through their drawers to find some to enter in the show. She is an expert. Her needlework is perfect – neat, detailed and beautiful with lots of complex stitches.

'We've got to put it in the show,' I tell her, 'it's bound to win, it's fantastic.'

John's dad wants to enter some of his roses and asks if I will arrange them in the vase. I don't know how to arrange flowers but I feel really special being asked so I try my best. He shows me how to put paper between them in the vase to help support them. We don't win anything with the roses but the embroidery wins first prize. It's like we're a little family, but only at weekends.

I come to see them on Saturdays and Sundays. On Saturdays I help John's mum get tea ready while John and his dad talk about which is their best breeding doe or whether they should buy in more stock. It's always the same tea: his mum opens a tin of salmon and a tin of corned beef and the four of us eat this with bread, marg and tomatoes. For afters there's a tin of fruit with Carnation milk and cups of sweet milky tea of course. After tea John might take me to the pictures or, if we've been at a show with one of the rabbits, we might stay in.

We don't talk about it or even think about it but it feels like me, John and his parents all expect that we will be together always, even though I'm not 15 yet.

Sometimes we have rows, though. His dad worries about this, too. Ironically, he told us that we better not fall out when we are out because he wouldn't want me to go off on my own as it's not safe for a lass walking the streets by herself. It feels strange to hear that Mr Jones cares about my safety, and sad when I think about my own dad, and having to stay out until 9.30 every night.

On Sundays I get two buses to Sunday school and have tea with Barbara afterwards. I love these teas. Barbara is doing a cookery course at night school in town so she is always making something new and wonderful. She lets me whip the cream for the chocolate eclairs she makes in her narrow galley kitchen and I measure the Camp coffee for the coffee and walnut cake. Her cakes are the only time I've ever tasted coffee. We eat in the living room at the dining table. There's only one living room at Barbara's. Hardly an inch of the white tablecloth is visible between the pretty plates of delights that result from Barbara's course. I feel loved here.

After tea I walk round to John's. It only takes five minutes. We sometimes go for a stroll in the beautiful dell where their rabbit hutches and sheds are. John holds my hand and it feels just right. He usually takes me home and sees me to the end of our passageway where we have a long snog goodbye.

The tinned teas at John's are wonderful because they are served with love and there is never any atmosphere there, or at Barbara's. Although these are the really special places where I have meals, anywhere at all is better than eating at home. It's not just that the slops are revolting, it's because of the tension and knowing I'm not wanted there. I even relish school dinners, unlike all of my school mates.

The only other place where I eat regularly is at my old primary school teacher Mrs Wressle's, where I still go once a week to help her with her housework and for tea. Her house smells of old wooden furniture and fittings that have been cared for and she has a silver brush and crumb tray on the polished oak table.

It's Wednesday, so after school I take the bus and go two stops further than my usual stop. I get off at the church, the one where Dad sent us to Sunday school when we first moved here, but when I told him we had to recite the creed and nod our heads in certain places he said they were like *bluddy Catholics*, and we never went back. Mrs Wressle lives five minutes' walk down the hill. Going to her house is a way of getting off the streets and into the warm. As I walk past the old Edwardian semis that are much bigger than our house, I wonder what it would be like to live in one of them. If I lived here, I bet I'd go to the high school, I'd have books to read, I'd learn things and be able to go to Guides.

Then I notice, There's something wrong on the other side of the road. A lorry's parked funny near the chip shop. I don't see it at first, but when I get past the lorry... Oh no. Oh please no... It's lying with its body making the wrong shape across the edge of the pavement; a thin stream of dark red has drawn a line on the tarmacked hill.

I feel sick everywhere. Nothing works. I can't make my legs go. I push my hands through the holes in my anorak pockets right into the front corners at the seam so I can pull it around me, hugging myself. I've never seen an animal even bleeding before and the poor dog is still, lifeless. My head feels foggy. I keep my eyes fixed the way I'm going. I've got to move. I've got to get away. The pavement under my feet looks nearer than it should. I lean on the garden wall of one of the houses.

I'm past now, I don't look back. It seems to take ages to get to Mrs Wressle's. I walk up her drive and hold onto the wall by her door, take a big breath and press the wind-up bell which responds with a deep *drrrrring*. I need to tell someone. I need someone to make me feel better, to take away the sick feeling I have, to comfort me.

When the door opens. I see no kindness or comfort in the old hooded eyes, just hardness and impatience. 'Whatever is the matter Susan, what's wrong with you?' she demands.

'Ah... an accident... a dog... bleeding... in the road, a lorry.

I think it's dead. Can I sit down please? I don't feel very well.'

'Yes, sit there,' she says, pointing to the old dark wooden dining chair in the hall.

I want her to ask me to lie down, to tuck me up in one of her spare beds under the gold coloured eiderdown with a hot water bottle. I want her to bring me some soup or even a cup of tea and put it on the crocheted mat on the bedside table. Barbara would do that and I know Auntie Pat would have done. But they're not here and I just have Mrs Wressle to turn to.

'Well if you feel unwell, you should go home.'

I'm stupid. Why would I think that she cares? Can't she guess what it's like at home? She has never asked and I'd be frightened to tell. Even if she knows, she obviously doesn't care. I realise in that moment that our Wednesday evenings are a one-way service. The old-lady pink bridesmaid suit she bought and the polite tea when I come to clean for her aren't a fair exchange for the years since primary school that I've been her child servant every Wednesday. She has to know from our clothes and shoes, that we don't have loving parents at home who will take care of us if we don't feel well.

But it's no good wishing for things to be better, or for people to be different. She doesn't want me and I have to leave. I step back out into the cold, lonely streets. I've no plans to meet any of my mates and, because I'm usually at Mrs Wressle's, there will be no tea at home and I wouldn't dare go there now anyway, so I'll go hungry.

I start to drag myself back up the hill, keeping my eyes to

my side of the road. Lights are shining in some of the windows of the houses I pass, they look welcoming. There'll be warm fires in the ranges. The kids will be coming home from school, there'll be nice teas ready. Their mums will be pleased to see them. Maybe they'll be having egg and chips.

OUT OF CONTROL

It's a Saturday. A long day to fill. I won't be seeing John until this afternoon when he's finished doing his rabbits, so I cling to the warmth of the bed. I'm 14 and I've survived her for about a year now. I'm lying in my bed under the sheet, blanket and eiderdown. I love the little window in here. It's not a sash like in the other rooms; it opens outwards onto the back garden. There used to be a picture on this wall of a beautiful little boy with a mass of blonde curls. It had a fancy gold painted frame. Dad said it was of him and that back then boys *did* use to wear long white dresses when they were little.

Usually on Saturdays the Hoover comes on in the room below my little partitioned-off bedroom and continues until I'm up and out. For some reason this morning is different. Instead I can hear the low rumbling of voices in the room below. Suddenly the raised bacon-slicer voice comes up through the floorboards and threadbare mat – 'Arthur, you will have to stay here to keep her in, that girl is *out of control.*'

The last three words are carefully tailored to take a slice right through all of me. I am so scared to do anything wrong that I measure my every action in order not to upset her but she still sifts through my life with a nit comb, twisting everything around so that it's me that's doing something wrong. Has she actually convinced herself (and Dad) that I roam the streets at night because I want to? If Dad believes all this crap is it because he's stupid, or is it easier on his conscience, or does he just not give a bugger?

Her instructions to me, relayed at high volume through Dad, continue: '...and she can get herself into the front room and wait till they get here.'

I've no idea who '*they*' are or why they're coming to see me. Oh dear Jesus protect me from this. I promise to pray every night before I go to sleep. Is she putting me away, back in the Home, or maybe a borstal for wayward girls? Do they have those? Another way for me to disappear and for her to save money to spend on them? Well, would it be that bad in the Home? It has to be better than here. At least we might be able to watch telly and they had all those books and the food was lovely. I know I have to get up now but when I swing my feet round to the floor it's hard to get them to do anything else. Slowly I put on the black skirt I made at school from a dress that I got at a jumble sale and the striped blouse from the catalogue that's a bit tight now.

It must be something very serious if it's the front room. I follow the order, without a word having been said to me directly I go to the front room. I sit there with nothing to do but wait. I just have to wait here alone for *them*, feeling scared.

There is only me in the house, and them, in the next room. Nicky will be 'playing out' by now. Arthur will have been out early doing his paper round before going to his Saturday job where he does the supermarket's accounts and then he'll be playing hockey somewhere in the afternoon. I hope they feed him at the supermarket.

There's just a wall and a door between them and me. I can't open the door, speak to them, ask what's going on. I just have to stay here.

My stomach churns. I'm hungry and I'm scared, anxious, alert. It's quiet in here. A car passes. I listen for the next one in the distance, hear it coming closer, then past the front window and quieter again. I daren't stand up. She'll hear the sofa creak. She'll know where I am in the room. The more I try not to think about what I must have done and who *they* are and why *they* are coming to see me, and why I'm *out of control* the harder it is to think of anything else. When was the last time I sat on this sofa? Was it one Christmas before she came? The cushion sags under my weight. The springs underneath are slack. That's our fault. When we were younger and Dad was at work, we kids would pretend we were Captain Pugwash and his shipmates and leap between this sofa and the armchairs, boarding a ship laden with treasure and fighting the crew.

Except for that, we only ever used this room at Christmas. Every year I helped Dad decorate the small artificial tree. Did we clip on the twisting red wax candles which he never lit or were they just left on when the tree went back up to the attic? On those happy Christmas mornings lying under the covers we had to wait till Dad lit the fire in here so the room was warm enough for us. Now the air smells a bit fusty. I shift around in my sagging seat. Some things in the room are still the same. The buff coloured lampshade with the hunting scene on Dad's bureau, the old tiled fireplace and, in front of it, the long pile half-circle of red mat covering the lino. They're the same as before but on the wall the plaster head of the Arab wearing a turban is hers.

I hear another car in the distance and the change as it gets closer but this time it doesn't go past, it stops outside our front wall. I daren't look. I don't want to look. I'm already frightened enough. I think she must have contacted someone from the 'authorities'. That man in the suit nine years ago who came to tell me that Mam was dead, he was from the 'authorities'. Our head teacher is from the 'authorities' and him getting involved didn't end well for me.

I hear car doors close but I can't see anything from the sofa through the lace curtains. I try to block out the footsteps leaving the car, walking along the stone pavement to our ginnel to get to the back door. I freeze as I hear voices from the living room. I crane to hear but I can't make out the words. The bacon slicer has been turned off for the visitors. The voices are low so I don't know if it's her, or Dad, or *them*. I don't want to be here. I want to scream and scream but they would lock me up then and I can't anyway, I am under her total control, like a robot. Then, just as my head is about to burst, the door opens.

Two tall strangers, one woman and one man, both wearing smart dark clothes and black lace up shoes, come in. They look like prison warders. Is she sending me to prison because I'm *out of control*? Oh God, please help me.

The woman is wearing black stockings and she sits next to me on the small two-seater sofa. It sags even more and I feel embarrassed for our family. I move my backside to the hard wooden rim to take my weight off the springs. The man sits in one of the matching armchairs. Dad, and her, stay in the other room.

The strangers introduce themselves as police officers. Is that worse than prison warders? The electric shock that results passes through me in slow motion. What has she arranged for me now? The female copper next to me shifts on the sagging sofa and I cringe.

'Your mum...' Aaaaah! I want to tell her she isn't my mum, she's an evil bitch who tortures me every minute of every day; even when she's not there she's in my head digging away at me with a pick axe, reminding me I'm nothing. But I know I can't say any of that so I stay silent, looking at the woman. My eyes must be wide with terror and hate, '...tells me that you sent a letter while you were at your Grandma's saying that she's like Lady Chatterley. Can you tell me something about that?' she asks.

What the hell is she talking about? Grandma, like Lady Chatterley?

'I never said anything like that,' I say, suddenly relieved to have something I can truthfully deny, but it's still scary. They must be here because the book has been banned and they know I borrowed a copy from someone at school. Can I go to prison for that? Can I be arrested or have my name put down somewhere on a record that will stay on my file for life? I've already been in trouble for shoplifting so they might not be lenient this time.

She opens a little flip top notebook and reads from the letter I'd sent to Arthur who hadn't come with us to Grandma's this time: '...I hope they don't find the Lady Chatterley book or they'll be having another baby...'

How could I be so stupid? She'd steamed open that letter just like she does with any letter that arrives for me. I thought I would be OK because it was to Arthur and she's not mean to him, but she could see it was my handwriting.

'Yes, I wrote that,' I respond, 'but I didn't mean it like she said.'

'Have you read the book?' Is that a note of softness in her voice? She does not sound as mean as I expected.

'No, everybody was talking about it at school and I borrowed it from someone but I thought it was boring when I tried to read it so I left it under the mattress in my bedroom while I was away at Grandma's.'

Really, me and my mates had just tried looking up the rude bits, but we couldn't find any or see what all the fuss was about so I didn't bother trying to read it.

'Do you have a boyfriend Susan?' she asks next, without asking anything else about the book.

'Yes, John,' I reply, not seeing the point of lying.

'And how long has he been your boyfriend?'

'About six months.'

When she stops talking my insides feel the way they do when Muriel's in the room and I'm paralysed because I daren't move or look anywhere. I notice the man out of the corner of my eye. He hasn't said a word. He's trying to look as if he's not watching us. I feel like the fox in that hunting scene in the lamp on Dad's bureau, every nerve alert now. I know I have to be on my guard.

There's a smell of sweet tea on the woman's warm breath as she says, 'Your mum [does my silent scream show on my face?] thinks you have been having underage sex and she wants us to take you for a medical examination by the police surgeon,' as if she's asking me what subjects I like in school.

Oh God! Jesus! She wants to have me internally examined to prove I'm not a virgin? That's worse than anything I could have expected, worse than anything else even she has ever done. Now I'm churning inside and hatred is burning all through me but I have to be wary. Like the fox on the lamp, I need to get out alive. I need to outwit my tormentor, Muriel.

'I'd like to ask you about some things that you write in your diary about John,' the policewoman continues, and I wonder why, after what she just said. She checks her notebook again. My diary isn't even a proper diary – just one of those pocket things that I use to write where and when the different subjects are at school. I keep it in my duffle bag. It's with me all the time except when I go to the toilet or when I have my bath once a week. She must have gone through it then. I don't dare say anything about her in there but now I realise how stupid I am to write anything down at all. How could I imagine that she wouldn't find a way to read it *and* use it? She is all over every part of my life.

'What do you mean when you say, "and then we made love"?'

Oh God, please help me now and I promise I will say my prayers every night. I frantically search for words. 'Well, that's what they always say in my brother's James Bond books when they are being romantic,' I say.

It feels like the policewoman's face has softened a little, as if that's what she wanted to hear. I've become very good at reading faces.

'OK, I think that's all we need to ask you,' she says finally, after writing something in her notebook. I don't know if she believes me; I didn't actually tell her any lies. But even if she didn't, I think I know that she understands how things are in this house. Then she says, 'Is there anything you want to tell me Susan?'

Oh, there is so much, so very much. How wonderful it would be to have someone who wants to know, someone who would listen, someone with the power to do something to help me. But why will this be any better than the letter from the head teacher? Can she save me when he couldn't? If she tries will it just make even worse things happen? There is only one thing I can think of that she might be able to do. I'm so desperate after what Muriel has asked the police to do that I dare to say it. I have to get out.

'Can I be put back in a Children's Home?' I ask her, because at Fartown Grange I was not anxious every day. I don't think about Nicky and Arthur or my Dad because they are no longer part of the tiny life I have when I'm at home. There is no one else in my world here, except her. I could even do the shared clothes from a box thing. I don't care about anything – well, nothing except escaping from her. It's more than I've ever dared say to anybody. No one knows what it's like here for me, no one except her. The policewoman seems to be on my side, and I have a chance to get out so I have to take it.

The policewoman leans in a little and there's the sweet tea smell again. 'That would be a big step, I think it's better if you think it over for a bit. If you still feel the same in a week come and see me at the police station in town. You can come and see me any time if you'd like a chat, my name is Sergeant Wood. Do you know where the station is?'

I tell her I do. I hope she doesn't know about the shoplifting.

'Don't I have to come anyway for the examination?' I ask. I have to know.

'No, that won't be necessary.'

I've won, I've won. I've turned it back on her. I'll wait exactly a week and then I'll go and find the policewoman and she'll save me. I'll be free! I'll go back in the home and there'll be parties and jelly squares and music and nice food and doorsteps and a holiday by the seaside.

The coppers get up and go back to the sitting room where Dad and Muriel are waiting. She probably had a glass to the wall. I'm left in the front room with all its memories of happy Christmases. I can't tell what the voices are saying in the other room, or their tone. It's just a low mumble. I know I have to stay out of there till the police have gone and then I have to get out. It's past breakfast time so I have no reason to be here. But the only way out is past her. I wait, anorak on, duffle bag in hand.

When I hear the back door close, I count to 10 then open the door into the living room. She's standing in front of the food cupboards. I wonder if the coppers saw the padlocks. I outwitted her, I survived, and now I've got a way out. Someone's on my side now and I can go to that policewoman whenever I need to. Muriel has once again shone a light on what happens in this house and once again the authorities have not seen things her way.

But they've gone now and I'm still here. I have to get to the back door. The living room is filled with the burning acid of her atmosphere. I try to get out. She blocks my way. She raises a clenched fist an inch in front of my nose. I can see the white of her knuckles. I don't care. She can't hurt me. I'm already dead.

The strength in Muriel's right arm had been honed manipulating monster machines amid the deafening din of the weaving shed. But I did not expect violence from her. Her more – far more – effective weapon of choice is psychological: disintegration from the inside, like putting a puppy in a micro-wave. Terror through menace and degradation until everything on the inside is pulp. The blow is to be no surprise. She wants the anticipation. She's showing me it is coming.

'I could bloody well hit you,' she seethes at me through her false teeth.

And I think, yeah, now they know what you're like and it's you that showed them. Is it because they were on my side? Is that what's riled you? Or is it because they're not going to examine me? What have you got to be angry about? It's me that should be raging and hitting you after what you just tried to do.

I know I'm not allowed to meet her eyes but I can't avoid seeing the fist and the bulging arm. My only feeling is hate. There is now no space for fear.

Then she does exactly what she said she would like to do. She pulls back her arm and punches me with all her strength. A dizziness passes through me and a dense hard pain shoots through my face to the back of my head. I don't flinch. I don't duck. I don't care. I'm beyond caring, I'm nothing. What's the point of caring if you have no power to do anything?

I say nothing. There's nothing to say. I don't leave. She hasn't told me to. She may not have finished hitting me. I'm helpless, paralysed, I can no more leave the room than if she'd put bolts through my feet into the flag floor. No one has ever hit me in the face, until today.

The man who used to be my dad is still standing in the background. I know he must mind about this. Did I see him flinch out of the corner of my eye? Imagined or not, I cling to this: I need him to know that I still exist and for him to feel ashamed of this show of brutality to his little girl. Are you satisfied, Dad? Is this life quiet enough for you? I clutch the flinch to my shattered shrunken heart as I slouch away on her command.

'Go on, get out.'

I make for the kitchen and the back door. Once I've passed the window and walked through the passage to the street at the front I can breathe again. I put my hand to my nose and there's blood. Yes! Great! Something to show the copper.

I set off down the hill from our house on my way to town feeling sorry for myself but relieved that I've now got a clear way out. She's done it now. I'll find the policewoman and tell her that I've decided and why. I don't need a week, my bloodied nose is my ticket out. I want to go back to Fartown Grange right now. I won't spend another day in that house. She's bound to take me now and maybe they can have Muriel up in court for assault. Then everyone will know what she's like.

A blue Reliant Robin has pulled up beside me. I won't look, it might be a dirty man trying to pick me up. But then Dad gets out. He must be on his way to work. He must have taken time off because she told him I'm 'out of control'. Can he just go back to work then as if nothing's happened? I stop there on the pavement just 100 yards down from our house and hold my bloodstained sleeve to my nose. This is the first time I've been with my Dad without her for nearly a year and it's the first time he's spoken directly to me in all that time.

''Ows tha doin'?' he says, and gives me half a crown.

Well how the bloody hell does he think I'm doing? He must be really worried if he's giving me money. He's never given me any more than my weekly pocket money. Is he trying to find a way of making it better?

'Where's tha off to lass?'

'To see the policewoman,' I tell him, dabbing my nose. 'I'm going to tell her that I want to go back to the Children's Home, now.' These are more words than I have been allowed to say to Dad in a whole year and I mean them with all my heart.

'Well I don't want thi ta do that,' he says, 'I want thi ta stay at home, for me, will tha do that?'

Why? Why does he want me to stay at home? To watch me suffer? And yet, in that moment everything else falls away – my daddy said 'for me'. I reach out and pull in these soft words that I weave around with love into my shrivelled self.

If I'd thought about it, I might have realised that they wouldn't want social workers and courts and the police involved in their business, hearing what happens under their roof. But I don't think. I don't care. I'm not even bothered about what she will do to me in the future. All that matters in this moment is that my daddy has asked me to do something *for him* and that's all I need to hear.

If only I had been Arthur. If this were happening to him would he have had the sense to set conditions before he agreed to go home? If I were like my big brother would I be confident enough to demand to be treated like a person, to be allowed to stay in and watch the telly, to be able to talk in the house, to have the same food as them? But I'm not a confident educated half-adult. I'm a lost little girl that loves her daddy because he was all she had for seven years. I think that if he told me I had to come back and eat sick for every meal I would, as long as he said it was '*for me*'.

'I want thi ta go back 'ome and apologise to tha mum and tidy up tha room and we'll 'ave no more talk a goin' ta t'children's 'ome.'

Me, apologise! For what? For her punching me in the face, the cow, the effing cow. I wash my daddy's words in my mind until they come out right. I decide that we must both know how things are, that we have an unspoken understanding of what's right and wrong but we have to keep her happy; she controls all of us, even him. I keep washing and washing his words so that I know he still loves me.

This is my only feeble attempt at any kind of open rebellion. I have nothing to rebel with, just a black hating heart which feeds my survival.

I do what he asks. I go back, into the house, find that cow and drown out the silent screaming inside as I say, 'I'm sorry Mum.' I have no idea what for, but it re-establishes her power and control. I go to tidy up my room, still hungry from missing breakfast.

* * *

If only I had left then, perhaps the authorities would have removed Nicky as well. But there was no escaping the bond forged in my childhood which had made my father's faults invisible to me. Like an indentured labourer, I was forced to work for the repayment of an undefined debt.

Even though Muriel's corrosive presence in our family had overshadowed the relationship Dad had once had with us children, the bond that was created through the time he was our sole parent acted as a protective rose-tinted caul through which we viewed him.

CASH COW, 1967

'How would you like to come to the mill where I work next week?' Muriel had asked me in the early days. She'd gone into the mill straight from school. 'I'm sure you could find a job there when you leave school.' No, of course I don't want to go with her to look at the weaving sheds, but just like the 'you will call me Mum' instruction, I knew I had no choice.

The roaring din of the weaving sheds was unbearable but the visit was very useful. It made me very sure that I would never, ever, work in a mill or any other kind of factory.

It's our second year of having her living here. In January, my fifteenth birthday comes. I get steamed-open and resealed (why does she bother to reseal them?) cards from Grandma and Auntie Dorothy. Barbara and John's parents give me cards and John gives me a lovely romantic one.

School has just started to get interesting; we did a Shakespeare play, *Anthony and Cleopatra* and I loved it, it felt like it does when we do art appreciation or music with Mr Wood, or when we did French. It finally felt like someone thought we were worth teaching something that stretches us, something worth thinking about.

But I'll be leaving school at Easter. My classmates are staying on to do their CSE exams in the summer, and the teachers want me to stay on, too. But I am not going to. I'll be the only one from the A stream leaving, but being the odd one out in my class isn't anything new. I'm also the only one not to do DS properly, the only one not to have gone on the school trip to Belgium and the only one to wear prison-warder shoes a size too small.

We don't take O levels at our school because it's a secondary modern – they are only for the grammar schools. It has been decided that the product of our school only needs to learn enough for us to get manual, unskilled or semi-skilled jobs. There are jobs waiting for us in the local mills and factories, or the boys can join the army.

However, exams are a moot point because there would be no question of me staying on. I have to leave and start earning money the minute I am legally allowed to, at the Easter break. Muriel expects me to get a job in the mill. Does she think I'll hand my money over to her to keep them while I eat workhouse food and roam the streets every night? I imagine she says to Dad, *'Well you've worked all your life to bring them up, now it's their turn to make your life easier love.'*

I would do it for Dad but not for that bitch and her kid – I'm not keeping them. I have no feelings for Edward. I'm not allowed to. We have no contact with him. There are two separate families in our house, one that lives in the light and another that skulks around in the shadows.

Muriel draws Dad's leash tighter. He has moved from a highly skilled job as quality controller at David Brown Tractors, five miles away, to an unskilled job on the edge of town, one mile away, making wooden boxes, all so that he can come home for his dinner. Presumably he had a drop in wages as a result, so he wasn't earning as much as he was at Browns. Maybe he was able to change jobs because of the money she saves on our food, or maybe he made the move because they expected me to make up the shortfall. But they're wrong. I can't wait to get out of here. Nothing changed after the police incident. She still controls everything, including, in my mind, our dad.

I've no idea how to get away, but I know I have to. Can I get a job and live on my own when I leave school? The Youth Employment Service (YES) comes to school to arrange jobs for the pupils leaving at Easter – the whole of the B and C streams who are already 15, and me. When it's my turn to go into the small office the clerk from the YES asks, 'Now what sort of work would you like to do?'

I've given up my ambition to be a vet. A teacher told me that I would need to have gone to grammar school and have A levels. So, I say the next best thing I can think of: 'I'd like to work with children.'

'All right, I'll see what I can do,' he says, looking through his index cards.

Before my next appointment I find out that you can get jobs 'living in'. On the next YES day, I wait with the other few early leavers who are not sorted out with a mill job or army career yet and when it's my turn I give my name and the man shuffles through his notes and then moves over to his index cards.

'Yes, you wanted to work with children, didn't you? Well there is a job here in a factory packing teddy bears.'

I think. *Duh!*

I say, 'Oh, well that's not really what I was thinking of. My friend told me that there are jobs where you can live in, do you have any of those?'

He faffs about with the little cards and eventually says, 'Well, there is one here for a job at a hotel in the Yorkshire Dales.'

Wow, I sit up straight and take notice. I bet they have farms there. I love the countryside. I can get away *and* live somewhere beautiful. My life will change. I'll get out. I'll be free and happy.

'That sounds good, what would that be doing?'

'It says waitress and chambermaid, live in, £5 a week, starting as soon as you leave at Easter. They want you to go for an interview first. You would have to take two buses,' he continues, reading from his little card, 'one to Skipton then another to Settle and they would pick you up from there. I'll phone them to arrange a date and I'll let your teacher know.'

Could my escape be so simple – find a job and move to a beautiful place? I won't be talked out of it this time, even if Dad asks me to stay *for him*. I'll never stay at home and work for her.

The job is in a tiny village called Clapham at The New Inn hotel. On the arranged date, I put on my least scruffy clothes, take a bus to town and then the buses that the man had told me to get. I'm allowed a day off school because our form teacher says I can tell all the class about it when I get back and that will be educational. I don't know if the school or YES write home but I don't say anything to them and she doesn't say anything to me. I might be late back so I tell her I'm meeting John, which I am. I would never dare to lie because she finds out everything.

NATURE AND PERVERSION

It's the final stop, the Settle Down Cafe, it looks quaint and there's a bench outside, I'll wait there. But just as I'm about to sit down a man with thinning black Brylcreemed hair, pot belly and three piece suit, shiny from ironing, comes up to me. 'Susan Cooke?' he asks.

I'm not sure whether to say 'sir' so I just say, 'Yes.'

'I'm Mr Price. Come with me.'

We go into an inn. It feels really special. I've never been into a pub before. This one is lovely with a big sweeping staircase up to what must be the sleeping part. There are animal heads on the walls and pictures of hunting scenes. We walk through the inn into a car park. You can wait in the Land Rover, I'm just about finished here.'

He puts me in the Land Rover and goes back into the inn. I haven't sat in a car since Dad's wedding day. It brings back memories but I feel proud of myself for finding this way out. I imagine how wonderful it will be to be free and live in the countryside, just like going back to the farm. Twenty minutes later Mr Price emerges from the inn and gets into the driver's side. 'Right,' he says, 'let's be off.'

Out on the road we snake our way in silence up the gorgeous hillside and I know I want this job. I know I can do it – it's housework, I've done that all my life. I don't care how hard the work is if I'm living somewhere as beautiful as this and not living *there*.

The white painted inn is at the centre of the village of Clapham. It sits just opposite a beck and a little humpback road bridge. There are quaint houses with pretty front gardens along the length of the beck. It's a dream come true. Ingleborough peak stands watch in the distance as I follow the manager into the dingy bar at the front of the inn. It's very quiet. I hope they still need me.

'Would you like something to drink?' asks Mr Price.

'Could I have a lemonade please?' I reply. I want a cup of tea but I don't know if you can ask for that in a bar and I don't want to be any trouble. The lemonade comes and after I've had a few swallows a glamorous, curvy, well-dressed and made-up woman who must be about 50 comes up to my little round table.

'Hello,' she says, 'I'm Mrs Thomas, I'm a friend of the owners. Would you like to come with me?'

I take another big gulp then leave the half-finished glass of sweet bubbles and follow her up the stairs and into one of the bedrooms. We make a bed together and then she shows me how to clean a room for a change-over. As we come out, I get a glimpse of the man she says is the owner. She doesn't introduce me as we pass him. He looks like Colonel Blink from the *Beano* – short, fat and bald, with a slicked down comb-over and three-piece suit.

She takes me to the kitchens and dining room and introduces me to the chef and the pot washer. She collects a tray of tea with a heavy silver looking teapot, hot water pot, cups and saucers, sugar and milk and takes this into the shadowy empty dining room and we sit down at a table in the window. Every place at each of the tables is set with cutlery and a red napkin standing like an upside-down ice-cream cone. There's a stale smell of food mixed with furniture polish and an old-houses smell. Tinny Hawaiian music plays in the background.

'You will get £5 a week all found,' she says after pouring me a cup of tea. 'We do silver service here but you will be taught how to do it. The area is a beauty spot popular with walkers and cavers and people on route to the Lakes. Now, do you think you would like the job?'

'Yes, I do,' I say trying not to sound too excited.

I've done it, I'll get away! I won't have to roam the streets in the cold and dark and wet or say 'mum' ever again to *her*. I'll never have to watch them eating luxury food while I eat cows' tails or pea and specs of ham soup or bite into oozing grease. Maybe I'll even go back to Huddersfield on my day off and go to school and meet Nicky and we will talk to each other.

And then, just as Dad's dream of a good life must have disappeared with Mam's death and then again with Muriel's pregnancy – just when I thought I was home and dry, the glamorous woman is saying something that spoils everything.

'You will have to accept the owner's strange ways,' she states, now that she has me in the bag.

I don't dare to ask what she means, nor does she allow me any time to do so. I'm 15 now and I know that her few well-chosen words mean that the man who will be my boss is a sexual pervert. He gets up to something dirty and I will have to accept it. What can I do with this information? There's no one I can tell. How can I allow anything to stand in the way of escape and freedom? I have to take this job. If I say anything at school they might not allow me to come and John and his dad would certainly have something to say. But what choice do I have?

The smartly dressed woman says goodbye and busies herself arranging a lift for me back to the bus stop in Settle, as if what she has just said is part of normal conversation. I try not to think about her parting words, but inevitably I keep returning to the phrase, 'strange ways' like a tongue to a sore tooth. My mind is made up. I'd rather be here dodging that greasy comb-over pervert than spend another minute at 'home', earning money for them.

* * *

I've done it. I've defied her, got a ticket out. I'll be free. If only I can get through the next days and weeks.

The bacon slicer constantly hums until the menace escalates, the atmosphere getting thicker, heavier. Then the slicing starts, always while I'm at the Formica table forcing down the cheap slops.

'You don't care about your father or you wouldn't be leaving' or 'After all he's done for you' and 'You could be earning much needed money. You're a selfish little bitch.'

These thick, slow, through-to-the heart slices are infrequent; there is more menace in the silence, the silence and the hum.

You would have thought she would have wanted rid of me but no, she had it all worked out. She could feed me cheap slops and never see me except for mealtimes so I had become almost invisible and of little trouble to her. In her mind, I was to be her cash cow, there to sweeten the life of the *other* family. Did she really expect that I would continue to live here and walk the streets until bedtime handing over my pay packet at the end of every week? Not a chance. If I leave, she has lost.

March comes. Not long till Easter now. I'm nearly free. I'm still here, still anxious, still afraid of doing something that might provoke an explosion, still at the mercy of the merciless. But I'm counting the days. Every endless day is a day nearer freedom. I try not to think about the pervert, or if I do I remind myself that I will have a better chance with him than I have here.

If Dad had really wanted me to stay that other time because he cared about me, then he would ask me to stay now. He doesn't. So back then he just didn't want to be *shown up*. I don't care. It's not his fault. I love him and I know he still loves us. It's her I have to get away from. She's older than him (I don't really factor in that it's only a year) so I know she'll die first, then we'll get our real dad back, the one that has to hide when she's here, and she's always here.

* * *

It's Edward' first birthday today. She's been crowing about it all week. I can feel thick wisps of hatred in the air when I come down for my sludge and plop. If there's to be cake and a candle it will just be for the gang of three, probably when we're out of the way after tea.

I've bought a card for the little brother I've never been allowed to touch or speak to. I want to give it to him, but how can I? I know I can't give it to her. Dad isn't here and I wouldn't dare bypass her by giving it to him anyway. Can I leave it on the table? No, that would ignite a searing explosion, screaming, accusing me of something vile, probably of never speaking to Edward. Give it to the baby to rip open? That would be almost like touching him, polluting him. There's no way out. The dense glowering atmosphere closes in, paralysing me. If I don't give it, she'll say to Dad that I ignored my brother's birthday and if I do, I'll be breaking the unspoken rules about contamination of the happy family by one of the unwanted leftovers.

I finish my porridge and slouch off, card in pocket. Maybe I can do something with it tonight when they're both there, at least then Dad will see I tried. I walk out into the drizzle, along the back of the two houses, through the shared passage that runs along the side of next door, out onto the street and suddenly I know what to do. I'll put it through the letter box at the front door. That way, I don't have to face her and she won't know that I've put it there until it's too late to do anything to me. It will be like the post coming. I know there'll be consequences when I get home that I'll worry about all day, but will that be worse than if I *don't* try to give it to him? Either way I'm for it.

I go around the house to the front door, open the flap and start to push the card through the letter box. When it's half way through I jump back in shock. She's waiting at the other side of the door.

'Take it back, just take it back now, how dare you try to give Edward a card, you wicked little bitch,' she screams, 'we don't want your stolen goods.'

I bought this card for him. I didn't steal it. I haven't dared nick stuff since I got caught. Dad must have told her about the shoplifting. What can I do? If I take it back, she wins. In that split second, perhaps because I'm almost free, I taste rebellion. I'm in a battle of wits and wills, the kind of battle I've already won once and I'm not about to back down. The letterbox is spring-loaded, so in order to take the card back I would have to push the letterbox in again from my side. On the other side of the door she's powerless to push the card back because of the strong spring mechanism. I know what I can get away with. I pull the card from right to left making sure that it rips through the middle. That way I'm doing what she said (I would be too scared to just leave it where it is), but I'm making sure that half of the card stays where I intended. I've done it. I've won. I leave for school cradling my small victory. There might be more screaming tonight, but she can't accuse me of not doing anything to mark my brother's birthday.

* * *

I struggle on through the suet of hours and weeks, towards my leaving day. I only have to be there at mealtimes. I know I can do it. My raft in this wide sea of despair is that I'm going. I cling to that. What might the pervert do, expose himself, grab me? Whatever it is, can't be as bad as quaking in these shadows. I'd rather be alone and starving than a dead shell with her picking at everything I do. But I'll be leaving everything I've ever known, including the good things in my life: Barbara, John and his parents and my friends at school.

It's my last Sunday school class and Barbara has organised pop, her homemade biscuits and cake. 'We've had a collection for you and we wanted to give you this present to take with you to your new job,' Barbara says for the children.

From the shape and weight of the gift I know it's bath cubes. I open it, ready to pin a big smile on, and then the smile turns real. It's a travelling alarm clock, something I really need. It's metal, folds out into a triangular shape and has a green vinyl covering on the case part. It reminds me of when Dad gave me the fantastic doll at our first Christmas back together in the lovely new house. I felt loved then and I feel loved now, by Barbara, and I know Jesus loves me, he loves everybody, especially children.

Before I leave, for some reason, Muriel gives me an oblong casserole dish and two tea towels, presumably for my 'bottom drawer', things to save ready for getting married. I feel like the Red Indians in the cowboy films who get beads in exchange for land. There's no mention of the Premium Bonds that Grandma Swift said she'd bought for us each year.

I'll be taking three buses to my new life so I put the casserole dish and other things I won't need at the hotel in an old suitcase. I have to lug it down our road and along the river to Maggie's. I don't know how I'll ever be able to collect it. John's family has no transport. We always go to rabbit shows on the bus. I'll be sad to leave John but I can't see anything beyond getting away.

Like Dad, John never says very much. He knows how hard it is for me at home and that I have to get away, though neither of us really understands what this means for us. I just assume we will still love each other and see each other when we can. We don't think that not having enough money for bus fares or enough time to make the long journeys will matter. We know we're committed to each other and we don't see beyond that.

School breaks up for Easter. It's hard saying goodbye knowing that my class will all still be together next term without me there, but because I know what it will mean I can do it. Miss Whittle has always been kind to me. She says she'll come and see me at the hotel and that she knows that I'm burning my bridges when I leave home. I don't feel like it's me who is burning bridges and nobody else has actually said that I can't ever go back home, though I know I would never go back there to live.

The next day Nicky is not there, Arthur is probably doing his paper round and Dad's at work. I wade through my last ever plop and dollop. I'll never have to sit at this yellow table ever again. Will I ever see Dad and Arthur and Nicky again?

She says nothing. She's singing one of her bloody Jim Reeves songs. I open the back door and look at our little bit of scruffy garden for the last time. I then head for the passage way and freedom with my little travel alarm clock glowing with Barbara's love from inside my suitcase.

PART THREE

FREEDOM

I've found paradise, in a big shabby room with bare floor-boards. It's just behind the kitchens and its warmth hits you as you step in. There's no yellow Formica table here – instead, a big old scrubbed pine one. No atmosphere, no slop and dollop, no sludge and grease. I can breathe. I can take up space. I can be seen. I'm alive. I belong. It's the staff dining room. I'm staff and I'm here for my breakfast. Chef makes bacon and eggs and toast and there's butter and jam and I eat it and I love it and round it all off with a lovely cup of hot, sweet, milky tea. How can food represent so much? Love, freedom, peace.

After breakfast my first job is to clean the two bars. There's nothing quite like a bar in the morning: empty, silent, gloomy. There's a sour smell of beer slops, a smell new to me but, just like the bacon and eggs, it signals my freedom. From 7.30, for an hour each morning, this bar is all mine. It extends from the rough flagged public bar for the farmers and keepers into the carpeted lounge for those that think they're better. I stand behind it wiping the taps. I replace the wet slops cloths, wipe down the bar and then clean out the fire grates, wipe down the tables in both bars then lift the stools onto them so I can sweep and mop the stone floor and vacuum the carpeted one. Then I move to the landings, corridors and stairs. After that it's time to serve breakfast. Then there's the bedrooms to change and clean. There's only me in the day time and a lad who comes in from the village to help with dinners in the evenings and at weekends.

Before serving lunches it's back to the warm cosy staff dining room. I chomp my way through whatever chef serves up: a thick gammon slice sweetly scented with pineapple or half a roast chicken with bread sauce with either spuds or chips or mash, whatever he gives me and the pot washer. There's no wrong side of the table here, no special food for people who are not me.

In my break from three to six I take the boss's Labrador across the gloriously wild hills of the Dales. Here there are no bleak pavements, just paths that feel like freedom. I run about taking in the trees and wild flowers. I take deep breaths, I sing, I shout. I'm free and it's so beautiful.

It's spring and this is the Dales so there's still a chill in the air. The next most important thing about being here, after the staff dining room, is that I can go back to my own warm room up in the attic any time I'm not working. And I can go into the inn without my insides turning to concrete as I approach the door. The only atmosphere here is the expectation of hard graft and my only anxiety is about the 'funny ways' of the boss. I've seen him in the bar of an evening and when I've collected the dog but so far there's been nothing weird.

My working day ends at 10 when I leave the dining room clean and laid up for breakfast. My attic room has a sink and two single beds. The toilet is along the corridor and there is a staff bathroom on the floor below where I dump the linen from the dining tables and bedrooms.

Mondays is linen sorting day and I have to count the tablecloths, put them into the wicker laundry basket and list them in the laundry book. I pick up the first tablecloth. I can't believe what I'm seeing, a seething mass of black is moving in the middle of the pile. I drop the tablecloth, scream. Huge black beetles run in all directions. I run as well; I run as fast as I can to tell my boss. The bar manager laughs. He's not interested. He expects me to get on with it, so I have to. I go back, making as much noise as I can, hoping the plague-carrying things will run away. I force myself to pick up each laundry item by the very corner and slide it into the basket without looking, trying not to disturb the cockroaches as I note all the items onto a list. I wonder what happens to them at the laundry.

My favourite job is serving teas for the coach parties that come through on their way to the Lakes. There's a room in the middle of the hotel that you wouldn't know was there. All the other rooms – dining rooms, kitchen and bars on the ground floor; guest rooms and the boss' private quarters on the first floor – are obvious and used all the time but this one is tucked away like a secret room in an old country house.

It is somewhere between all the other rooms. It's huge with a sloping wooden floor and massive beams. It feels special because we only use it when we are expecting a coach party.

I challenge myself to get rid of the queue really fast. I plan well. I set out all the cups and saucers and plates of boring dry coffee biscuits. I turn on the urn in good time and put a little milk in each cup. Then I listen for the coach pulling up in the car park so I can mash the tea in a huge aluminium pot and make coffee in the tall pot. I leave enough time for the coach trippers to go to the lavs and then I start pouring the tea just as the first ones arrive. I time myself on the wall clock to see how fast I can serve them all. I refuse to allow a queue to form. I aim to get better each time there's a coach for tea.

At night, in my lovely warm attic room, I brush my teeth. I'd never done that at home. Dad didn't believe in dentists and toothbrushes. I wind up my little travel alarm clock on the chair next to my bed, ready to wake me up to start again tomorrow. I think of Barbara and John and I go to sleep not knowing if I'm happy but certain that I'm relieved.

Every Saturday at three I can get a ride into Settle, the nearest town. I bank most of my nearly five pound wage in the post office. Our wages are made up partly from tips and are never over a fiver, usually less. The smart made-up woman who interviewed me didn't mention I'd be cheated as well as perved. I keep a bit back to buy stamps for my letters to

Grandma and John and Barbara and sometimes I buy a single to play on the record player in the staff dining room. The first one I get is Englebert Humperdink's *Last Waltz*.

From my first wage packet I send money for my siblings. A week later I get a reply along with one of the 10-shilling notes that I sent. Amongst the small talk it says, 'I'm returning your 10 shillings because you couldn't be bothered to speak to anybody when you were at home, so don't try to bribe us now.'

The Japanese Flag and the Listening Tom

More girls have arrived from nearby towns and cities for the summer season; the restaurant is busy and the rooms are booked. I've got a room-mate. We're a family with Chef making meals for all of us. One of the girls is sacked and has no money to get back to Liverpool. I give her my Post Office savings book. The police bring it back. I tell them she didn't steal it. I hope she's managing.

One day, in our afternoon break, all the young waiting staff go across the humpback bridge where we can get down to the beck. We build a dam. It's really narrow, but we manage to swim three strokes to the other side. I'm having the sort of fun I haven't had since I used to play with Arthur and Nicky, before she came.

I've left my flip flops on the bank and, after we all clamber out, the male waiter throws one of my flip flops into the beck. What a pig. I go in to retrieve it and step on a broken bottle. Blood pours out of a deep gash on the sole of my foot. We wrap a white towel round it and when I take it off it looks like the Japanese flag. The doctor is sent for and I have to stay off my feet for a few days until it's healed. The waiter has to do my work as well as his own – ha ha! It's great being looked after by my room-mate, eating in our attic room until I can hobble downstairs to the staff dining room for meals with a big bandage on my foot.

I go down for breakfast one morning when I'm better and Chef hands me a tray of food. 'Take that up to the old man,' he says. 'Oh, and he's not in the flat, he's still in bed, the door on the left opposite the flat.'

Is this it? Will he *accidentally* expose himself when I deliver his breakfast tray, or try something worse? I look up at Chef – there's no indication from him of this being a set-up. He's no friend of the boss. I've got this pot of hot tea. If he makes a grab for me... I'd like to... but I don't know if I'd dare. Where would I go when they kicked me out? How would I live?

I stand outside this room that I've never entered before. I've never been asked to clean it or change the bed. I knock at the door and wait, giving him a chance to get decent. I can hear crackling and a muffled strange sounding voice from inside. 'Come in!'

He's in bed, wearing striped pyjamas, and only his top half is above the covers. Thank you God! The long bit of his comb-over is hanging the wrong way. The smell of sleep is hanging in the air. In the room there's just him in a single bed, a bedside table and next to that a metal box about four foot high and two foot wide sporting rows of switches. As I go in, he reaches up and flicks up one of the switches and the crackling and muffled voice stops. So he does spy on us. That's one of the rumours confirmed.

Chef, when he's been drinking, has shown me microphones hidden in the kitchen into which he shouts obscenities when he's the worse for wear. I've seen the same things in the private dining room, the staff dining room and there's one on top of the wardrobe in the honeymoon suite. I put down the breakfast tray on the bedside table and nothing happens. I return to the staff dining room for my breakfast, feeling relieved.

There's another rumour, though, which worries us waitresses much more than wondering if he has a bug in our bedrooms. We've heard that his perversion is something to do with him making us strip off. My room-mate and I can't find the bug in our room but we bravely insist in loud voices that if anyone tells us to get undressed in front of them, we will refuse to do it. We don't have long to wait before our resolve is put to the test.

It's bank holiday weekend, our ranks have swelled and we are preparing for the lunchtime onslaught in the dining room, making sure all the red ice-cream cone napkins are folded and in place and the salt cellars are full. We chat happily as we work.

The manager comes in and says, 'Now girls, go to the private dining room, the boss wants to see you all.'

Oh God. Oh no! This has never happened before. Is this it? A cold shiver goes through my body right down to my aching feet. I look round at the others: blank faces, panicked eyes, cornered, stunned, beasts in an abattoir, knowing there is no way of avoiding what is to come. I don't usually take any notice of the canned musak playing vaguely Hawaiian tunes but now, in the instant silence, it's all I hear.

The small private dining room, at the back of the main restaurant, seats about eight. It's occasionally used by groups of male diners who seem to be pally with the boss. Otherwise it's just for storage. We file into the small room in silence, unable to force a half smile onto our anxious faces as we look from one to the other for the reassurance that we're all in this together.

The eight of us wait in the small room, each silently willing the others to a level of defiance none of us dares ourselves. Then the patterned glass door with its pale-yellow privacy curtain opens and the boss steps in, breezy and businesslike, his waistcoat buttons straining over his pot belly, bald head shining through the gaps in his greased comb-over.

He's holding something.

'Now girls,' he says, 'take off your uniforms, I want to make sure that you all smell nice for the customers.'

Not one of us dares to say no. How can we? Our food, our income, our home is all in the hands of this man. I bet none of us is feeling homesick for a loving family – there's a reason we've all taken this live-in job in the middle of nowhere. We each take off our red tabards then undo the poppers on our blue overalls allowing them to fall to the floor.

In anticipation of just this sort of event, that has been a

threat in the back of my mind ever since that first interview with Mrs Thomas, I'm wearing a skirt under my overall. But I'm the only one. He can't say anything because it's our underarms he plans to dab. Everyone else is now in their bra, knickers, tights or stockings and suspenders. I'm 15, most of the others are 16. Colonel Blink is over 60.

We're standing in a semi-circle at one end of the little room, in front of the boxes of napkins and other supplies. He shakes the bottle he's holding onto the palm of his other hand and says, 'Now lift up your arm.' He moves along our line patting each girl's underarm close to her breasts with the scented liquid, dab, dab. 'And the other one,' he says, and I watch as each of my friends compliantly lifts their arms one at a time as he douses each armpit with the freezing cold fluid. Then he's in front of me.

'I've got my skirt on sir, because I'm indisposed.' Why am I explaining? He's the one in the wrong. He ignores my intrusion into his sordid fixation.

The liquid is shockingly cold. It doesn't make me feel fresh and clean but used and dirty. Some of the girls have started to put their overalls on again. When he gets to the end of the line, the dirty old man says, 'Come on now, get back to work, the customers will soon be here for lunch,' and he leaves.

Thankfully this is the only time this happens. If we'd known that we would have been glad to get it over with, but we lived in constant fear of it happening again. Just as I did with Muriel, we tell no one because we are certain that no one will care and that no one will do anything. We finish getting dressed and step out into the fray of the bank holiday rush taking our shame with us.

FIRST VISIT HOME, 1967

Nine months after beginning at The New Inn, the owner has sold the business and a new family arrives a few weeks before Christmas. I tell them that I cannot work at Christmas because I am a Christian. The next day I'm told I have to leave and I will get a week's pay, £5, in lieu of wages.

There is nowhere to go but Grandma Swift's. She welcomes me back to the extended family and, this time, perhaps because I am paying my way, I am not expected to skivvy and I am really grateful that I still have a home to come to. Without her would I be on the street? I pay her board from my unemployment benefit. I spend my time helping my lovely Great Aunt Florrie with her cleaning jobs and charity work. She's soft and gentle like Dad's mum, Grandma Cooke, who I can just remember. I also get to see more of Auntie Grace and my cousin Corrine who live just across the road.

I had only had one day off a week at the New Inn. Never enough time to think of anything but a walk up to Ingleborough caves and babysitting for the estate's under keeper and his wife who I had become friends with. Now I do have time, and I decide I want to visit my real family – Dad, Arthur and Nicky.

I've no plans to see John. After I'd been in Clapham a month, he wrote dumping me because we live too far apart. His rejection compounded that of Dad's. I was heartbroken and cried for weeks whenever I thought about him. Then, just as I was beginning to get over it, he wrote to ask if we could get back together. The anger I could not direct at my father was released onto John. How dare he! I was not prepared to take him back.

I refuse to give up on my family though. So I swallow my pride and I write a 'Dear Mum and Dad' letter. I know that to see Dad, Arthur and Nicky without her would be as difficult as removing the eggs from a baked cake, so I will have to do it on their terms. It's just after Christmas, so I buy presents for them all – well, Dad, Arthur and Nicky. I tell Auntie Grace. She says that I have to take a present for Muriel as well. I remember Edward's birthday card. I just can't do it. I take none at all.

I choose to arrive on a Saturday dinnertime when Dad and the boys will be there. What will happen about food? Will we sit around the yellow Formica topped table and pretend to be normal? I'll take a pie and eat it on the way and say I've had my dinner. I know I have the security of Grandma's to come back to but I still have to force myself to go.

It's three buses and a 50-mile journey but I've been doing it since I was seven. I eventually arrive at the passageway and get the familiar leaden feeling in my middle, but I have to go in for Dad, Arthur and Nicky. At the back of the house the tiny garden looks tidy. The small piece of grass that used to be kicked up in the old days from us playing ball games or wars with armies of little plastic men, is now neatly mowed.

She sees me pass the window and comes to the door: same limping gait, same Vitapointe hairdo, same C&A Stepford-wife clothes and pinny. Plastic words are said and I go through the tiny stone-floored kitchen where I spent so many hours making our food and washing up for the five years before she came, over the stone step and into the same lino-covered living room.

'Now you go out and play,' Muriel tells Nicky.

No! I scream inside, that's who I've come to see. How dare you! Does she think I want to see her? As usual Dad says nothing and Arthur is nowhere to be seen. Muriel is telling me about Edward. *I don't want to listen to you, shut up, shut up! I want to go after Nicky and talk, be together, offer comfort and the only thing I have, money* – but I can't. And what about Arthur? They haven't mentioned him.

Now they're talking about John – they don't know we broke up. Dad's actually speaking. He's going on about his expectation and dream of walking me down the aisle. It's his ideal vision of what a dad with a daughter should do. He wants to be the proud father, giving me away in virginal white. He thinks that John should be the man I marry – because he was my boyfriend the pair of them were convinced I must have had sex with him.

'But John wrote breaking up with me,' I plead. I don't tell them about the letter asking to get back with me.

'Well, let's go up there and see what's ta do,' Dad insists. They must have planned it all before I came, as a means of still controlling me, making me acceptable somehow, washing away the *wayward* girl she said I was that day when the police came. The idea that my only experience of sex was with John shows how little they know about the dangers of the streets.

I'm crawling inside with the thought of seeing John again. It will be so embarrassing, but I have to go along with it, I have to stay friends with them. I haven't been able to see Arthur or Nicky properly yet, but my dad is actually speaking to me.

We walk out onto the stone flags of the back path where, in pre-Muriel days, we kids once had a brilliant water fight. I got Arthur with a water-bomb and he sprayed me with a hose attached to the kitchen tap and I ask, 'Where's Arthur, is he playing hockey?'

'Don't mention that name in this house again,' Dad booms down at me as we stand under the window of what used to be my bedroom, 'he's no son of mine.'

I'm shocked to hear him condemning the son he was once so proud of and fall immediately silent – you don't question Dad. How could that have happened, Arthur no longer the shining boy? It must have been something massive. I'll somehow have to find out Aunt Dorothy's address and write to her. I know she had the transport café in Kirkburton but I never knew the address there. Arthur was always her favourite so she'll know what's happened.

I get into Dad's car for the first time since the day he got married and they dropped me off at Maggie's after the wedding. I'm sure he won't be taking me into town for the bus to Barnsley later, clearly this journey is far more important to them. The trip to John's only takes five minutes, not like the hour it used to take me on two buses. They both come in the car of course. The inner circles of hell would give out ice cream before I would be allowed in the car, or indeed anywhere else, alone with my dad.

We arrive outside John's parents' tiny cottage. I'm flushed with embarrassment as I knock on the front door. His kindly dad, with his huge head, silver brylcreemed hair, pale puckered skin and the same big nose as John, comes to the door, bending under the lintel. In the year before I left home, this man cared more about my safety than the man whose house I lived in. John isn't in (phew!) but his mum and dad say it's lovely to see me, they miss me and they'll tell him I came round and please to come back again soon.

We drive back to the house and I navigate my way through the minefield of small talk until teatime. I'm safe so long as I just sound interested in what she's telling me about their life, Edward, and her being a lay preacher at church. I talk about my job at The New Inn and Dad says that the former owner (pervy Colonel Blimp) used to work for David Browns. 'He were t'catering manager there but he were dismissed because he were up ta no good wi' some of t'woman staff.'

So Dad had known about this man's reputation when his 15-year-old daughter went to work for him. This is the first time he has mentioned it.

I now seem to be allowed to exist in their world, at least for the length of my visit – perhaps because I am no longer a threat; I'll be leaving soon.

When we've finished, I say I will have to be getting back and, somehow, I manage to give Dad a hug which feels funny as the last time we got anywhere near each other was when he intertwined my fingers at his wedding three years before.

ARTHUR

It's difficult to say how it came about that I no longer spoke to Arthur and Nicky or Dad. It was just like everything else that changed – it was in the air and became part of us, like a virus becoming part of a living cell. In the beginning, when Muriel first came to the house and told us we had to call her 'mum', we talked to each other about it after she had left. But that was the point, she had left. Once she was living with us, there was no escape from her all seeing, all knowing 'Big Brother' control of our lives.

Arthur's separation from us was perhaps more noticed by us than by him. He was 16 when they married and, though we still had fun together at home, he had already begun to build a separate life by this time and seemed to have an easy relationship with them. He was earning, He told me many years later that:

'In the end I was working two evenings a week, Saturday mornings and all-day Sunday. As well as the paper-rounds I worked in the newsagents in Lockwood, run by a lovely Polish chap.'

He played hockey on Saturday afternoons; we saw little of him. Over the summer he had a job at C&J Hirsts a textile mill in Longwood. Though he received pocket money back, his earnings from all these jobs had to be turned over to Muriel for "safekeeping – until you're old enough."

'It was when they wanted me to work Saturday afternoons, too, that I got upset. There had already been a falling out with Muriel and Dad when Muriel had stated that I wasn't Dad's. Aunt D was having none of it. Apparently, Betty had spent several weeks living with Aunt D before the wedding and knew exactly what was going on.'

Before Dad had brought Muriel into our house, the three of us would go roaming together in the woods or up Castle Hill – an Iron Age hill fort that dominates the town, later topped by a Victorian memorial tower. At home we would mess about playing games which involved rampaging through the house or using the Formica table for table tennis, golf in the back garden or touch-and-pass or French cricket on the rec. Arthur and Nicky played around in the house with their tiny plastic armies and I made our food and looked after us. When Muriel came, all that changed. It was her house now, not ours. Arthur said:

'My recollection is that Muriel was OK (at least with me) during the first year, but everything changed with Edward coming along. On raising a topic with Dad when I got back from school one day, for example, the sort of thing I'd always been able to do before, and my subsequent logical question, Muriel intervened with "Don't answer your Dad back", and that as they say, was that.'

It is difficult to know why Muriel felt she needed to separate us from each other, but each of us as an individual child was certainly easier to control than if we were a unit.

The trouble we had caused Dad before the advent of Muriel had usually arisen from our combined activities: Arthur pushing Nicky down the stairs so Nicky's bum went through the pane of glass back at the lovely new house; the smashed leaded window at this one when I threw a big wooden mill bobbin at Nicky who ducked; Dad having to take Nicky to hospital because of the encounter with the rusty railing that they were throwing spear-like down Castle Hill; Dad coming home to a half front tooth missing after a play-fight; the shoplifting incident, me running away. Muriel's iron grip put an end to all that by putting an end to who we were. Children that have no will do not cause damage, or play or run away, they just shrivel up inside.

Perhaps it was too late for her to remove Arthur's will. His self-assurance was derived from his academic and sporting achievements and the full support of Auntie Dorothy. Dad was not very good at expressing his support. He would never have gone to any of our schools. It was Auntie Dorothy who attended parents' evenings and gave him money for good school reports.

Muriel's tactics didn't even need to be divide and rule. There was no need to tell us to stop speaking or associating with each other. She just crushed my will so completely that I was so cowed that I knew it was not my place to speak. The rule extended to not speaking to her (unless in response to a question or to ask to leave the table) or Dad or any of my siblings. I was as lonely and isolated inside the house as I was when I was outside on the streets every evening.

Muriel's complete control over us allowed her to have an easier life and to live a fantasy in which it was just the three of them – her, Dad and Edward – without any interference and minimal financial burden from the three unwanted step-children. It seemed that, by being older and more independent, and something of a golden child, Arthur avoided a lot of the treatment that I received from Muriel. That was until something happened that created a life-long rift between father and first born, and resulted in Arthur leaving home for good. It was 50 years before I found out the detail of what happened when they tried to interfere in my over-achieving brother's education and sporting life.

* * *

While I'm laying the foundations for a great future in the catering industry, things are not all Cling peaches and Carnation milk at home. Muriel seems to be torn between making arrangements for clearing the nest and feathering it. Perhaps because they were denied my earning power, or just because they would have done it anyway, they crank up the pressure on Arthur. It seems that they actually believe we should pay wages to them as a fair exchange for her dedicated care over the previous two years.

Dad was always very much against me getting educated

because of my sex. His father had been the same, refusing to allow Auntie Dorothy to be educated (he, like Dad in relation to me, could see no prospect of return on investment) and this was probably at the root of why Dorothy was so supportive of Arthur. Dad felt very differently about his first born. He was inordinately proud when Arthur got into the grammar school, although he had only scraped a place. However, his grades were soon the best in the year. He achieved eight O levels, six of which were the top grade. Though he failed French first time round.

Despite the fact that we only had the immersion heater on for one hour a week, had no new clothes or proper shoes, nor any proper holidays and Dad never went out, Dad told me that he would pay for a tutor if mathematician Arthur needed one to pass his French O level for university entry. This is a massive commitment from our dad and showed just how much he values Arthur's educational achievements. He would be the first of either of Mam's or Dad's family to go to university. But, Arthur being Arthur, he passed French in the Autumn resit.

'Once tha's a big shot tha can tek me ta pub and buy thi old dad a pint,' he had said to Arthur, when we were still a family.

Despite all the jobs he is doing, Arthur has exceptional success at A level, five A grade A levels and three top grades in special papers. His teachers expect him to go to Cambridge. He expects to go to Cambridge. His dad had once wanted him to go to Cambridge. In order for him to take up his place, however, a parent would need to sign his grant forms. But because of the fall out over Arthur not working on Saturday afternoons, our blinkered, obstinate father is refusing to sign the grant forms so that the application can go ahead.

The Local Education Authority (LEA) are so concerned that a deputation is sent, and this time, on the only ever occasion any of us can remember it being used, the Education Officers are allowed to use the front door. Once again, the hunting scene lamp, Dad's bureau and the sagging three-piece suite of the front room witness the authorities struggling to understand the mindset of this couple.

'We think it would be a shame for your son not to go to Cambridge, Mr Cooke,' says the LEA officer. 'His achievements are so exceptional, that even if he were to leave now there would be a place for him to read mathematics at Manchester University. If he stays on for another year to do the Oxbridge Entrance Exams, it's almost certain that he'll go to Trinity College, Cambridge.'

'Well, that's not summat we can afford, we 'ave another two kids to think about,' says the man who used to be our dad.

'It's very likely, Mr Cooke, given his academic achievements,' the LEA officer continues, 'that Arthur would receive a scholarship from the university and if not, then would get a local authority grant and I believe he also has the support of his aunt.'

'That would still mean we would have to keep him for the next year when he could be bringing in a wage,' Dad says, without Muriel's mouth even moving.

'I believe that Arthur is already earning,' the LEA officer proffers, 'both before and after school as well as at the weekends, which is more than most boys, but he still has the best marks in the school, so I think that he could continue to do this without detriment to his studies. It's unthinkable that he could leave school now. I would urge you to give the matter some serious consideration. This is an exceptional lad you have, Mr and Mrs Cooke, and it would be such a shame if he were not able to fulfil his potential.'

'Aye, well, we'll think it over,' says Dad.

'This is my telephone number if you have any questions,' says the LEA officer, giving Dad his card. 'Please ring if you want to discuss the matter further.'

With that, the meeting is over and the visitor is shown out of the (sticking from under-use) front door.

Muriel does not attempt any physical assault on my six-foot, five-inch tall brother and he's too self-confident to be easily emotionally manipulated. The most effective way to control and diminish Arthur is to take away his education. She had left school to work in the mill, so why shouldn't Arthur. The pair's resolve is undeterred by the visitors' arguments.

The school summer holidays arrive and Nicky is sent to Grandma Swift. Arthur's teachers hope for a miracle. Nicky enjoys the respite, the pigeons, pigs, dogs and hens, Uncle Cyril's stories and plenty of tasty food. Arthur no longer goes to

Grandma's, he stays at home to work in the textile mill. He is not allowed to be in the house while the nuclear trio go to stay with Muriel's sister for their holidays, so Aunt Dorothy and Uncle Jimmy take him in. As Arthur's educational champion, Dorothy is in turmoil over her protégé being forced to leave school.

Dad, Muriel and Edward return home from their holidays rested, happy and carefree, already anticipating a better holiday next year with the extra wage packet coming in. Tea made and eaten, little Edward fast asleep in bed, they are just settling down to a cuppa and an evening in front of the telly when there's a knock at the door.

'Now who can that be?' says Muriel. 'It's all right love you put your feet up, I'll go.'

It's Uncle Jimmy on the doorstep with Arthur. They haven't seen Jimmy since the refusal of the loan but they are expecting this visit. Muriel wonders why Jimmy didn't just drop off Arthur to save them both the embarrassment of speaking to each other. Why has he come to the door with him? Jimmy ignores Muriel's menacing signals to leave and pushes past her into the tiny kitchen and through to the living room with Arthur in tow. After exchanging a curt greeting with his brother-in-law, he announces, 'T'lad's coming to live with us, we've come to collect rest of his things. We'll keep him so you don't have to worry about finances and he can continue with school.'

Muriel is momentarily struck dumb with shock and amazement as Jimmy marches past them, an anxious Arthur in his wake. Then, gradually the pressure cooker bobs and hisses and the safety cover comes off the bacon slicer. Passive, quiet-life-man Dad looks at his wife. Jimmy and Arthur make their way through the front room and up the stairs to collect Arthur's books and meagre belongings.

If it had truly been a matter of financing him through the last year of school then university, surely Arthur leaving home would have been received like fish and chips as a mid-week treat, but no, the pair have been thwarted. Muriel's strategy was short-sighted, the second cash cow is about to be lost. Back in the living room with a few stuffed bags and the suitcase that Jimmy brought with him, the pair make for the back door.

Arthur hesitates. For him alone, of the three of us kids, his life, apart from the food, had remained much as it had been before the arrival of Muriel. He has no great desire to leave what for him is still a cosy home. Dad appears to be finding the parting as difficult as his son. For reasons of his own, he takes Arthur into the front room and shows him two florins (English pre-decimal two-shilling pieces) and says he is keeping them for him. Although Arthur didn't ever get the coins, this gesture seems to be our inarticulate Dad dredging up the love that the lost, pre-Muriel father, still feels for his son.

Arthur, now taller than his dad, his eyes glistening, meets his father's sorrowful gaze and knows that boats have been burned.

'Come on lad,' Jimmy says to Arthur, 'it's the only way tha can stop on at school.'

The two head for the kitchen and the freedom of the back door, but Muriel is not finished. The last words that Arthur hears as he leaves his dad and his home forever, are hers: 'You're not even Arthur's son anyway! Your mother was a loose woman and was pregnant before she got married.'

Two hearts were broken that day. Arthur was to remember leaving home as the most emotional experience of his young life. Dad was later to tell the adult Edward, that Dorothy had stolen Arthur from him.

Undaunted by the pair's stubbornness with regard to the grant forms, Auntie Dorothy hires a lawyer and applies for legal guardianship of her nephew. As part of the case, Dad and Muriel have to admit that they do not know the whereabouts of their 16-year-old daughter. By this time, I was living in Morecambe and had found no reason to tell Dad and Muriel where I was. Arthur's only involvement is a simple yes in front of a magistrate that he agrees to the adoption. This is then granted to Dorothy and Jimmy and Arthur's academic future is assured.

* * *

Of the three of us, only Arthur, who had always had the protection of his life outside home, was able to see Dad for what he really was. He felt contempt for a man who had sold out his kids. Sadness tinged his contempt because he remembered, just like we do, that Dad 'used to be a really nice guy'.

The Drudge

Dear God, help me now. I said I wouldn't work at Christmas in the hotel because it would be an affront to you. I lost my job so you must have a plan for me. You gave me the power to say what I wanted. I know I can't continue festering at Grandma's. I'd like to go back to the place where we had the farm, on the North Yorkshire coast – I was once happy there. I want to look after children. Please help me.

The Youth Employment Service finds me a family in Bridlington who require a mother's help. I have to go for an interview but they say that I should take a suitcase, because the family have had girls go for interview before but when they had been offered the job and supposedly gone home for their things, the interviewees never returned. If I'd been a bit more mature, I would have realised that there must be a reason for this. Instead, I just hope for the best, like I did when I knew I had to work for a pervert.

At my interview I immediately understand why the other girls never came back. The parents are quite old, they are retired. She is in her forties and he is in his sixties and they have a seven-year-old girl. They say that while they are deciding whether they want me I have to do their washing up. Every surface of their huge kitchen is covered with pots and pans swimming in grease and covered in burnt on grime. It looks like they've been keeping it for days. If I didn't have my suitcase with me, I would have said I needed to go home for my things and I wouldn't have returned either.

Then the mother shows me my room. It is more beautiful than anything I have ever seen. There is a glass-topped dressing table with a long gathered curtain across the front which matches the curtains and bedspread and there is a rag doll on the bed. My feet sink into the soft thick carpet. I can't imagine that I could find anything better, so I stay.

I soon discover that they think that a mother's help is another name for slave. Being in service must have been like this, but at least I would have had other servants to talk to. I work from seven in the morning until eleven every day, even longer than at my job at the inn, but here there are no other young people. In my three free hours each afternoon I wander aimlessly along the seafront.

I can only cope with cleaning their large rooms, clothes, pots, pans, ovens, windows, car, caravan, cutting their lawns and hedges, doing their washing, ironing, cooking and baking because I believe that Jesus will eventually save me and, in a way, that's what happens.

Although my wage is £2.50 a week (half of what I was paid at The New Inn) there are many weeks that I am paid nothing and still work 13 hours a day, seven days a week. Three weeks' pay is docked because I burn part of one of the old man's bri-nylon shirts while ironing it.

The wife takes me with her when she is collecting for the Lifeboats. I have to wave a collection box in the shape of a rescue boat under people's noses. I think this must be the first time the wife notices or cares about the condition of the near-rags that are all I have to wear. She finds a solution. She will sell me some of her old clothes.

'But I can't afford them,' I say, because I'm too callow to tell her I don't want them. I wouldn't be seen dead in her cast-off twinsets and old lady dresses and skirts.

'That's OK, you can pay me a bit each week.'

Just like the 'bring your suitcase' ploy, there is nothing I can say to this, and anyway, I have no money for real clothes.

Knowing that I now have no money at all coming in, she suggests I find a summer job for the three hours I have off each day in a cafe or ice cream parlour on the seafront. The old man finds out.

'No, she works for us, she can't have a job anywhere else,' he says, and that's that.

I feed them every meal. It begins with a cup of tea and toast in bed first thing in the morning and finishes with their supper of cornflakes and Carnation milk while they are watching the telly in the evening. When I make batches of their favourite Viennese whirls each week I force down as many as I can to make up for not getting paid and for everything else that's missing from my life. It's the only weapon I have and it feels like I'm being kind to myself. I yearn for the life that I'm not living, meeting other young people and maybe even going out. I put on three stone and get piles.

* * *

Growing up, I had mixed feelings about my big brother. I deeply resented the way that Auntie Dorothy favoured him and how both she and Dad supported and encouraged him with his education, while mine was seen as pointless. But at the same time, I really admired and looked up to him. Now we are both free agents, I will be able to make contact and meet up with him again.

I manage to find Aunt Dorothy's address and I begin to write to him there. It's summer, he's on vacation from Cambridge and he's staying in Goathland with the Youth Club. He arranges to come to see me in Bridlington. My diary from that day says:

Arthur, that is all I have been thinking about all day… I phoned Goathland after receiving a card from him. I said I would meet him at 12 noon. He called back saying he's coming here. I love him as much as myself, so much that I can't explain. He sounds so different that I am frightened to see him. He's 6'5" and I love every inch of him.

And the following day:

Arthur came, he's fascinating and marvellous and I love him so. He pretends to have no sentiment, so as to make me feel better. I took him to

Sowerby Park and took four photos of him and he has one of me. I showed him all the letters from home.

The 'no sentiment' that I wrote about was in relation to our father's rejection of him. Although Arthur had always had the support of Auntie Dorothy and Uncle Jimmy and the gleaming spires and glamour of Trinity College, Cambridge, on his horizon, he had still lost a father that had once loved him. Our father's transformation and rejection of him must have hurt him as deeply as it hurt me, but his solution was to take a pragmatic approach and move on.

When it was time for him to leave, it was heart-breaking to have to let him go again. I felt just like the little girl of six who would wait with her big brother for his bus back home after he had visited me at the foster family in Deighton 10 very long years earlier. We had each been through so much since then.

The two of us look out from the photos, him with his cheap clothes and me with my old lady twinset and skirt, overweight from all the buns. We're poor, but we're free and, at last, even if it's just for a day, we're together.

YOUNG AT LAST, 1968–1969

After I've been with them for about nine months, the family move to a much smaller house in Morecambe. I move with them, help them with the cleaning and unpacking and once they are settled in, I am told that they don't need me anymore. The husband gives me a week's notice. His wife, embarrassed, helps me secure another job.

After days of panic, in a strange town, scouring newspaper ads and making phone calls from telephone boxes, I manage to find a perfect job in a nursery in Heysham and a big, light, airy bed-sitting room in a leafy district just outside Morecambe town centre. It takes only one week for me to realise that independence is expensive. By the time I've paid my rent and bus fares to work I have only enough money left over each week for one packet of cereal and one bottle of milk.

I reveal my plight at work and my employer tells me her mother has a boarding house where she needs someone to clean the bathroom, stairs and landings and keep the Rayburn going. She lets me have a grotty little bedsit there for reduced rent. I also iron (more carefully) for two of the male boarders, babysit for an agency three nights a week and look after the two children of a hairdresser on Saturdays. I get lunch at the nursery with the children and eat meagrely at home. I survive on the edge. I'm 16. I have five jobs and I am utterly alone, except for Jesus.

I go to chapel every Sunday and I feel part of something. I crave a family and, despite the kindness of the people I meet, I still feel like an outsider. The minister and his wife take me under their wing, along with an elderly blind lady, Auntie Joan, and her dog. We are invited to tea with them every week, just as I was with Barbara. When the second Christmas of my freedom comes into view, the minister uses church funds to buy me a return bus ticket to Grandma Swift's.

Religion is all I have. For the past year I've been thinking of becoming a missionary. Over a cup of tea, Morecambe's Methodist Missionary Society representative tells me that I won't be allowed to go out and *save* the poor little heathens unless I have a profession. This meeting is the pivot that changes my life and my fortune because, before I can learn a profession, she says I will need an education.

There are three choices of profession for a girl of my class: teaching, nursing and secretarial work, and only one of these pays a wage while training. So I have no choice but to opt for nursing, even though I know I do not want to wipe other people's backsides.

On the two nights that I'm not working at one or other of my jobs, I take the bus into Lancaster to the College of Further

Education. The requirements for nursing are at least two O levels in English, maths or the sciences. I choose English literature and English language because I think they are a good place to begin and I still retain a terror of maths.

I felt cheated of an education at secondary school so I am excited to be starting on this new path. Since leaving the New Inn, my life had been utterly boring – first at Grandma's and then in Bridlington. Now, at 17, I am taking control of my life, taking it back from Muriel who had driven it off course. I am utterly determined to succeed. I don't care that I work so many hours, as long as I am doing something for me, something that will make a difference in my life. Going to college will be the thing that makes that difference.

* * *

Eventually I make friends with the girlfriends of the men I iron for at the boarding house, Marlene and Lynne, and my dreary life transforms into a whirlwind of delights. I have my first real friends since school. We go out together when I'm not working or at college and, because this is a seaside town and they have rich boyfriends, we have an amazing time: big band nights, PJ Proby, Tom Jones and The Beach Club. Sometimes it's just us girls but when we get to the The Beach Club we sit at round tables with their own little lamps and the girls' big builder boyfriends and watch the cabaret acts. I never question why I should be invited. I'm just accepted as part of the gang. We do our make-up and hair together and talk about things that the girls read in magazines. I feel alive for the first time in a long time and, perhaps for the first time ever, I feel young. Now I'm part of something; these two lasses from Lowestoft are my new family.

My friends are planning to work the season at the new Pontins Holiday Camp in Heysham that their boyfriends are building, a short bus ride from Morecambe town centre, and they suggest I join them. So, when it opens, the boyfriends get me a job in the nursery with Marlene, while Lynne is hired as a chef in the kitchens.

I have a place to live, a ready-made community and things to do. I love it. One of the other nursery girls lets me ride her horse on the beach; a bunch of us have an evening with cider and a ouija board. I get drunk – another first. I'd never had alcohol until I met Marlene and Lynne. Arthur comes on a visit with some of his old school mates. At last, I'm living a young person's life. I fit in. All my food and accommodation is provided and I'm still doing the babysitting and childminding so I have spare money. The girls help me to choose clothes. I'm reborn, I own my world and my life has direction.

An Education, 1970–1978

When I finish my O levels at college (and provided I pass), I will be old enough to begin my nurse's training at the next intake. The Missionary Society has given me a list of recommended training hospitals. I also look into the option of joining the army to train as a nurse. I want to see the world, but I decide to start with London and apply to Bethnal Green Hospital, one of the ones on the recommended list.

When I go to the interview, I only have one O level. I had to re-sit the language paper. I have always had difficulties with spelling. And so the course tutor says I would therefore have to sit an IQ test, which I do.

'Well I'm pleased to tell you that you got all the questions right,' the tutor tells me. He then goes on to say, 'You should really be applying to the London Hospital. They usually require three A levels for nurse training but with a score like this you would certainly be accepted.'

It's no good, it's too late for that. I know I cannot go back to doing five jobs just to keep a roof over my head while I go through the complicated application process and wait for the next intake at the London. So I stick with my current plan and, shortly after my eighteenth birthday, I begin my nurse training.

All our training is marked out in blocks of six weeks each. We spend the first six weeks in study block. The course content is challenging and I am apprehensive, but because I am learning from scratch in a supportive environment where the tutors and the consultants who teach us are capable, somehow something clicks into place and I know I can do it.

The teachers expect me to succeed and I do. I'm soon top in every topic and helping some of the other students to understand the nuances of human physiology. The low academic expectations that I had been drip fed all my life fall away. I had worked as a domestic drudge since my mother's death when I took over as mum of our little family, and now I am being paid to sit in a classroom and learn. I can't believe it. My self-esteem doubles, triples and quadruples in this environment and my capacity for learning becomes my new identity.

As I step into this new and very comfortable mantle, the religious one falls away like the protective shell of a chrysalis. Free of all those negative beliefs about myself, I can fly. I don't need to believe in God because I have begun to believe in myself. I lose all interest in becoming a missionary. Education becomes everything. I decide I want to fit more GCE classes in around my 40-hour day and night shifts and I do much better at my next two O levels.

Although I am very keen on the learning side of nursing, I am not enamoured of the practical side of what I recognise immediately is a gendered occupation. I don't understand why we are learning so much about medicine and surgery and anatomy and physiology in the classroom and then acting as manual labourers in service to a medical elite on the wards. Why are highly trained people giving bed baths, changing beds and doing bed pans? My feelings about nursing are very mixed. I love being in a community but I hate the wards.

We live in the nurses' home with a home sister to watch over us. I have a group of ready-made friends, lasses from southern Ireland. There are also nuns and some girls from Africa, but they keep in their own groups. So I decide that the only way I can get through the next three years is to focus on the positives.

I look at the programme of our training that has been marked out on a chart for us. Study blocks punctuate practical training on wards, then it will be six weeks each in casualty, theatre and our two options: specialisms that are not covered at this hospital. I will choose paediatrics and ophthalmics. I love theatre and casualty where I feel that my training and skills really matter. I love the study blocks and I am still keen to work with children.

When it comes to it, I excel at Moorfields Eye Hospital too, where the surgeon doing strabismus corrections lets me scrub in and help with the calibrations – the other nurses call me the squint queen. I fall in love with colleagues, all doctors, three times – but my adolescent experience does not stand me in good stead when it comes to building positive emotional relationships with men. I feel I want to be them, or at least be doing their job, as much as I want to be with them.

I've never accepted my lot in life – well, not the lot that said I am *only* working class, *only* a girl and that I will get married and be a housewife and mother. I raged at the injustice of my brother getting an education and me being denied one and I was resentful that I was treated differently at Grandma's. I spent so many years being bored and unchallenged that I was rampant with desire for achievement from the time I left the New Inn. Perhaps it was Muriel's suppression of my spirit that caused it to bounce back like a diving board does after the diver launches themselves into the air.

I take A level English in my second year of training and get an A grade. The first person I tell when I get my results is my big brother. Now there is no stopping me! I sign up for another A level and I apply to university. Marx, Engles, Durkheim, Greer, Gavron, de Beauvoir and John Stuart Mill have replaced Jesus in my life and I see my previous religious beliefs as little more than a class stockade and emotional prop.

I go for an interview at Sussex University to study psychology, but though I am by now an academic whizz, I have no finesse. I am still the working-class lass that I always was. The interviewer tells me that he thinks that my A grade was a fluke and my application is turned down. I feel it will be more sensible for me to choose, instead, to go to a university that does not require an interview.

I score the best ever marks in my hospital's nursing finals. I am awarded the hospital gold medal on the strength of this but it is taken away when, immediately after my State Finals (SRN), I give Matron my notice. We are expected to give six months back to our training hospital after qualifying as a staff nurse but I want to get out as soon as possible and my contract says that I only need to give one month's notice, so that is what I do. When my results for the State Finals come through I will be able to get a job anywhere but, in the meantime, after working my month's notice, I find a nine-to-five office job to tide me over until it is time for me to take up my place at university. The office job is another first. It's the first job I have had that was not manual labour. My result for my second A level, studied in the margins of my job and nurse training, come through and that is also an A grade.

As a child I had wanted to be a vet. Then, when I was 16, I wrote in my diary that I would like to be a missionary doctor in Vietnam. Now I realise I would have liked to pursue a career in medicine, but I still find it impossible to shift the terror of *boys'* subjects, like maths, physics and chemistry, that had been ingrained in me. This and poverty ensure I never make it to medical school.

* * *

I take up a place at Keele. It had just won *University Challenge* and it has a foundation year in which I can study all the subjects I missed out on at school. While doing my combined honours degree in psychology and sociology I work every vacation as a staff nurse in London and, because I need to prove everyone in my childhood wrong, my higher second-class degree is followed by a fully funded Doctor of Philosophy place at the London School of Economics.

My opinion of myself had begun to change following the nursing school interview. Since then, I had flourished and each academic success had fed the next. Something as simple as getting continuous As for essays in nursing school fed my growing sense of confidence in my academic ability, which spurred me on to get A grades at A level. It was more than that though. I also needed to prove I was worth something.

I applied for a DPhil because it was, to me, the pinnacle of academic achievement. I needed to prove myself, to myself and to all those who had written me off: the system that assigned me to secondary modern school, my dad who thought me not worth educating. Perhaps I had to show Muriel that I was better than her opinion of me, and in doing so I assumed I would cast off the shadow of her destruction, but I never could. The anxious adolescent inside me still lives in fear of her. I even fear women who remind me of her, women who try to put me down, women who are dishonest and sly – women I know not to trust.

My thesis title is 'The Correlates of Gender Role Innovation' – in other words, what factors prompt someone to choose to work in an occupation which is predominantly populated by the opposite gender. However, by the time I get to the LSE I'm used to such an intensity of working, learning and achieving as an undergraduate that I am bored and I know I cannot stretch out my research for three years.

I am also finding it hard to live on my research grant. I become deeply depressed. Perhaps it's because I am home and dry. I've got my degree and I have been accepted at one of the most prestigious universities in the country. Or perhaps it's because I have too much time for reflection. In any event, something has to change. I cannot go on. One day, while looking through the window of a dress shop that sells clothes that I cannot afford, I know I have to give up my research. I've been poor all my life and I've had enough of it.

I got into the LSE, having turned down several other offers, including Oxford, but now I know I have to get out in order to ensure my survival. More than anything, what drives me to make this massive change is boredom. If I had still been in a campus university and had the support of my peers and been engaged, challenged to work, I could probably have stayed on.

I am unable to face my lovely supervisor, so I write a note for her saying I have to leave and I push it under her door. Her response is a kindly and empathic reply, she insists she understands and that I can return at any time.

I come to understand that the next stage is to get a graduate trainee job with a big company. I arrange interviews with the 'Milk Round' (when companies visit universities looking for high quality graduates). Even though part of me knows my worth by now, the other part still listens to the voices that have always put me down – because I am me, because of my gender, because of my class. If only I had *known* that having all that life experience, including running acute surgical wards and responding to emergencies in casualty and theatre, had prepared me as well as any other graduate who had experienced only the production line of academia.

I attend several interviews, some of which are in glamorous hotels where we stay over for a series of selection tasks. I get several offers. Though still there is a nagging voice that says, *Are the offers because I am applying from the LSE, rather than because I am competent and capable?*

I am invited for a second interview at Ford. My anxiety and what is now called imposter syndrome kicks in, so I arrange a meeting with one of the university careers support staff and I ask her, 'Why do you think they have invited me for a second interview? It's nearly all men who work there. I'm worried that I won't be able to do the job.'

'Well they wouldn't be wasting all this time and money inviting you for a second interview if they thought that. You must have really impressed them.'

Her kind words convince me to at least go for the interview.

I do some research and, at this second meeting, I am able to tell them all about value for money when purchasing a Ford; cost of servicing and car parts and reliability and also about the experiments with doing away with the production line at Saab Scania, the Swedish motor company. I choose Ford Motor Company's fast track graduate trainee programme because, amongst the offers I have, it's the brand that I see as being the most prestigious.

The graduate intake is not until September, so I have the summer to earn money. Just for fun, I take a stop-gap job as a staff nurse in the medical centre at the Pontins holiday camp in Lytham St Annes, Lancashire. At the age of 27, astonishingly only 10 years on from when I was in a similar camp in Morecambe, I'm back, just a little further down the same coast. And I enjoy the work even more this time, because I have a chalet to myself and I'm in charge. I have a ball!

THE REUNION

I had taken on the role of mother to the family after Mam died and part of this was looking after the baby. I had asked if I could be the one to tell Nicky, aged just three, about Mam's death the year after we had been separated from her. I took Nicky to school and cooked for all of us. I did write to my siblings and forced myself across the burning coals of Muriel to see my Dad, Arthur and Nicky. But it was not until I was 20 and nursing that we were eventually able to meet up away from Muriel.

Nicky came to London with a mate and they visited me in Bethnal Green. We had a party at my small bedsit under a railway bridge on Hackney Road and Arthur joined us. It was the first time the three of us had been together since I, then Arthur, had left home. We got on well together, despite now being worlds apart.

We had fun. Nicky mixed up a powerful cocktail and served it from a teapot. We all found somewhere to sleep on the two double beds and, best of all, we reclaimed our sibling bond that day, the bond that had been broken seven years earlier when Dad had remarried and chosen his wife over the welfare of his children.

Art was not always easy to communicate with. Though once when I asked him, 'Why didn't she mistreat you?' he emphatically responded, 'Because she was out to get you, love.'

Dad relied heavily on both Arthur and me before he remarried. Arthur was in charge when Dad was not there, he shepherded us safely on the three buses we took to Grandma's every school holiday and he paid the mortgage for Dad each Saturday. On the other hand, he was often in trouble and Dad would 'give him a good hiding'. When he was only eight, Dad kicked him up every step in the little slum in Leeds Road for some misdemeanour or other.

Despite being older when Mam died and when Dad re-married and not suffering to the degree that I did at the tongue of Muriel, Arthur's life could not have been easy. For example, Dad would insist on cutting Arthur's hair himself in a military style that bordered on the Peaky Blinders. Very short back and sides with a mop on top. I really felt for him having to go off to school looking like a new army recruit. Dad was not really aware of what clothes we needed or how fast we were growing. Consequently, my enduring vision of young Arthur, is him walking along Tunnacliffe Road to catch his bus to school with what must have been a unique hair cut amongst his peers at New College and trousers two inches above his socks.

And yet, when the time came for his entry into the previously alien world of the middle, and later, upper classes, Arthur was self-assured. He flourished academically and in sports and had a host of friends both at secondary school and when he went up to Cambridge.

Although I was sometimes deeply jealous of my big brother when we lived at home, I also admired him, revelled in his successes and yearned to walk in his academic footsteps. His visits to me where I was fostered on that grim council estate had been the lifeline that kept me attached to our little family.

If I were to sum up my relationship with my big brother after we had left home I could do it in six words: *he was always there for me.* He visited me in Bridlington and again when I moved to Morecambe, always maintaining that lifeline that meant we were family. Once he was up at Cambridge, he invited me to the May Ball. Although I felt awkward and out of place with no idea about needing to wear a long dress and not having any money to buy one, my big brother's confidence shielded me. Arthur was completely at home, his name printed on the brass plate of the entrance to his hall in Trinity College. This was his metier. His seven years at grammar school and the continuous praise of our aunt had prepared him very well.

One year, when I was working as a staff nurse in London during my uni vacation, he had just come down from Cambridge and was living in the smallest bedroom of a shared house in Golders Green. He suggested I come and stay with him. I was working days at Hampstead General and he had a temporary job as a night security guard in the West End. We did what is now known as 'hot bedding', taking turns sleeping in his bed. When he had a night off, we would make up a bed for me on the floor.

He soon got a job in the software industry and while I was living in London and he was a bachelor working in Amsterdam, I was a frequent visitor to his beautiful house on the canal there. When he was in London we would go out together. I chose alternative theatres – the Peckham Palace or the Hackney Empire – or I would meet him at the Island Queen in Islington where he was table football champion. (I drew the line at Luis Bunuel at the National Film Theatre on the South Bank, though.) On these nights out, after a few pints, he would invariably carry me on his shoulders and I would feel on top of the world.

In my first *proper* job, at Ford, when I was earning enough for a mortgage, it was Art who offered to lend me the deposit, no questions asked. It was me who insisted on paying interest.

* * *

So much happened to Arthur and Nicky and I separately – things that the others did not know about at the time and couldn't have dreamt of discussing while we lived under Muriel's rule. It took many years for all of the stories to come out and, over time, as we compared our experiences, there were a great many revelations. For example, it is a full 50 years after we have left home that I discover that Art had never known about the police visit and that Muriel had punched me in the face.

I am with Art and his lovely wife Kate in a restaurant in Soho. As they make their way through what they describe as an excellent bottle of wine, the conversation turns to our time with Muriel. I'm embarrassed as I tell my brother and sister-in-law why the police had been called in and what was planned. I feel my voice catching in my throat. I notice that my big brother is taking off his specs to wipe his eyes. Seeing that he cares makes my own eyes fill and, looking across to Kate, I notice that she too is moved by this new revelation.

But there is to be a further disclosure that I find soothing, because of my brother's then response to it. I am amazed to find that the 17-year-old Arthur had been a witness to Muriel screaming at me the day I tried to give Edward the birthday card.

'I was just coming downstairs. I couldn't believe that someone could behave like that over a kid just trying to give her brother a card. I was really shocked.'

These words offer some kind of vindication. Part of me has believed, as she had always insisted, that it was me who was bad, that everything was my fault. His shock at the time underlines the effectiveness of Muriel's compartmentalisation of her cruelty. Apart from this one occasion, my big brother had been totally unaware of what my life was like back then. The birthday card scene had been a pocket of very private and personal pain for 50 years. As with most child abuse, only the perpetrators and victim are aware of what is happening. Control is communicated in nuances, fear is atmospheric.

In our family, the only witness to our stepmother's cruelty was usually, but not on this occasion, the man who used to be our dad.

PART FOUR

Golden Handcuffs, 1978–1982

Although the first three years of my life after leaving home had been precarious, I had survived and grown. Nursing had been a useful step. The knowledge and experience I gained was invaluable and my qualification kept me solvent through my university years. Getting accepted at Ford felt like a massive achievement. This working-class lass had broken down yet another glass door. This was a man's job in the man's world of the motor industry.

I start at Ford in 1978, one of three women out of an intake of around 100 graduates. I am thrilled to learn that, during my induction week, I am to stay in a hotel. And not just any ordinary hotel but a wonderful medieval one. I am paid so much that eventually I find myself at a loss as to what to do with it all. Parsimony, stinginess, call it what you will, but it had been essential to our survival as a working-class family and the habit is hard to shift.

All through my life I'd had to learn my place, put up with my lot as a working-class girl. Nursing was very much a job for women, in service to the male doctors. University felt like a place of greater equality, but even there an English tutor felt it appropriate to comment that he hadn't expected someone like me to read the literary section of *The Times*. Here at Ford, in this dynamic company, where we call our bosses by their first names, I expect equality and, mostly, that's what I find. I am, however, occasionally jarred out of complacency when I discover a few areas where the light of gender equality was yet to be shone and I feel duty bound to challenge the outmoded ideas that still fester there.

My first encounter with these outdated ideas is during a presentation in which scantily clad women advertise the Ford Parts division. Although I must have sounded quite timorous and shaky when I stood up to speak, I am compelled to point out that we could not hope for women executives like myself to be taken seriously if we are still using such outmoded advertising.

Fortunately, I have no further encounter with this division of the company but then, when I had been with the company for about six months, I am selected to go on a course to learn about the leasing of Ford vehicles – in other words, paying for them on a hire purchase scheme. It is held in a modern hotel on the river in York. Apart from one other woman, the audience and tutor are all men. Many of the students are from the dealerships who sell our vehicles. As the teaching day was over, the man who is leading the course *accidentally* shows out-takes from an advert. In the version that made it to television, a model steps out of the sea, rather like Ursula Andress in the Bond movie *Dr No*. However, in the snippets he shows, one after the other, the model's bikini top is dislodged by waves as she emerges. I feel hot inside and stunned by this blatant expression of arrogance and objectification of women. I stand up before I know what I am going to say and blurt, 'If you want to continue showing these films, then I will leave the room.'

'Oh, sorry, that must have been on the tape before I taped over it with the presentation. It wasn't supposed to be there.'

These meagre attempts to raise the awareness of the male establishment at Ford are hard work. It would be easier not to speak out, but if I did that then the burning I feel inside on these occasions would not have gone away. I would be left with a sense of having been demeaned and done nothing about the injustice. I had never been able to speak out about the damage that Muriel had wreaked upon my life, but the burning anxiety I was feeling now was the same feeling that I had back then. Now I can speak out, and it is perhaps because of my earlier experiences that I feel compelled to do so.

I don't know if my objections to the half-naked models had any effect beyond the rooms where I expressed them, but there was one area in which I know my arguments did have a lasting impact. Every year Ford was represented, along with all the other vehicle producers, at the International Motor Show at the NEC in Birmingham. As the event drew nearer, my male colleagues became excited about the prospect of attending and it's clear that everyone else in the office is going, apart from me. When I ask them, my workmates seem taken aback. I may as well have been a man asking to be a beauty contestant. It is taken for granted that the show is a male domain.

I screw up my courage and approach my manager in his glass office. He switches off the cricket on his portable radio. I swallow and state my case.

'I think it's unfair that women are not allowed to go to the motor show. I don't understand why.'

'It's for your own protection, it's not a suitable place for women. I like women, my secretary is a woman and so are the two data inputters.'

'Don't you think it is important that Ford should show in practice that it is a dynamic go-ahead company that employs women executives, a trendsetter in the industry? We claim that our cars are first class, shouldn't our public relations be giving the same impression about our work practices? The sixth floor [senior executives] have recruited women in the company at this level. I am here because of their policy. So surely, they would want us to be visible beyond these walls, to the industry as a whole – and what better place than the Motor Show?'

I have no idea whether my arguments had been successful until a week later when I and two other female colleagues in different sectors of the company get our invitations. This year, for the first time ever, female executives from Ford go to the NEC to mingle with customers, observe the scantily dressed models draped over sports cars and listen to the obscene ranting of the comedian at the evening reception.

After a year in logistics, I apply for a job as an account manager in fleet sales and move sideways to what many of my friends see as a peach of a job. Here I encounter not a jot of sexism. My patch is London and the south east. My expense account opens the doors to all the best restaurants in the West End, to floating boats moored in the Thames, a barge in Camden lock and at the invitation of one of our customers, a gentleman's club in Mayfair. I mingle with the buyers and directors from some of London's biggest companies. But rather than revelling in all the finery, I am ill at ease and think... is this it, is this all there is?

In the summer, I take groups of fleet buyers on the company yacht down the Thames from the Embankment, ostensibly to tour the plant in Dagenham but often the Thames Barrier is down for testing so we go in the opposite direction, to Kew. I usher my brood of buyers into the magnificent gardens and on the return journey we drink champagne, eat chicken salad and take turns at the wheel wearing the captain's hat. The nagging voice floats through the alcohol – *is this all there is?*

I make a presentation to sales staff and fleet buyers at a conference in a glitzy West End venue. It's high end stuff and I finally feel I'm being stretched. After hearing me speak and chatting with me over lunch, one of our biggest northern Dealer Principals (the director of a company authorised to sell our vehicles) rings my boss to let him know that he regards me in high esteem. His exact words are, 'That lass of yours (yet again I was the only woman in our division), is like shit off a shovel.'

I can choose the guests for my table at our Christmas party at a swanky Mayfair five-star hotel. The ice sculptures, the welcome cocktails, the room set out with 20 perfectly dressed circular tables looks like a reception for the Oscars or a party set from a costume drama.

I'm here, I've made it! I'm no longer the desolate 15-year-old who mumbled Pet Clark's song that miserable night walking between the gas lamps beside the Colne River in Huddersfield, when I was in danger of disappearing altogether, melting into the rain-soaked flagstones. Now, in my late twenties, I am downtown, these are the bright lights!

I'm out of the shadows but I still carry my loneliness.

Nobody Home

With just the three of them at home now, Muriel, Dad and Edward moved to a smaller house. They vacated the place where Auntie Pat had taught us card games and how to cha cha; where, as a single parent, Dad had given us such brilliant Christmases and where we had once all sat round our yellow table having lovely teas and Sunday dinners together. They move to nearby Taylor Hill, still in Huddersfield.

In 1981, I'm staying at Nicky's for a few days when Dad and Muriel pay a surprise visit, turning up one day without having arranged a time. I'm not sure if I was in or out of favour at the time, but they would not have been expecting to see me.

The last time I had seen them was the previous Christmas. I had popped in for tea and it had gone well. I had learnt how to make small talk and put on a plastic front. I always recall a particular part of the conversation from that evening.

'Well next time you come up,' said Muriel, 'you will have to stay with us.'

I almost choked on my Christmas cake. Rather than respond to these astounding words, I said, 'This cheese is nice, is it Caerphilly?'

Today, on the occasion of this visit, having had no contact with them apart from the odd letter over the past couple of years, I am, as always, civil to them.

I am sitting on the living room floor, Muriel and Dad are on the sofa facing me. This woman in front of me holds no particular fear for me as an adult and I am on safe, friendly territory at Nicky's house. The effect of the aging process on Muriel and my independence have diffused her capacity to reduce the adult me to a quivering victim, at least on the outside. And yet there are associations with the Vitapointe hair, and every other unique facet of Muriel's appearance, which ignite a part of me that is still a pathetic cowering child that, despite the adult I have become, I am unable to exorcise. For that child she remains all mighty.

Dad, his Brylcreemed hair as black as ever, now has a prominent (and ironic) widow's peak. His legs are splayed to accommodate a huge belly – too much rich food and indolence having taken their toll on this once handsome man who, well into his remarriage, had been broad shouldered and well-built but never fat. The couple are talking about Muriel's thyroid medication. 'Every time I take a tablet, I ask the Lord for healing,' she says.

'Ah yes, our bodies can do amazing things and we can heal ourselves sometimes and not need tablets.' My adult self knows about the placebo effect.

'Ah, tha's talking about, mind over matter,' Dad says, 'but what *we* mean is the power of the Lord.'

Oh no, he's got it too, he's really got it. Religion had always been the muzak running in the background of our lives: Sunday school; 'your mam is in heaven'; Dad banging on about walking me down the aisle in white; all the weddings and funerals at Grandma Swift's being in chapels – and the unspoken assumption that we were chapel people, Methodists, members of the church of the working class. But in pre-Muriel days, I had never known Dad attend a church service himself, even at Christmas. The background tape has become a deafening brass band drowning out reason and any possible counter-argument. I feel disgust.

'I don't agree with you. I think our minds can be very powerful,' I say with all the confidence bestowed on me by my – in my view – superior education. Dad could strip down an engine, build almost anything and tell you everything about tractors but he had never taken to education. Somehow, here on Nicky's territory, where I feel at home, where I am not at her mercy, a part of me feels confident. It is really unfortunate that I use that confidence to argue with a dad that I have under previous circumstances not been allowed to exchange a word with. I have not allowed for the superiority that can be derived from religious dogma.

'Dunt tha believe in the power o' the Lord?' Dad brays at me.

I have no fear of my father. 'No, I don't believe in God any more,' I say to him.

With that, he leans forward, pushing his large belly even further between his splayed legs, and says, 'Tha mun believe lass, tha mun believe!'

Oh dear, I think, and for the first time I realise that the dad I love is no longer there. My adult self can now, at last, see no purpose in trying to continue a relationship with a man who is not there. This religious fervour is much more effective in allowing me to shrink away from him than his complicity in all the cruelty doled out in my most vulnerable years.

And yet. Even though my adult self is appalled and turns away, the little girl inside still reaches out, beseeching. That part of me still blindly clings to the memory of when Muriel was in hospital and we temporarily got our old Dad back. That part remains convinced that one day she will be gone for good and he will magically revert to his old self. While my adult self understands in this moment that my old loving wonderful dad is lost, too far gone down the rabbit hole of fundamentalism and Muriel, my child self cannot let go and yearns for him with all her heart.

On the surface at least, my adult self wins out. From that day, following that exchange of words, I see no point in communicating with someone who was now just an empty shell. I stopped writing to them and saw no reason to visit.

* * *

On a future visit to Nicky we discuss what has happened to Muriel's treasured son, Edward.

In 1985 he had acquired a shotgun, sawed the barrel off and, along with a mate, held up a nearby petrol station and made off in a stolen car. He was caught, convicted and was now in prison.

I ring the probation service. His probation officer is pleased to hear from me, no doubt hoping that I would become involved with Edward's rehabilitation, but all I want to know is the length of our half-brother's sentence. I remember writing the number eight in steam on the kitchen window of Nicky's house. He had been sentenced to eight years. I find great satisfaction at this turn of fate. Sadly, I don't see Edward as anything belonging to me – I had never been allowed to do that – but simply as part of her. I see the incarceration of her precious progeny as karma for all the harm she heaped on us.

A Wish List, 1982–1988

My mother's untimely death gnaws at me. I'm getting closer to the age she was when she died. I'm finding my job at Ford vacuous and undemanding. Is this what I really want to do with the rest of my life? Just as I realise that I can no longer tolerate the golden handcuffs shackling me to a soulless job, the recession hits and I know there will be a long wait for a move upwards.

It's a hard decision. I have already walked away from a promising academic future and now, having procrastinated for a year, I resolve to abandon what for some might seem to be a perfect career. In my own mind I've proved to myself that I am worth something after Dad and Muriel suffused me with worthlessness. I've shown them – even though they weren't looking and didn't care and probably wouldn't understand anyway. What would have mattered to Dad would have been a commitment to Jesus and him walking me down the aisle wearing a white dress. Good grief, my mother was pregnant by him when they married!

Despite everything, it matters to me that they understand that I'm worth something, but it's a battle I fear I am never going to win. I got into the LSE and now I have proven I can work in a prestigious, male-dominated industry and perhaps that's enough. Perhaps as importantly, I'm financially independent. I sold the flat and progressed to a four-bedroom house which I've filled with lodgers who will pay my mortgage when I leave.

So, despite the protestations of my manager, I walk away.

*   *   *

I make a wish list. First on my list of things to do is to find a therapist to get me through the creeping fear and guilt that I am feeling as I approach the age my mother was when she died. I come at the problem from every possible angle – psychological, spiritual, intellectual. I throw myself into various therapy workshops; learn and practise co-counselling; work with a therapist, but nothing helps. I never stop seeking comfort from food and I remain anxious.

I study the epidemiology of breast cancer and, as a result, become a vegetarian. I join a group which explores ancient matri-archal and matrilineal cultures and the sacred feminine. I take courses in creative writing, sculpture, ceramics, philosophy and Swedish, and decide to fulfil a dream that grew from studying the egalitarian culture of Sweden when I was at university. I become fluent in Swedish and blag my way into a job as an English teacher in Sweden. Once there, I find the 18 hours teaching English each week insufficiently challenging – even though I'm also taking lots of advanced Swedish lessons – and leave after a year.

Back in London, I continue to see a therapist. I indulge my wish list further with a visit to Battersea. I adopt a puppy whom I call Freja because I collected her on a Friday. I find new housemates through the feminist magazine *Spare Rib* and create my own fabulous family.

Janice is the most amazing and flamboyant person any of us has ever met. All the housemates want to be her. We love her and she loves pink. Not girly pink or baby pink but bold, in-your-face, bright, brilliant, gaudy, shocking pink. When she came to see the room, she pleaded with me to allow her to paint the huge bay window frame and sill, the picture rail, skirting and door, pink. She can take up the carpets and put in pink ones for all I care. I just want her as part of my new family.

Janice is a 'lipstick lesbian', slender and pretty, with long, dark, wavy hair with a pink streak and ribbons – a female Boy George. Her on-trend clothes are always black. She's a hairdresser and her sparkling glamour infects us all. She puts a blue streak in my hair. She is our hero, taking on the world with pink.

We become a flamboyant family. We have a fancy-dress party where everyone comes as their (female) hero. For Winter Solstice we deck out a Christmas tree with fairy lights and light a fire in the living room grate. Janice paints all our faces and then dons the Santa outfit I found at a jumble sale and we take it in turns to sit on her knee by the fire and tell her what presents we want. This bliss banishes my hurts like a mummy kissing a child's grazed knee. I'm held in a haze of love in my home and I want it to last forever.

Even when I get cross, Janice gets round me. The house-mates tell me a light bulb needs changing. 'You do it, I'm not your mother,' I say, in the remnants of my northern accent, and from then on Janice leaves notes around the house addressed to Our Mutha.

We cannot be Janice so we settle for basking in the corona of her brilliance, hoping that her sparks will make us as shiny and wonderful as she is. Occasionally we pile in the back of her shocking pink VW Beetle and set out for revenge against the patriarchy. We commit drive-by cat calls on unsuspecting men shouting 'Pubic face!' if they have beards and 'When's the baby due?' if they have beer guts. Then we quiver and duck down below the windows if we have to stop at nearby traffic lights.

On Saturday evenings we all go up to Racquets, a women's club in Islington where we dance and jostle the night away to the likes of Franky Goes to Hollywood and Chrissie Hynde and The Pretenders.

During this delightful time, I consolidate the remains of my wish list. There are three more things I have to do: the first is having a daughter and this outweighs everything else tenfold. The others are to return to Yorkshire and focus on self-healing through psychotherapy. Despite seeing a therapist every week for a year, and also trying out psychodrama, spirituality, re-birthing and a host of other therapies, I feel that all I've ever done is to wade around in the mire of my distress, never finding a route to dry land. Above anything, I needed to separate myself from my mother. Having someone to talk to about this had offered stability but not transcendence or closure.

A friend tells me about art therapy training. She cannot apply because although she has a portfolio of artwork, she does not have a year's clinical experience and a related degree. I realise that I have all those things. Doing art therapy training would give me a year of free therapy and hopefully bring me solace, alongside learning how to help others with their issues.

Sheffield University accepts me for post-grad training and, after a struggle, I get a full grant. I buy a tiny dilapidated cottage for £5,000 in Meltham, the picturesque village in the Huddersfield moors where Dad used to work at David Browns Tractors. Coming back to Huddersfield feels right, especially this part which is associated with happier times. The *new house* we had lived in is just a few miles away and this is where we used to come to Dad's works Christmas parties when we were little.

A year later I graduate, but my emotional baggage is still firmly intact. I build up my own private practice and teach at a local further education college. I find a partner through advertising in a newspaper and I have a daughter, the very best thing in my whole life, ever. I call her Phaedra, after the pre-patriarchal Cretan goddess of light, because she has such blonde hair.

Despite moving back to Huddersfield I have no contact with my father. Of course, there was no way that he would be in contact with me, that would have to be through her, and the last time I wrote to them it was to say I was moving back to Huddersfield and doing a post grad course in Sheffield. Muriel replied asking when I would be getting a proper job, so I didn't bother after that.

In the back of my mind I am still biding my time, waiting for her to go away so we can have our old dad back.

EMPATHY

Just before my daughter was born, I'd bought a bigger house to accommodate the three of us. It's in a leafy suburb of Huddersfield, not far from Netherton where we first lived in the new house and I went to Sunday School. I invite Nicky and family and Art along with his wife and two girls to my daughter's naming ceremony. I want to invite Barbara, my ex-Sunday school teacher, but I haven't seen her for many years. She had moved and I have to ask around Netherton in order to find her. It's a small friendly village and she has lived there all her life so it's not difficult.

Barbara now has a husband and two grown-up boys of her own. Over tea in her living room she tells me of a little girl who had problems at home. Barbara took her in and almost brought her up. I found myself wishing that she had done that with me. My adult self knew that the circumstances were not the same – when I was having problems she was much younger and single and had her mother to care for and a full time job – but that does not stop my child-self anguishing over what might have been. Barbara, along with Auntie Pat and

Auntie Grace, had been a kind stepping stone in a dangerous river. Barbara had been the kindest. It is important to have her here at this special time.

The relationship with my daughter's father, does not last. I need support and help doing the hardest job I have ever done and he is unable to offer either. I ask him to leave the house. I make sure that the two continue to see each other either by paying for his fares and booking his tickets so he can visit us, or by taking Phaedra to visit him and his parents.

*   *   *

When Phaedra is almost three. I'm sitting on a bench watching her play on the swings in the park just opposite our house in a quiet cul-de-sac in Beaumont Park, Huddersfield, when I get chatting with another mum. She invites us back to her nearby house. We drink tea as the children play happily in the garden. My new companion talks about being a teacher and where she used to work before leaving to have children.

'Oh, you were a teacher at Denby Dale,' I say. 'I think my Dad worked at that school. His name was Mr Cooke, he was the caretaker.'

'What? Oh no! Were they your parents?'

I could see she was struggling with difficult feelings.

'Well, Dad was, Muriel was our stepmother. We had a really hard time with her, that's why I'm not very clear about them working there. I haven't seen them for years.'

There is no immediate reply, so I take my eyes off the children racing around the garden to look at the woman opposite. I hardly know her, so I'm surprised to see that her eyes are full and tears are leaking down her face.

'Oh, I'm so, so sorry,' she says. 'I can't imagine how awful it must have been for you having that woman as a stepmother and having to live with those two.'

Her face tells me she can imagine only too well.

I explain a little of my story. 'It was awful,' I say, 'but I survived. There were three of us and we all managed to get out in our own way.'

I'm intrigued. Why is she so upset? I ask, 'What was your experience with them?'

'Well, they had their own bungalow on the premises, but they seemed to think the whole school was theirs and that the staff, the children and even the head were an inconvenience that they had to put up with. They wouldn't take any instructions from anyone, even if there had been a spill and something needed cleaning up urgently. It was their looks and body language and the atmosphere that was so unpleasant. Mrs Cooke would even tell the children off in a really nasty way if she didn't like the way they were behaving. In the end we all dreaded coming into school knowing they would be there. The head talked to the local authority and they had to take unprecedented legal action to remove them.'

NORMAN, 1991

I have decided I've had enough of Huddersfield and its provincial town attitudes. I've been back for five years now, and I feel isolated and lonely. Sometimes I sit in the car when Phaedra and I come back from being out and cannot face going into the house because that will be it for the day – I will not see anyone else. I know once I close that door, there will only be the four walls. I have one lovely local friend, Jane and two friends from London, Viv and Sioned who occasionally visit and I see the occasional psychotherapy client. I can be there for my clients but there is no one there for me. My main feeling is of desolation.

I question how we have created a culture in which every woman is in her house alone, cooking her own food, doing her own dishes and looking after her own children, in isolation. Surely our lives were never meant to be like this? We are human – we crave community and the support of our peers.

I yearn to replace the wonderful micro-community we had in my house in London. I've heard so much about Hebden Bridge, about how a whole estate from Islington has moved up there and how trendy it is. I resolve to take Phaedra and Freja there in search of the wonderful life I had in my final year in London. After lots of visits to view houses and to the lovely paddling pool and swing park they have there, I finally find somewhere. We move to Hebden Bridge and I let my house in Beaumont Park.

We've been in our 1930s three-bed semi overlooking the town for only a few months when, one Sunday afternoon, there's a knock at the door. Phaedra is playing upstairs with her stuffed animals and Freja is keeping an eye on them all. The steps up to our house and the steep hill we live on just out of town mean we never get unexpected visitors.

I reluctantly abandon my solitude and open the door. The stunning view of the magnificent Calder valley, with the town crouched in its lap, is partially obscured by a glamorous looking stranger. 'Hello,' she says, 'I'm sorry to drop in on you like this but my name is Anne and I have your brother in the car.'

Brother? What's wrong with him, why hasn't he come to the door?

'I'm his wife,' she adds.

I'm even more confused. Art lives in Heidelberg and is married to a Dutch woman.

'Well, it's your half-brother actually, Norman. Your mother had him before she met your dad,' the well-dressed woman continues. 'We left a message for you with your estate agent in Huddersfield and when we didn't hear from you, we thought we'd better come and find you ourselves.'

I am speechless. Phaedra comes down to investigate just as Norman himself arrives at the door. He is tall and wiry, dark hair, not fair like us, no dimple, that's a Cooke feature as well. Instead, he has the deep-set Swift eyes and rounded nose. With Anne by his side, he seems completely relaxed.

'Well, come in, come in,' I say, directing them towards the living room.

'I know it may seem strange finding you after all these years, but Norman is almost 50 and we recently got married and I'm interested in genetics, so I suggested we research Norman's family of origin. You don't seem too surprised by our turning up like this.'

Well I am – and I'm not. I offer them tea; they don't want it. I tell them about the rumour we heard on our visits to Grandma's. We all knew that Grandma's two youngest children that she had brought up were actually my aunt Alice's children. But there were rumours of another two who had been adopted. I knew for sure that one was another of Aunt Alice's children, also born before she married his father. I had been asked by my cousins, his siblings, to visit him where he now lived in Doncaster and he had made me very welcome. It appeared that the rumours had been correct and that the other adopted child had been my mother's.

'So, it wasn't just Norman that was adopted. I suppose that's what it was like then,' says Anne. 'Shall we continue talking over lunch? We wondered if we could invite you?'

I leave Phaedra to entertain them with her chatter and go upstairs to get changed. I'm in a whirlwind. Mam's son here to meet us. I feel sad for her that she's not here to see him, to know how he turned out, that he found us and he's OK.

I take them to our favourite local gastro pub with yet more stunning views over the wild Pennine moors. Even Heathcliff would have felt at home here. It's a lunch of discovery and sharing of timelines. I want to know anything Norman can tell me about my mum and what happened to her when he was born. Any little thing that will bring her closer to me across the yawning emptiness of all those years.

'We did all the research at St Catherine House [the public archive until 1997] and you were the only one we could find. We got your Huddersfield address from your Auntie Grace in Conisbrough.'

I feel so sorry for Mam; these days of course there would be no question that she could keep her baby. I torture myself with the thought that they were so close to each other at times. Norman was 16 when she died. As a lad he'd cycled to Conisbrough Castle, within a mile of Grandma Swift's. I tell him about our lovely Great Aunt Florrie who ran a little shop from her living room window, just opposite the castle. He remembers buying sweets from her. If only... if only so many things.

Norman tells me how he discovered he had been adopted. Lily and Joe had been advised that 14 would be the right age to tell him about his adoption but his birth certificate was requested at the age of 11, for transferring to grammar school.

For fear of anyone finding out, Joe and Lily sat me down and told me amid much emotional tears. They asked me if I remembered Auntie Betty, which of course I did, they told me that she was my birth mother. They also told me that Betty had lived with them for a number of weeks before my birth and a month or so before the due date both went to live in Sheffield, where I was born in the Jessop hospital.

Previous to all that, when I'd be between six and nine years old, I collected stamps, so I was always looking for documents which included a stamp as most did at the time. I got lots of Victorian stamps from my grandfather's papers after he'd died. At the time, I noticed a number of papers and letters, etc, that included the name Swift, but not my birth certificate. Anyhow, suddenly they were all moved, no doubt hidden, and I never saw anything again but retained the name of Swift in my memory.

I reacted positively to begin with and did well at school until adolescence when the wheels came off so to speak. I would have been 14 and did not see the point of school and was generally very mixed up. I left school at the Christmas after my fifteenth birthday and started at Wharncliffe Woodmoor Colliery, I was there for four years before I started to realise I was capable of better things. I think it was knowing a lad who was at university that started me studying at home for GCE "O" levels. I couldn't go to night school because of shift work. What finally clinched it was when a lad my age was killed by a runaway mining truck loaded with rocks. I took a warehouse job with a food distributor in Barnsley. When I became their buyer, I gave up my "A" level studies. Eight years later I became Trading Director and I've had a very successful career in grocery wholesaling. When

I retired, I was Chief Executive with another large company.

I got most of my information about Betty from Elsie, who was my adoptive mum's sister and Betty's best friend. All she would say about my biological father was that he was an officer and Scottish, though I have no confirmation of this. I had a feeling that Elsie knew more than she was letting on but, despite my asking many times, she would always fall back on the fact that it was so long ago. It was Lily who told me that she had asked Betty to stop coming when I was three because she was worried that I was becoming too attached to my 'Auntie Betty' and it would be confusing for me as I got older.

It breaks my heart to think of Mam having to say goodbye to her son for the last time. Something she would have had to do again, with us, 13 years later, on our last visit before she died. I look at my lovely daughter and know how impossible it would be to think of her in a Children's Home, or with another family, or just not with me. But my mother lived in different times and Grandma felt she needed to protect them all from scandal and shame.

Norman has heard all about Grandma Swift from his adoptive family. He calls her 'Catherine the Great' because of her ruthless power-wielding. After a lovely lunch together, the four of us and Freja make our way back to the house to drink tea and continue our conversation. I bring my new brother and sister-in-law up to date on his other siblings and relatives and then, after telling me about their visits to Mam's family in Conisbrough, and Dad's in North Yorkshire, Norman says something and it's as if I've been driving at full speed on the motorway and suddenly a wall appears in front of me.

'We went to Lebberston where you lived when you were young,' Norman relates. 'We asked at the village post office and they directed us to people who had known your dad. He's a real legend around those parts – they said he could stop a tractor with one hand!'

'Aw, that's lovely,' I say, feeling pride in my dad as a young man. 'It's a shame I haven't seen him for so long, it's just that he doesn't seem to be the same person any more. Muriel has such an influence over him that it's like he no longer has his own personality. He's gone really religious.'

Norman seems to be looking at me in a strange way. After a pause he says, 'I'm sorry, but I thought you would know, your dad died two years ago. He had lung cancer.'

The moment freezes. My mind shoots back to that visit to Nicky's house, when I realised that the man who had struggled to keep us all together when so many other single fathers might have given up on us had become an irretrievable religious dogmatist. I was sitting on the floor then, as I am now – on the thick, broad mat in front of the gas fire in my new house with my newly found half-brother. The world is standing still once more.

How could she not tell us he was sick, or that he was dying, or even that he had died? *How could he die?* Inside, all of me is screaming into a long lightless tunnel. She was supposed to be the one to go... anywhere, just go... so we could have our real dad, our old dad, back. I had always been so sure, certain, believed with all my heart, that would happen. That there would be a time.

I can't bear it, it can't be true, it's not possible – she was the one that was supposed to go, not him, not my daddy. We had to have a chance to make it all alright again, to get back the kind, fun dad who loved us.

I drag words out from some part of me that is still in the room: 'No, no, that can't be right, I would have known, somebody would have told us. People can't die without their children being told.'

'I'm afraid it is,' replies Norman, 'I have his death certificate here. We even went to see Muriel but she didn't let us in, she's remarried now and didn't want her husband to hear.'

Inside there is only turmoil and disbelief, but on the outside part of me is there, functioning. I don't know how. I mouth pleasantries to my new brother and his wife. They depart for their journey back to Warrington. I manage to keep a kind loving face for my sweet daughter. Talk, eat, keep busy, keep it together. What would I do now if I didn't have my little family?

I get Freja's dinner and ours while Phaedra chatters. After we've finished I take Phaedra up to bed and read her a story. I usually lie with her until she falls asleep, but tonight I leave her with Freja to cuddle while she's nodding off. 'Mummy will be back soon sweetheart, snuggle up.' I'm drowning in pitch made of hate and anger. How evil can one person be? Dead for two years and she's never told us. What about the funeral? She even kept him all for herself after he died. This is worse than anything else she's ever done and she's the one that goes to church. And she's married again!

The devastating news churns round and round in my mind. How can she still be alive when he's dead? It was all going to be all right again, just like it had been before she came, once she was gone forever. Run away, run over, whatever. Gone out of our lives.

She'd said long ago that we wouldn't get anything when Dad died. Why would she say that? I didn't want *stuff*, I wanted him. But now I think it would have been nice to have something of his. I think of the lamp with the hunting scene from the front room or that old picture of him that had once hung in my bedroom. Is that why she didn't contact us, because she thought we would want stuff, money? Or was it because she was ashamed – because of what we might say.

And what about Dad's only sister, Auntie Dorothy, why hadn't they even told her? I hadn't been in touch with them for some time. Dorothy had remarried and gone to live in Spain, but Arthur had said she'd been back for a few years. If Dorothy had known she would have found and told all of us. Muriel had kept us all out of Dad's final months weeks and days, kept him all to herself and Edward, even for his funeral.

And what about Dad? Didn't he have a yearning to see his eldest son? Even Uncle Jimmy, Dorothy's first husband, had hung on to say goodbye to Arthur when he was close to death and there was no blood between them. Had Muriel's poisonous words convinced Dad that he was another man's child?

They could have found me, surely. Maybe they'd heard I was a single mum and didn't want to be tainted by contact with me. Did she want to keep up the lie that it was just the three of them – her, him and Edward – right to the end? Has she no compassion, no morals? Did she believe her own lies about us not caring about him? All these thoughts come and go like food on a sushi belt, round and round appearing and being replaced by another over and over.

She'd saved the deepest cut till last.

I have to talk, to tell someone – that'll help, won't it? I ring Arthur and Nicky. I'm glad that both have partners so they'll be supported, not like me, alone.

Arthur always advised me not to bother with Dad after I left home, but he had Auntie Dorothy and Jimmy to love him, I had only the gap left by Dad. I can't believe they didn't even tell Dad's only sister. Had they alienated everybody so much that they didn't dare approach anyone, even when he was on his death bed? Did they think we would say good riddance and not bother coming to see him?

My big brother gives nothing away in his tone or words but I'm certain none of us will escape the impact of our father's death and exclusion from it. There will be no redemption for us now. Our remaining parent stolen away by death with no funeral or letting go or saying goodbye. We were cheated out of our mother by cancer, then cheated of our dad's death by his second wife.

An image takes over my mind. I'm hammering six-inch nails through her face. I've never imagined doing harm to her before because I was so terrified of her and rebellion was beyond my reach – but this is different, this is not just treachery, it's murder. Without me even knowing, she has stolen my father for a second time. I can see her I-have-the-Lord-on-my-side smug face. I don't think of ripping out the Vitapointe hair or smashing her on the nose like she did to me. What I think of, and cannot stop thinking of, are the nails driving through the flesh and the bones of her cheeks, as I pound them with a hammer again and again.

But I never get out the hammer and nails that are in this scene that runs constantly in my head. I don't smash her door down and knock her to the floor. The adolescent me that yearns to wreak revenge is too cowardly. I'm not brave enough to go round there on my own, there is no one to come with me – Arthur is in Germany and I've only just met Norman. When it comes to standing up to her, I am still the cowed child that was told to call her mum.

Then it gradually dawns on me… that it was all my fault.

Dad in later years had always had Ladas and before Muriel came his cars had sometimes been odd colours. We had one that he painted pink. I'd seen a yellow Lada near my house in Huddersfield a couple of years ago as I was driving in the opposite direction to an important meeting. I knew from Nicky that their last known address was in Denby Dale, half an hour away at the other side of Huddersfield, so there was no reason for our paths to cross, but my intuition had bristled on seeing the gaudy coloured car. Could that have been them? Were they coming to tell me about his illness, his looming death? Were they coming so he could see his little granddaughter before he died? To ask for help? To say goodbye?

Why didn't I turn my car around?

Why didn't they leave a note?

I imagine the scene: 'Shall we leave a note for t' lass, to say we've been an' leave our number?'

Muriel would surely not have been able to tolerate Dad leaving me a note in his elegant hand. Surely she would never have stood for him signing it 'Dad'.

Did she reply, 'It's God's will, Arthur, it's His will. If He'd wanted us to see her, she would have been here.'

And did Dad reply, 'Aye lass, I'm sure tha's reet?'

But I was there. I just didn't turn around!

What could we have said? Would it all have been too hard? Would the news of his terminal illness have been too much for me to bear? Would there have been recriminations, an attempt to shame me for having a child and separating from her father? Would I have dissolved into victim mode? Would he have banged on about their Lord?

But *my* dad would have met *his* granddaughter and bounced her on his knee and seen how beautiful she is and everything else would have fallen away. The tears and sobs fall from me as I play this missed meeting in my mind.

Dad never met any of his four granddaughters – was Muriel a fair swap for all of us: Arthur, me, Nicky, five grandchildren and a sister?

A LITTLE GIRL'S DADDY

I flail around for comfort. I find a bereavement counsellor. She only wants to talk about her own widowhood. I go to a service at the local Methodist church. People are just interested in judging my previous absence and establishing a commitment to future attendance. Remembering the kindness I received in Morecambe, I ask the Methodist minister for emotional support. He has none to offer. Instead I ask him if he has contacts with the Elim Church in Huddersfield. Yes, he has. Can he find out whether Dad and Muriel tried to find me? Yes, he can.

'But how will you feel if they *didn't* try to find you?'

Oh, if only… that would be such a big thing, such a weight lifted, to know that it wasn't my fault. But I can't tell him that. I want him to tell me the truth, not what he thinks I want to hear.

'Yes,' he tells me the following week, when I steel myself to ring him. 'They had tried to make contact.'

No, no, no. I have to live with knowing that it may well have been them that day – and a couple of days later in a different place. The second time, too, that sixth sense that we call intuition nudged me to take notice of a similar looking car just a few miles away amid stunning Yorkshire country-side. Had synchronicity placed us in the same location at the same time, twice? The local beauty spot of Holme wasn't somewhere I would normally go. Was Dad taking a last look around, bidding farewell to the hills and trees and was this a second missed opportunity to make contact with him? I was free that day, I could have followed the car until it stopped. But I was still not brave enough to be in her presence. Anyway, what was the urgency?

The Methodist minister also tells me that Dad died in Kirkwood hospice and, desperate for anything that might bring me closer to him, to give me some sort of closure, I go there.

First I visit Auntie Dorothy, who I haven't seen for several years. After a few years in Spain, Dorothy now lives back in Huddersfield with her second husband, Bill. I hope that my aunt and I can find mutual comfort in talking about the situation.

We talk, but I'm not sure either of us is comforted. I have my three-year-old daughter with me and a little friend of hers so I am trying to make sure I don't get too upset. For me, just talking about the situation is like slightly undoing the screw top on a bottle of fizzy water that has been shaken vigorously. My aunt has other things to worry about. Always slender, she is now almost emaciated, periodically inhaling from an oxygen cylinder. She is 76 and smoked almost as much as her brother, but she's still alive. Dad was only 64 – the origins of illness are not solely physical. I ask if she will come to the hospice with me.

'I'm too poorly to do anything that will be upsetting, Sue,' she responds, and I understand that she cannot enter into my desolation. We reminisce about what a good dad he had been before Muriel came along and we talk about how awful Muriel had been, but the screw top remains under immense pressure.

The nurses at the hospice are kind. I meet the one that was with him when he died.

As I hear her story of his death more tears pour out of me than I knew I could cry. I sob and groan from depths that I thought had been emptied already as I ask her why the hospice hadn't enquired whether he had any children. Someone has to be responsible. I feel lost, wild and confused as I tell her that dying people should have the names of their children tattooed on their foreheads.

The nurse listens patiently and says that his religious beliefs were a comfort to him at the end.

Did religion also blanket over the absence of his children, grandchildren and sister? But I don't think any of this, I think instead of how excruciating it must be to die because you can't catch your breath, like someone is trying to drag your breath away from you until the sea-saw tips and the thief wins. No breath left to groan or whisper the names you gave your children, knowing that God will be waiting with His scales. Was that how it was for him? Or did he just flow towards the light on a cloud of Brompton's Mixture, knowing he would meet his Lord and be enfolded into His loving arms?

WHAT DOESN'T KILL YOU... 1992–2007

'How long did you live with Muriel?' an otherwise ineffectual therapist once asked me. This was back when I lived in London, when I first started my long journey through therapy, trying to make sense of it all, trying to find some sort of escape or resolution. I had been to her trendy Scandi-minimalist – before Ikea was even heard of over here – lounge in Hampstead about 40 times. Once a week, 40 hours at 50 quid a shot, plus an hour's journey each way on the tube. I was two grand lighter but I still hadn't made much of a dent in the weighty baggage of my youth. I didn't know if she was keeping me sane or if I was just indulging myself, poking a sore tooth.

But then this question stopped me in my tracks.

Me: mug of herbal tea in hand.

Her: Rogerian empathic expression.

And the world stood still.

I was Saul on the road to Damascus. I struggled wordlessly with a monumental revelation. Surely it was all my life, all my childhood. Was it really only two years? That can't be right. How could she have done so much damage in only 24 months?

Somehow those two years of emotional agony had infected the years before and after like watercolour bleeding on wet paper. In my mind she had always been everywhere I ever was, and am. Now, with this short question, I found a parenthesis measured in years.

We lost the idyllic farm life by the seaside when I was four. A year later we lost our loving mother when she became too ill to live with us. When I was seven, my dear, sweet, soft grandma and her dog went too and I had to finally accept that my mother wasn't coming back. I survived all this because I had a rock to cling to, a constant and loving father. Then, six years later, he went too when he brought a woman into our home who turned my world to terror.

As if to balance things up, my adult life has been filled with gains – my wonderful daughter being the greatest of these. Education opened the door to affluence, and by 30 I never needed to work much ever again. I could care for my daughter, see therapy clients, sculpt and write, but it was never enough.

So many therapists and friends over the years have tried to point to my father's role in the misery inflicted on his children. I was never able to see it. I clung desperately to the version of the daddy who disappeared when Muriel arrived – the daddy that gave me an ice-cream float and fixed my skates and made Christmases magical, Bonfire Nights special and played Mischief Night tricks on us. That's the daddy whose brand is burned into my heart, the one that I knew would come back as soon as she went.

I don't see the dad who condoned and was complicit in the callous cruelty perpetrated by the woman who, contrary to her initial claim, was the blueprint of a wicked stepmother. I don't see an ignorant, stubborn, bigoted, selfish man who betrayed his children, I see only the daddy who lifted me in the air by my elbows and sang with us on day trips.

Is it just some of us that inhabit the space at the edge of a precipice of despair with a powerful vortex at its base? Are all of us or just some of us constantly scrabbling to keep out of the crevasse? Did I focus on achievement to avoid the edge? Sometimes – most times – I find the psychological or metaphysical muscles I need to help me to cling on or to scratch my way back up from the abyss. I find it easy to understand this in others because I know it is true for me. I try not to have expectations of myself. I try to flow. If I need to get lots done then I do it. If I need to relax, I read or watch a complex thriller. I keep very busy – I have to, or the vortex beckons. Keeping plates spinning is my therapy.

I have wonderful friends, but that's been hard, too. I have had to learn how to trust people and not to reject them because of some imagined slight on their part or dissatisfaction on mine because they have not lived up to the unreasonable standards I have set for them. Only people like Jane, who can offer me unconditional acceptance and love, who can see beneath the surface of my occasional grumpiness and neediness, have stood the test of time.

None of the therapists I tried after leaving Ford were of any help, and nor was the year of therapy whilst I was training to be a therapist myself. But I had to try. I couldn't give up on myself or she would have won. And I would have been utterly crushed by the final act of annihilation, not being told of my father's illness, impending death, his passing or his funeral.

After Norman told me the news, I lived moment to moment. I wasn't really there in my life. Living was too raw, but I went through the motions. I took Phaedra to a play session and broke down in the teepee. Liz, one of my two best friends in Hebden Bridge, was there with her daughter. She told me about a therapist in Blackburn. She is South African, she tells me, and that may be the reason for her completely different approach.

So, once a week, while Phaedra is at school, Freja and I make the trip over the county border and this wonderful woman guides me back from the edge of the precipice to safe ground. She painstakingly works to show me how my shroud of victimhood and hatred for Muriel are intertwined and helps me to release both. She suggests that I work with Shakti Gawain's book, *Creative Visualisation*, which exhorts its readers to become the conscious authors of our own destiny. It was something I had been doing subconsciously all my life but now I was being encouraged to act consciously.

The hardest part would be to let go of my hatred of Muriel. I don't think that's the same as forgiveness. It's more that what she did no longer matters to the same degree. It partly diffuses her power over me.

As I put the parts of this philosophy that I feel comfortable with into practice in my day-to-day life, I soon discover that if I think happy, I am happy. If I decide that there is something I really want in life, it comes. If I vacillate, nothing happens. I learn to radically alter my beliefs and my life.

Despite the reality that other people are able to see. I had been able to block out the man my father had become, because when Muriel was in the hospital our old dad had re-emerged, so my child's mind had reasoned that he must have still been there, somewhere, hiding away from her. Now all hope of that loving father is gone.

Somehow, with the help of this wonderful therapist and Gawain's book, I manage to glue a new reality over the top of the pain and the minced raw-meat of my being, so that I can edge up, out, and clear of the precipice. I am perhaps hoping that this sticking plaster will let the wound underneath it heal, but it feels like adapting to this new world will be a struggle.

* * *

I'm feeling unsettled in Hebden Bridge. One of my only two friends here is moving to Cockermouth in Cumbria. The other issue is my daughter's schooling. I am determined that she gets what I was denied, that there will be no limits to her hopes and dreams and every opportunity to fulfil them. After visiting the local junior schools that have places, I discover that Hebden

Bridge cannot offer this. We visit several schools in Huddersfield and find an excellent one in Berry Brow. It is only infants but she has a year left and that will give me time to find a good junior school. My house in Huddersfield has been rented out so it's easy to move back into.

While in Hebden Bridge I trained as an Ofsted inspector, but I plan to do only a few inspections and spend the rest of the time with my daughter, sculpting or writing. Instead I am inundated with requests and I find the work enjoyably challenging and rewarding. School standards are close to my heart.

Back in Huddersfield, Freja, our beloved dog and a central member of our little family, is dying. On her final day I wrap her in a blanket and carry her around our local park, where she had been our fielder when we played cricket and flown after us as we sledged, all collapsing in a heap together at the bottom of the slope. She has been my child, my mother and my best friend for 15 years and my heart is broken when she leaves us. We bury her in the garden. Norman comes over and digs her grave.

I set up my own inspection contracting business. It thrives, and in the midst of my inspection empire building, Phaedra turns 11. In order for her to attend a single-sex secondary school, we move to Leeds and, at the last Christmas before the new century, we eat our dinner off packing boxes. In the evening we're invited to a party at a Georgian style mansion, the home of one of Phaedra's new classmates. Everyone is too busy enjoying themselves to notice that I am a pretender, here only by virtue of a daughter for whom I will brook no class or gender disadvantage.

Until now, I had worn my class on my shoulder, as an identity chip, but I've jumped ship. Phaedra's friends' families are surgeons, academics, lawyers, editors and accountants, and in my new executive role, with an income to match, I'm passing as part of the Leeds establishment. I've navigated yet another major step away from the girl who had a weekly bath in Daz and wandered the streets in danger of disappearing. Now I have a role, status and 500 ex-head teachers and local authority education advisers working for me.

Six years after beginning work on inspections I decide I want out. The business is valued at £2.5 million, though I've vacillated too long to be able to sell it, as Ofsted is changing how inspections are to be conducted. For the second time, I release myself from a pair of golden handcuffs and step out into an unknown future. There is something I am still yearning for but I don't know where to find it. I do know it is not in running a business that takes up so much of my time. I have made enough money now for my daughter's future to be secure, so I can afford to follow my dreams, even if I don't know what they are yet.

I know that I am drawn to exploring more spiritual avenues, like those I had encountered in Shakti Gawain's book. Taking control of my life in this way is appealing and then, just as the book teaches, if you focus on something really closely and you know that you want it, the universe will conspire in your favour to provide it. And that's exactly what happened next.

My very best friend Viv, who I met through a women's group in London after I had left Ford, is visiting for the weekend, as she does regularly. We take our new puppy, Daisy, out for a walk and on our return I find a flyer on the doormat:

'Shakinashram, Weekend Retreats in Glastonbury, at the foot of Chalice Hill, meditation and contemplation. One massage and one session of reiki included, along with breakfast, lunch and dinner. We serve only raw food.'

I know I want to go. Viv immediately offers to take care of Phaedra so I book a place.

* * *

As we sit in the beautiful ashram gardens in Glastonbury eating a surprisingly good raw food vegan lunch, a parade of women dressed in reds and oranges with garlands of flowers in their hair pass by. It's the week of the annual Glastonbury Goddess Conference. I chase after them and find myself on the top of Chalice Hill watching a sacred ceremony accompanied by drums and didgeridoos. I'm so enraptured that I fail to notice the soft interior of a cow pat oozing over the top of one of my Birkenstocks.

The whole weekend falls beautifully into place, including the raw food. The flavours, textures and variety are enticing and everyone talks enthusiastically about the science and philosophy that surrounds it. The health boost that raw food offers really feeds into my early-death avoidance mentality that is so tied into my mother's death at 33. Since I left Ford and did all the research and changed my diet, I thought I was doing as much as I could to prevent myself from getting breast cancer. Now I discover that I can do so much more.

I learn that the wholefood vegetarian diet that I thought was healthy is nothing of the kind when compared to the super health-enhancing nutrition offered by a raw food diet. I have the typical symptoms of peri-menopausal women who eat a standard Western diet: fibroids, intermittent very heavy bleeding, night sweats and hot flushes. I've been overweight most of my life but especially since I stopped breastfeeding. I have used food to compensate for unhappiness and there are still serious issues that I have to root out if I am to stop hiding inside my fat.

Back in Leeds I discover an eating disorders group. The facilitator asks us to draw a scene from home where we are sitting around the dining table. I draw the yellow Formica table and old hardboard repaired chairs and, without warning, a demon that I didn't know was inside me takes over. It begins to scratch and scrape the coloured pencil round and round the drawing of the yellow table, making deep grooves, destroying the paper, destroying the table in the picture. All the while uncontrollable deep sobs wrench themselves up from inside me and tears pour onto the tortured paper. I leave the group still feeling shaken and I don't return. It's the wrong forum for that particular scab to be picked.

When I was a child at Grandma Swift's, there were constant

mentions of my 'puppy fat' from Grandma, who herself had the figure of Queen Victoria. My older cousin said I looked like a 'fairy elephant' when I put on a particular dress. I was probably not overweight, though I was certainly sturdier and twice the height of my more delicate female cousins of the same age. In this atmosphere of female body shaming, I overheard a conversation:

'Mrs Pike has lost a lot of weight, there's hardly anything left of her,' Grandma said to a visitor one day. 'She as thin as a rake.'

'Has she been ill?' the visitor asked.

'She's got cancer,' Grandma replied.

'Oh, I hope I get that,' I said to my cousin, convinced that it was more important to be slim than chubby looking, whatever the cost.

Now, as an adult, I am convinced that my association of losing weight with cancer and death is keeping me fat. One of the techniques I learnt from reading Shakti Gawain's book was to create a vision-board. I sit on my bed with a stack of magazines and a piece of cardboard. I take a page from a magazine that features a lithe, healthy-looking woman in a yoga pose and carefully replace her face with a photo of my own. I am now the very healthy-looking, slender yoga practitioner. I then focus on the picture with my face beaming from it and tell myself I am slim and *very healthy*. I follow this routine every evening.

Alongside this practice, I immerse myself in raw food culture and the gym, massage, acupuncture, country dancing and jogging. Within nine months I have lost three-and-a-half stone and achieved the body in the picture. I become an evangelist for raw food. I write books, run workshops, organise raw dinner parties and give the proceeds to animal rights charities, appear on TV and BBC Radio Leeds and a journalist gets me to feed him on an exclusively raw food diet for a week for the *Yorkshire Evening Post*.

Moving Down
South Again, 2008–2013

My daughter wants to be a vet. I am determined that she will be able to fulfil this ambition, all the more so because it was denied to me. She takes up a place at the Royal Veterinary College in London, so I decide to move to Brighton. I have discovered that it is the hub for raw food. I have been to a raw food festival or two and met some lovely people who live there.

In an effort to return to the happy days of my very early years with Mam and Dad, I am determined to buy a farm. I don't want animals, just land and woodland, a farmhouse and a barn. It's not just a carefree happy time I am seeking to recapture, I also want the kind of place that would have been perfect to invite Dad to visit. If things had been different, I could have offered him the opportunity to return to the countryside in his retirement, but because I cannot do that for him, I want to do it for myself. If he were still alive, if he could have been the dad he had once been, I would want him to say, 'Aye lass tha's dun reet well for thi sen.' (Though perhaps he would never be able to say that about a *woman* owning a farm).

While I search for the perfect place, I begin a year-long course on the ancient philosophy of the Kabbalah, run by a psychotherapist called Lilith. All the populist books about manifestation are rooted in the ancient teachings of the Kabbalah. The course intends to give us a deeper understanding of ourselves and the mysteries of life and the universe. It includes the study of sacred geometry, the planets, psychic journeying, quantum physics and how to manifest our desires.

We do guided meditations on each of the spheres of the Great Glyph, the Tree of Life which is at the heart of Kabbalistic philosophy. Lilith guides us through the meditation and then we're free to allow our imagination to create what happens until it's time for us to *return to the room* and take turns to describe our journey.

As we are arriving and settling into Lilith's front room at one of these gatherings, something enormous happens. Someone has brought a bunch of Queen Anne's lace to decorate our little altar. I'm transfixed, terrified, disgusted; bile rises in my throat. I'm no longer a mature, powerful, refashioned woman who creates her own destiny.

I snatch up the talking shell that we use so that each member is listened to without interruption. I vomit distress. Tears pour down my cheeks, adrenaline floods my body with heat and makes my voice quiver. I'm poised not for escape but self-destruction. Those flowers, the same ones that I picked and gave to my mother before she died, the flowers that are called

Mother Die, have dislodged my carapace of self-assurance and released a pus of festered fear and dread that is pouring out in an unstaunchable torrent. I'm terrified for the mother of the woman who picked the flowers. Someone suggests that Lilith keep them. Oh no, no, no! Lilith is the group's mother, Lilith will die. Lilith will die! My terror only subsides when another woman offers to take the flowers away with her and throw them into the sea to cleanse and disperse any negative energy from them. At last I feel calmer.

The adult me can understand that the danger of confusing the benign look-alike Queen Anne's lace with the deadly poison hemlock is the reason for that particular superstition. Like the saying that diamond creases in table linen are harbingers of death was invented to frighten maids in service into taking proper care of the laundry, and the one about whistling women and the devil was a metaphor for keeping women subservient – but logic is not at work in the mind of my five-year-old self. To her it is all very simple. I had murdered my mother when I picked these same flowers for her.

I have a one-on-one therapy session with Litith to try to address some of the trauma that was stirred up at the sight of the flowers.

'What do you want to say to me, darling?' Lilith asks, having taken on the mantle of my 32-year-old mother.

'I don't want you to die Mam, please don't leave us,' the infant pleads. My childish tears flow; I implore, beseech, reach out with my love, like a magnet to connect and keep her close. Lilith skilfully guides me through a loving parting. I don't know if the child will ever accept that she is gone but the adult, reluctantly sensible, makes an effort to let go, breaking the connection with my hapless, helpless, hopeless dead mother. Is that it now? Am I healed? Can I just be someone else, that person I could have been, leave behind the wounded infant and battered adolescent that take up so much of me?

* * *

Always seeking spiritual growth, ayahuasca is the next potential source of solace that I stumble into on my path through life. This powerful hallucinogenic drug is made from a South American vine and used by indigenous people in sacred ceremonies for healing, increasing intuition, creativity and attuning to nature. Also known as Mother Ayahuasca, the vine from which the drug is derived is seen as a goddess by its traditional users. It provides dimethyltryptamine (DMT), a potent psychedelic of the tryptamine family, the chemical responsible for sentience. All animals produce DMT in the pineal gland when we are born, when dreaming, and in torrents when we die. DMT tells us that Mother Nature can be kindly.

I have almost no experience of recreational drugs but, because of its spiritual associations, I have considered taking this one more than once. It had been offered at raw festivals and I even took some home once but was afraid to take it alone. I seemed to know, somehow, that the drug could help me and, because I believe in synchronicity (Jung's meaningful coincidences), I became alert when someone I knew told me about a *tea party* he had attended. Tea party, apparently, is code for an ayahuasca ceremony. The man who tells me about his experiences at the tea party recounts how he met the Goddess of the drug. She was dressed all in green and decorated with her sacred vine. I am sold! Just like when the opportunity was presented for the ashram retreat in Glastonbury, I know this is the right thing to do and I book a place on the next tea party ceremony.

* * *

I'm alone amongst others who all seem different, knowing, or with friends. Twenty of us, dressed in white, at a secret venue in Norfolk. At 60 why am I still seeking something? Am I just entertaining myself? Women are practicing yoga – show offs. People are chatting to each other. No one talks to me. I don't have a place here.

Eventually the time comes and we assemble in a circle inside a large marquee. I'm anxious, lonely. It's my turn. I sit on a far too low cushion opposite the shaman who ceremonially measures out the liquid I must drink before the ayahuasca. It stops the stomach neutralising the drug. I return to my mattress and attempt to drink it. It tastes foul and bitter, more foul and bitter than any medicine any child could ever imagine.

After all the show offs and people who are here with friends, or have been before, and perhaps a few others who feel as lonely as me have had their go, it's my turn for the actual drug. I force myself to drink. It is even worse than the first goblet, worse than dragons' faeces. Will it be worth it?

I arrogantly imagine that because of my raw diet and preparatory fasting that I will not succumb to the expected vomiting. I'm wrong. Very wrong. Each encounter with a psychedelic vision is accompanied by a rising nausea that finds its expression in the sick bucket that each of us is supplied with.

A musician sings *ikaros*, songs specially formulated to enhance the drug's effects. He has a backing chorus of retching and vomiting. I chuckle to myself at this. Some of those around me struggle with demons, others giggle, speak in tongues or talk to whatever they are envisioning. As the effects wear off the tinkling bell signals the second round.

I follow the same procedure for three nights on my first stay but I am disappointed. I believe I have not had the nurturing that the people around me have received from the voluntary helpers. I was cold. The man next to me always turned towards me to throw up. I am overwhelmed with fury. A barrage of bitterness and bile is released by the drug. The drug provides a conduit to the anger I could not express as an adolescent and it cascades out of me. I vent my fury on the organisers and the shamans for not looking after me properly. The following night I'm given hot-water bottles, a woolly hat and bed-socks. I refuse to go to the first sharing meeting and at the second one I express my fury. I count all this as probable progress, but I know there is still more to learn.

There is the opportunity to return for a second retreat. There will be no marquee. It will be summer so I will be warmer. The experience is better. On the final round of the final day the drug takes me beyond the psychedelic and the visceral.

The shaman tells us that we do not choose to come, She, the Goddess, calls us. Well, I want to meet Her. This is the reason I'm here. In my head I ask if I can see Her, the Lady of the Vine, Mother Ayahuasca. Surely tonight, my last chance.

Then the vision comes.

A figure appears from the shadows in the corner of a small dark room, but it is not Her. It's my daughter. Our communication is wordless. Intuition takes over from conscious mind and love passes between us. When our communications are complete my daughter's image fades and a second emerges.

It's my mother. She's wrapped in swaddling bands, a conflation of corpse and infant, blanket and shroud. A surge of love and pity swells inside me. I become mother to my mother. I feel the full weight of not having been able to comfort her when she was dying. I'm not sad. The Lady of the Vine gives me what I missed, what I need. I hold my mother's body, love her, rock and soothe her like a baby in my arms. Love flows between us. After the longest time I'm content to leave my mother. There are no tears. The experience is monumental, invaluable, comforting.

As my mother fades a third figure appears. I'm not shocked or at all concerned to see that it's Muriel. I don't question how my higher self wants to use the valuable time I have, with the effects of the drug about to wear off.

The source of Muriel's predilection for control and abuse is probed for me whilst I look on, impassive. Would she have worn callipers as a child because of her polio? Was she teased and bullied at school? Did she feel sexually unattractive during adolescence as a result of her disfigurement and limp? Is that why she felt so threatened by my blossoming adolescence? Was it Muriel's lack of any control over her life as a working-class mill girl that had hardened her heart? Did she cleave to religion when she discovered the power of the righteous?

The three women in my vision are utterly passive but this encounter with Muriel helps me towards forgiveness and empathy and perhaps even gratitude for the contribution my stepmother made to the woman I have become. Feelings in me shift and settle.

FINDING EDDIE, 2016

Edward grew up to be a tall and gangly blonde with straight toes – no too small shoes for him. There was never any bond between him and us, nothing at all. It was purposefully prevented. To me, he was her. To him, I was a distant, never-spoken-of, mysterious older sister.

I was curious to meet Eddie, writing this memoir had made me aware of the gaps in my knowledge of him. I had no contact details for him but found out that he was setting up a tattoo business. In 2016 I discovered that he had a Facebook page for his tattooing, so I got in touch with him through that.

* * *

We arrange to meet up in his hometown. My wonderful friend Jane, who I have known for 30 years and stay with in Huddersfield two or three times a year, drives us there. I bubble with excitement and anticipation the whole two hour journey.

Jane and I think an hour will be enough for the meeting so I pay the parking meter accordingly and we walk the short distance to the cafe.

It is a beautiful summer's day. The cafe is in the centre of town. One thing I notice about Eddie and Paula, sitting outside so that they could both smoke, is that they are extremely popular. People are constantly saying hello to them as they pass by.

Eddie is now 50. The last time I saw him he was about nine, that Christmas when I visited them, while I was at Ford. There had been little interaction with him back then.

I want to know more about the brother who had grown up to look the spit of our dad, right down to the widow's peak. He is well over six foot, well built, dresses like a biker, has myriad tattoos, a warm open face and a great sadness behind his eyes. He is keen to get to know me and we both have lots of myths to dispel. More than anything, we discover a sibling love for each other.

After an hour Jane and I go back to the car to drive it to Eddie and Paula's house. We stay for a further four hours.

Despite Edward – as he was called back then – being what we thought of as the spoilt one, who benefitted from everything that we were denied, I wondered if he was the most badly destroyed of all of us. We older three siblings grew up with our father's love until Muriel arrived and we have subsequently managed to piece our lives back together. Eddie had only known the attenuated version of our dad. He had lived with the pair for longest and he had no external reference points or wider family. It hurts him that he is on the outside, not a full part of the family with the rest of the siblings. Muriel's lovely sister, Gwen, who I had only met once and who had seemed entirely normal, open, warm and honest, had died when he was around five.

Many of the things that Eddie told me at that first meeting were complete revelations.

When I got to about 12, they didn't want to know. They had no time for me, they were just interested in the church. They had a shrine in the house. The church members would come round for bible readings and services. When the organ went on, I went out. Dad got to be worse than Mum. He would sit in the kitchen reading the bible, and I mean reading it, from cover to cover, while he listened to a tape of Mum preaching.

I was in a right state because of bullying at school. I was a big lad and they all taunted me because they knew I wouldn't fight back. Mum said I couldn't because I was a Christian. It wasn't until Dad said, 'Niver thee mind what thi mam sez, tha fight back an' I'll stand behind thee.'

That was in the last 18 months of school. So I stood up for myself against the bullies and I went from the bottom set in everything to the top set.

I knew I had three siblings. I shared a room with Nicky at one time. I kept asking why we never saw any of you. I never got any real answers. Once Mum said, 'Because they're rich and we're poor.' Another time she said something about you and Lady Chatterley's Lover, *but she didn't explain anything. Dad never spoke anyway, but he did once say that Auntie Dorothy had stolen Arthur from him.*

There was never any question of me staying on at school. I was expected to leave at 16 and get a job. I was set on as a mechanic. Somehow, I got into violence, probably because I was so mixed up inside. I put a gun in my mouth more than once. I didn't care if I lived or died. I hadn't for a long time.

Neither of them noticed anything when I got the shotgun. I sawed off the barrels and hid it. I was 19. I don't know why I did the robbery. Aggression had become a way of life and I suppose, yes, it may have been a cry for help or a way to get out. People don't understand what aggression is like. It's the feeling you get when you come down from it, everything falls away, you can relax.

Yes, the shotgun I pointed at the cashier in the petrol station was loaded. I don't know if I would have pulled the trigger. I don't know if I cared. It was as if nothing mattered. It all went wrong anyway. There was nothing in the till and the getaway car we stole was an unmarked police car.

I did it with a lad from work. I insisted on taking all the blame and said I didn't want any leniency. He got a bit less than me. I got time for the firearm and the robbery and the car theft. In the end I served four years, eight months. I was in young offenders for the first bit, then Wakefield maximum security with murderers, rapists and serial killers like Denis Neilson and Arthur Hutchinson, but they were scared of me. They preyed on the vulnerable and weak but I had been into violence. Perhaps they saw me as ruthless. They knew I had taken a loaded shotgun and was prepared to shoot someone in the face. To them, I had no moral scruples. So nobody bothered me.

I decided that the only way to get through the sentence was to play by the rules. I'd always drawn and a lad in there taught me to paint. One day, about 18 months before the end of my sentence, I had a sort of epiphany. I woke up and I was scared for the first time. I felt real fear about where I was and the men around me and I clearly remember

*thinking, 'I'll have to keep a lid on this.' So I managed to get through
to the end and got my parole. Because my sentence was longer than three
years it will always be on my record. I can never apply for a job without
declaring it. So, I've mostly had to be self-employed.*

In her time in our family, Muriel had tackled my school, the
police, Arthur's school and the LEA, the courts, the adoption
services and being expelled from a number of religious cults.
Through all of this there was never any real impact on her.
But in the Criminal Justice System she had met her match.
If the Fates or Karma, or even her Almighty God, had been
able to choose one thing that would punish Muriel more than
anything else then it would be this, her treasured and once
cosseted son being locked away from her.

I was once at Auntie Dorothy's when Muriel and Dad
were visiting and she held forth about what had happened
to Edward. 'They can just come and take your son off you,'
she said to no one in particular, and no one in particular
listened, or cared. In truth, because of my feelings about
Muriel, when I first heard about the sentence I laughed. I
was elated. For me, her son was part of her and, back then,
I hated her with a vengeance.

Poor Eddie. Each of us kids had found our own escape
route. His had perhaps been the worst.

Dad had been dead for 26 years. I asked him what he
remembered about it.

I'd only been out two weeks when Dad died. Yes, I think he was waiting for me. I was let out of prison once to visit him in the infirmary when his heart had stopped but that was a year or two before he died.

When he was dying, I heard Mum beg Dad with tears in her eyes, more than once, to let her contact you three but he wouldn't. He was a stubborn man. He said, 'If they didn't want me when I was alive, I don't want them now I'm deein.'

No, she couldn't contact you after he died because she believed in the afterlife so she thought that Dad could still see her and what she was doing, so she wouldn't go against his wishes. Though after he died, she lost interest in religion.

I always thought that there was a reason for all that bible study. Now I know some of what happened, I think they may have been trying to atone for what they had done to the three of you. There must have been some reason why Dad became so fanatical, and when I hear about how it was for you three, well that would explain it.

While I found this gratifying – that Eddie at least thought that Dad turning to God so fanatically was an attempt at expiation, an acknowledgement of wrong doing – I still found it very difficult to listen to what Eddie was saying. I also found it hard to believe him, especially after hearing competing information from the Elim Church elder about them trying to find me. I had been so sure that it had been Muriel's influence that stopped Dad from contacting us but perhaps he *had* been afraid of his chickens coming home to roost, his badly done by children telling him some home truths.

When Dad died, I lived with Mum. I got a job and we shared all the bills for everything. Then she found another man and he moved in. I suggested we split the bills three ways, but they insisted that they pay half and I pay half. He could be violent. They went off to stay in a caravan one weekend and she rang me to go and collect her. When I got there, she was out on the street. He'd been hitting her. I banged on the caravan door but there was no answer, otherwise I would have given him a thrashing, even though it might have threatened my parole. They got divorced soon after.

Muriel had married Dad precipitately after the death of her first husband. She was with her third husband when Norman had visited her. After her divorce from the violent husband, she moved to Lancashire to be near Eddie and married for a fourth time. Our dad had been just one in a line of men.

The fourth husband used some of her funeral insurance to bury her and then absconded with the rest, so she lies alone in an unmarked grave.

Epilogue –
Pearl in the Oyster

A woman once told me that our life traumas are like grit thrown in our path to create beautiful pearls. I wondered if she would spout such blasé tripe if she'd walked my path. Only now, so many years later, can I accept the metaphor. Perhaps my complicated childhood gave me the impetus to succeed in life.

I'm no longer the sad girl who had only Jesus between her and utter desolation. Now I'm the author of my own destiny, I am God. I determine my life. I no longer stumble, nursing my afflictions, I lead, like Eve in Eden.

But a pearl is not the best metaphor for what the grit of a tainted childhood creates. I am no pearl. I grew a defensive shell of a personality in order to survive. I became a shape-shifter: on the one hand a pathetic victim safer in its own company, living the learnt but now unnecessary frugality that our father bred into me. The other part of me is an over-protective, high-achieving mother figure, determined that neither my daughter nor I will be limited by family, education, gendering or class. My experience and education made me a radical with challenging opinions but with a core cowed by conflict or ridicule.

If Dad had not brought Muriel into our family, would I have stayed with him as he had once said I should, taking care of him and the house until I married John, and became what? Would I have been happy? Would I have seen or experienced very much at all beyond our small town?

Perhaps there is much in my childhood that I should be grateful for.

Author's Note

This memoir began as a story of resilience, survival and achievement, written by a journeyer throwing off the constraints of class, gender, abuse, neglect and poverty. But as I wrote, another story emerged, one that I had hidden from all my life: that of a father's complicity in the disintegration of a family and the blighting of the lives of all his children.

The legacy of my early experiences was pity for my mother, hatred of my stepmother and an inviolable attachment to my father, who in a feat of reverse alchemy had become callous and uncaring. He silently stood by while the woman he had brought into our home rapidly separated sibling from sibling and father from children, whilst calculatedly dismantling my own very existence. His *volte face* is hard to explain given that, in the aftermath of my mother's death, he insisted on continuing to be our dad, bringing us up himself at a time when it was very rare for a man to be a single parent. Nor was he any ordinary dad. He was a fun, kind, committed and loving father to all three of us.

His faults were his stubbornness and his limpet-like insistence on 'a quiet life' and I believed that this, along with the persuasive poison that our stepmother, Muriel, presumably poured into his ear, was the reason why he did not intervene in her brutal coercive control, bullying and abuse of his children. It may be difficult for a reader to understand that I did not hold our father responsible for what he allowed to happen to us at the hands and tongue of his new wife. But in fact I think it would have been much harder for me to tolerate my life with Muriel if I had ceased to believe that our father was just as oppressed and controlled by her as we were.

Unravelling my blind devotion to my father whilst writing this book has given truth to Alan Bennet's words, 'You don't put yourself into what you write, you find yourself.'

* * *

To tell this story, along with my own experience, I have used dramatic licence to relate scenes that have been reported to me but I did not witness. I have also included retrospective conversations with my brothers about our experiences as children and adolescents. At other points I bring my adult voice to comment on the unfolding story. I have used dialect when relating the words of my father and grandmother. My mother, Betty, would also have spoken in South Yorkshire dialect but, sadly, I have no memory of her voice so I have used standard English for her speech.

Unfortunately, there are many questions to which I do not have answers. I was only five when our mother was taken to live with our grandmother following radical surgery for breast cancer and we were put in a Children's Home, so the timeframe around these events is hazy. In the course of my research, I was told Fartown Grange Children's Home records were lost when, in 1974, Huddersfield joined with Dewsbury to become Kirklees, so I do not know how long we were in the Home. Despite making an appeal through the *Huddersfield Examiner* and finding some helpful contacts, I am unable to be absolutely clear on timings. I know we spent a summer holiday and a Christmas at Fartown Grange, and it was there that I was told of my mother's death at the end of March 1958 and that we left the Home not long after that. So I believe our stay there would have been at least eight months.

Clearer sources for my story are, along with my own experience, those of my siblings, my maternal grandmother Catherine, my father's sister Dorothy, my older cousin Pat and official records. Due to the candid nature of this memoir some individuals have chosen to be excluded from the narrative and I have therefore honoured this decision.

Acknowledgements

A book arises from the mind of the author due to the influences that surround them and the support that they receive in their endeavours. I am grateful to my daughter for all the joy she has brought into my life and to my siblings for all the assistance they have given me, not just with practical matters like dates but also their openness in talking about their experiences. Meeting two new brothers later in life has been a blessed and enriching experience.

I am eternally grateful to the Further Education system that provided me with the stepping stones and gateway to an education, when either my dad or the 1944 Education Act and its enforcers had written me off. It was also, a kind and patient Further Education tutor, when I was 50, who eventually removed my terror of mathematics sufficiently for me to gain a top grade GCSE in the subject.

My very precious friend, Jane Mellor, kindly and eagerly assisted in tracking down information about Fartown Grange Children's Home in the 1950s, and was able to root out, with the help of the *Huddersfield Examiner*, some now treasured pictures of myself and my siblings during our time there. These revealed that the house parents had given us some very happy experiences at a time when we otherwise might have felt desolate and abandoned.

The Arvon Foundation course on memoir that I attended was pivotal in helping me to take my work seriously. It was there that I met the journalist Ben Sharratt whose exchange editing had the same effect. I am fortunate to have Sally Holloway as a friend and member of our two-woman writing 'group.' She has been unstinting and unflinching in providing constructive feedback of my work, guiding me when I have been too engrossed and encouraging me when I have been too ready to give up. I was blessed to find Julie Fisher who provided a magnificently astute manuscript assessment and signposted me to some useful writers of memoir and teachers of our craft. Above all, Julie, like Sally, encouraged me to have faith in my work, to know and believe that once it was suitably honed, it was just a question of finding the right fit. That came with Judith Murdoch, the literary agent who recognised the worth of the writing and did a brilliant job of marrying me up with the right publisher. In the literary engine that is Mirror Books I have found the individual and interdependent parts to be not only erudite and as sharp as Shakespeare's wit but also empathic and aware. Central to the book's current shape, comprehensibility and coherence is Liz Marvin, who, in her structural editing, acted as a magnificent reader's advocate.

ACKNOWLEDGEMENTS

Finally, I would like to thank the family, my mother, father and siblings, of my early years, whose loving presence provided the firm foundation that ensured that I survived and went on to thrive, despite the tribulations of my adolescence.

Also by Mirror Books

Stella's Story
Louise Allen

*"Stella is just like a tiny bird. This is my first impression of her.
A quiet little sparrow of a girl."*

In the first of a new series *'Thrown Away Children'*, foster mother Louise Allen
tells the true story of Stella, a young girl scarred by an abusive past.

Named for the lager that christened her, Stella's life is characterised by
dysfunction and neglect. Her mother abandons her as a newborn and in the
'care' of her father, Stella is left with no food, water, clothes or warmth.

Louise becomes Stella's foster carer and is determined to give the girl a
better life. But when Stella has a startling response to having her photo
taken, it is clear that the effects of her abuse run deep.

MIRROR BOOKS